Also by Alan Cheuse
Candace & Other Stories (1980)

The Bohemians

John Reed & His Friends Who Shook the World

A   NOVEL   ✳   BY   ALAN   CHEUSE

Apple-wood Books, Inc.
Cambridge/Watertown 1982

The author would like to acknowledge the work of Granville Hicks, Robert Rosenstone, and Barbara Gelb, without which he could not have proceeded with such deliberate speed. He would also like to thank the staff of the Houghton Library of Harvard University.

The Bohemians © 1982 by Alan Cheuse

ISBN 0-918222-32-X

2   3   4   5   6   7   8   9   10   BP

The Bohemians

For Fathers and Sons—
Phil and Josh

Reed was a Westerner and words meant what they said.
            —**John Dos Passos,** *USA*

Do I contradict myself?
Very well then...I contradict myself....
            —**Walt Whitman,** *Leaves of Grass*

Part One

WESTERNER

On the eve of the 4th of July we put our shoulders to it and pushed off into the river—four boys, each dressed in his own version of a pirate costume, and a dog. Cliff, the tallest of our band, sported a kerchief of flaming red that he tied around his thick neck; Sox showed his style by wearing ragged old Sunday trousers, Bates by his knife, a wooden-handled affair borrowed from an older brother who had bargained it away from a Klamath artisan, and I covered my head with a spanking headdress from a Filipino chieftain, which my Uncle Ray had brought me from his last Pacific voyage. It bore feathers from a bird named Paradise.

"You're quite a sight," my father said. The festival spirit had infected him. He wore his woodsman's coat rather than his courtroom togs, but he held back from the actual labor of shoving our raft into the water.

"'Light winning makes the prize seem light,'" he called out to our backs as we huffed and puffed and slid our beautiful creation—the work of several weeks—into the moving stream. His voice resounded richly and deeply across the waters. It was the right voice for my Papa, fitting his thick brownish-red moustaches and his warrior-like stride the way a deep growl fits a bear. It pricked me to push all the harder, so that our raft, quite heavy at first, finally started sliding toward the edge.

We had built the craft with my father's help, in the attic of Grandma Green's big house atop the woody hill overlooking the confluence of this moderate stream, the Willamette, and the mightier Columbia. But let me not speak badly of any river! The Willamette was a perfect size for boys our age, with its woods and respectable current, and some of the places that we had mapped for ports on our little holiday journey called out to me with all the vigor of our broader, more ancient neighbor to the north, mother of cliffs and winds.

"And push, mates!" I yelled, feeling our craft grumble against the small stones along the shore.

"Here, Jack!" Sox called.

"Hey, ho!" sang Bates.

"Heave ho!" grunted Cliff, face flamed up to the shade of his neckerchief as he pushed with all of his might.

"Good show!" called Papa from over our shoulders as we felt the bulky raft pick up speed. Something twanged in my gut like a fiddle string snapping, but on I pushed and pushed. Somewhere in the next moment the pain passed, and I could feel the craft sliding fast, and then suddenly it sliced into the water and took on buoyancy in our arms.

"Hold it there!" I ordered, grabbing for the rope we'd tied to the stern. A little dynamo of fur and motion, Cliff's mongrel pup—his name was Hairball—leaped past my hand and caught the rope in his teeth and started chewing. We laughed and laughed at the doggy's sailorly antics, loading our provisions and setting the oars in their make-shift locks, hauling up our sail in a hundred and fifty shakes of that same dog's tail.

Our horse whinnied from the woodside, telling Papa how anxious he was to pull the wagon home. Through the trees I could see his bony brown figure, tail flailing incessantly against the flies. The beast was nervous, the opposite of Lee Sing, our ageless houseman and cook, who had remained stoic throughout the preparations for embarkation, dreaming perhaps of the time he had boarded an ocean-going ship on the other side of the Pacific and sailed for Portland. Little did he know then that his fortune would become entangled like an old rose vine with that of the Greens, whose daughter my father C.J. had gained permission to marry from flamboyant Grandpa, the man who founded our city's waterworks and rode about town in a coach and six, wearing a coat of the finest sables ever hauled over the ocean on ships from China's northwestern neighbor.

But then Lee Sing always appeared to be at least half-dreaming, viewing the world through eyes that even when opened wide seemed no more than slits in his yellow rough rice-paper face.

"Mastuh Leed," he called to me from the embankment, "you want to sail to China? See wall where Lee Sing born? Ha, ha!" He clapped his hands together as though applauding me in a play.

"Then you going long way!"

"I know it's long," I called back to him from where I stood knee-deep in river water, making a last-minute adjustment of our wondrous home-made rudder.

"No, not long! Long!"

"Wrong!" my father translated.

"Oh, wrong," I said. "Wrong! Long! Yes, a long way and a wrong way, Lee Sing!"

"What's he saying, Jack?" Cliff asked from his perch atop the rear of the vessel, his hands quickly inventing knots.

"Oh, he used to tell me bedtime stories about the Chinese village where he was born, 'under the shadow of the Great Wall,' he described it. When I was small, that was the place I always said I wanted to see."

"Oh, and he's hollering now about us going the wrong way from China?" Bates put in from the water on the other side of the craft.

"Long way, wrong way," I imitated Lee Sing's sing-song voice, finishing up my work on the steering part. "Maybe I will get there some day, boys. But for now it's upriver to the camp!"

And my friends let out some of what they took to be warlike whoops.

We had arisen that morning in darkness. Leaving behind mothers and little brothers and grandmas, we hitched the old horse to the wagon that we had loaded the night before and rode on down to the river, listening to the groans and creaks of the wooden cart and the clopping and snorting of the horse as we made our steep way downhill like choristers waiting to chime in with our parts. We did sing a few tunes in barbershop harmonies, though our voices—still high and girlish, threatening here and there in their vocal vagaries to sink like sacks full of stones—could not do real justice to such songs. When Papa joined in, the melodies deepened and stretched right. Lee Sing had remained mute, not an uncharacteristic role for him. It was only when we got ready to push off, under a sun that broke through an eight o'clock mist, that he showed his bone-white teeth in a smile and burst into a chant both rare and appealing.

Pool for the shore, Chlistin!

He sang his hymn while standing a pace behind Papa who took out his handkerchief and waved us *bon voyage.*

Pool for the shore, Chlistin!
Pool for the shore, Chlistin!
Heed not the lolling wave!

"Follow your map and don't be delayed!" Papa called from shore, yanking from his pocket a gold watch that glinted gloriously in the sun. "We'll meet you tomorrow at the old campgrounds past Oregon City!"

We'd already tossed the knife for our turns at the oars, and my luck was to take the rudder and stand like some bold captain as Sox and Cliff rowed us into the current. And so I waved back at Pa for quite a time, until he and Lee Sing became no more than reeds at the sparkling shore, and then we turned a bend and they were gone.

"Pull for the shore, Christians!" I urged our crew. "The farther shore, boys!"

Cliff wriggled his long nose at me.

"Don't get carried away, Jack," he said. "Not until you've had your turn at the oar."

Bates, squinting like an Indian in the sun, looked to the map and then to me and then to the map again.

"Well, me hearties," he croaked, "pull hard and the gold will be yours."

I pulled hard when my turn came. I loved the battle against those places where the current ran strong enough to push us back unless my comrade and I worked together to keep us moving ever and ever upstream. Our rhythms became entwined with those of the river, our forcefulness over-matched its own. When we sailed into a section where a small island, say, divided the often placid stream into several stronger roads we took the westward side always, enjoying the wind that picked up in those corridors.

Salt sweat poured down from the headband that held my pretty feathers, and the flavor, when it reached my lips, set me to hungering for the lunch Lee Sing had prepared. By the map, though, we had hours to row before we made our first port of call. Cliff hummed to himself off-key but quiet enough not to disturb me. Sox, when he wasn't rowing, played silently with Cliff's pup. Bates whittled away with his Indian knife on a nice piece of cedar he had withdrawn from his pack.

To pass the time I admired the trees, the cabins we'd spy here and there along the shore, imagining stories for each of the inhabitants going back before the times of the first white explorers. And when we passed slender canoes with holiday voyagers, young couples or boys and girls no older than ourselves, now thwick, now thwack, my blade flashed in the sun and I leaped from craft to craft, rescuing damsels and children, pups and maiden aunts from the Scyllas and Charybdises and whirlpools and sea monsters—what, so far upstream?—the small commercial boats that chugged back and forth from the logging camps to town, though there were fewer of these than usual because, I surmised, of the coming on of the holiday.

The woods grew thick and great enough in places where the bank steepened to mask even the climbing sun. The nasty flies didn't seem to care that we had put city life behind us and deserved some peace from the usual round we led, pacing the raft as we steered out into the broad center stream. The muted gush and splash of our oars mingled with the sharp, but never piercing, cries of birds both foreign and familiar. Once I even thought I heard a rooster just beyond the curtain of trees on the opposite bank, but wished the sound immediately away—who cared for the noises of barnyard life, the boring round of the settlement, not to mention the city, when we were off for forests and the unfamiliar? For old time adventures! time before this modern time! for the days of hidden gold and pirates who pierced the air with cutlasses and their ears with dangling rings and gems on precious thinly-beaten wires of purest metals! for old time whalers and Sinbad sailors! for great squalls and Great Walls! for a territory where school children turned into Saracens and windmills to ogres with a turn of the page!

As if he'd caught the scent of my imaginings, Hairball began to yip and yowl about the deck.

"Injins!"

Cliff got to his feet with a motion that dipped the raft toward starboard.

"Git your guns out boys! We're gonna have a fight on our hands!"

He dropped to one knee and scouted along the shoreline. His hand shaded his eyes, and he struck a pose like that of the very people he'd now engage in battle.

Hairball kept up his yapping, dancing at the raft's edge, then skipping back when the backwash from the oar splashed him, and then back again to the edge. Sox and Bates got into the spirit of things by yipping and hoo-hooting like red men, though since they both held oars in their hands they couldn't do it as properly as they should, with full clapping of a hand over the mouth formed into an O so as to make a tube of scary echoes, and so they sounded more like Hairball than anything else.

"Jack, you cover the far shore!" Cliff gave me the order. "Sox, Bates, you boys row with all you got! We're outnumbered, but we can run it if you put all your life into your oars!"

He used his hand to form a gun which he held out before him—a revolver, I could see, from the shape of his hand—which was a mistake since if there were hostile red men tracking us along the shore line he'd surely need a fast-action repeating rifle to hold them off. "Pow!!" he shot. "Pim!! Ping!! Pow!! Pow!!"

"Ooof!"

Sox slumped at his station, letting the oar slip from his grasp. While resting his chin on his chest, he reached over the side and splashed water over his ragged trousers.

"I'm hit, boys, I'm hit!"

"Lord God A-Mighty!" Bates sighed, sounding like his mother at a Sunday church picnic.

"Jack, you better start shooting!" Cliff yelled.

"They ain't shot at us," I said. I was enjoying the sudden turn of things, the way we were moving freely in the stream, until I noticed that despite Bates's best efforts we were about to head back along the way we'd come.

"They sure as heck are shooting, Jack! You start firing at them before they git us all!"

"Aw, Cliff," I said, "I can't shoot at Indians." I squinted into the sun and inched over to take the oar from the slumping Sox. "Move over, mate, and I'll help out."

"Aw right, then," Cliff announced, still pretending to fire at invisible targets along the shore, "and Billy, you git out your gun and help me."

His story back in place once more, Cliff broke out into a smile and slaughtered Indian upon Indian while I helped Bates turn the raft around—it was harder than it looked to turn against the current, however gentle the flow—and skedaddle so we could put the red men out of range.

Bates soon tired and Cliff slipped alongside me to take his place at the other oar.

"What's wrong with you, Jack? I always thought you was a brave boy, but there we was under ambush and you never so much as raised a pistol at them redskins! Too much of them Chinee songs on your brain?"

"I got nothing against fighting, Cliff," I said. "It's just certain fights I don't think are right."

"You say that, Jack, and you can think it's smart, but just wait till them redskins are shooting fire arrows at your family's house and trying to scalp and skin and you-know-what your mother. And then you'll see how much you'll hang back."

I laughed as I rowed, because it was my mother who might have made such a serious and unreal speech to me, and I laughed harder when I pictured hostile Indians, of whom there had never been more than a handful in these parts of the woods, coming up to the door of the Green house and asking for mother so they could tie her up and do the you-know-what to her—was it kissing? It was more than that, but exactly the mechanics of the thing eluded me as yet—and me standing back—this was Cliff's vision, remember?—and allowing them to ravage and pillage.

"I'd kill somebody if I had to, Cliff," I said, trying to overcome my jocularity. "I make up stories all the time where I'm killing monsters, ogres, evil genies, and evil pirates, of course—"

"Of course," Sox broke in, kneeling near us to listen in while Bates still scanned the shore.

"—but I just don't think it's right to kill Indians. I used to, but not any more."

"Is that 'cause of what your father's doing?" he asked, more respectful than I had ever heard him.

"Uh huh. They are a poor and sorry lot, fellows, let me testify."

"Well, there is all kinds of people," Cliff said, "and so I reckon there is all kinds of Indians. If the kind that attacked us was the poor and peaceful sort then we wouldn't have shot at them. But the peaceful kind wouldn't shoot at us first, would they?" His voice turned triumphant as he figured this point. "But now what if there was bandits, Jack? River pirates who wanted to attack us and scalp us like the worst of them Apaches from down south? Wouldn't you help us fight against those?"

"Yeah, Jack, would you?" Sox put in. "What if us, your friends, was held at gunpoint by these pirates, and you just came swimming up to the raft and had nothing but the knife you carried in your teeth? Would you slice their throats to help us get away?"

I had been rowing so hard that my headdress had slipped down over my ears, and I could see from the corner of one eye the bedraggled feathers tilting out from my scalp. With one hand on the oar, I adjusted my exotic crown with the other, smiled at my friends, and said, "Would I, boys? Oh, wouldn't it be swell when I did!"

Hairball rubbed up against me and gave me a keen little puppy smile.

The ambush had tired us out—and our hands by this hour felt as though they'd rowed us halfway to Lee Sing's homeland. We cheered when around the next bend we saw the low flat beach which on our map was called "Settler's Shores." Grass grew right down to the waterside. Had it been located in a civilized place it might have been a park. We rowed up to the bank and tied our vessel to the trunk of a small tree whose bark was scarred with hearts and arrows and many pairs of intertwined initials. Other folks, older and out for adventures other than our own, had moored here. But while we ate our sandwiches of bread and cucumber, washed down with lemonade from one of the many jars in our hampers, the glade remained quiet. Only Hairball's snuffling noises and our own earnest chewing competed with the gentle susurrations of the noon wind in the oaks along the bank. It had been a long morning, and harder work than we had imagined. While the other boys stripped down to their nothing-at-alls and waded out into the river for a swim, I lay down on the grass and took a nap.

Although I'm a big dreamer, this time I didn't dream. And I don't remember how long I slept. But it seemed like only a moment before I heard Hairball yip-yapping in my ear. I opened my eyes and saw the boys about halfway out into the water, their tanned bodies gleaming like polished logs in the sun.

Were they the object of the little puppy's excitement? A rustling, louder than the wind but softer than the clatter of pine cones falling into a thick bed of needles, made me turn my head from river to shore. No more than four feet from me, a rattler, thick as a double lariat, wearing burnished copper scales that glowed gloriously even in the shade as though from some inner fire, had coiled itself, bobbing its jewel-eyed, spade-shaped, slithery-tongued head up and back and down and up—as if entranced by some unheard tune that Hairball, brave little Hairball, was singing to it above the noise of his barks.

"Here, Hairball," I whispered to the pup. He ignored my call but the snake looked at me as surely as if he understood American talk, ceasing his little dance to pose as still as if he'd turned to stone—except for that slithering, forked tongue.

Had I grown up in a household where hell-fire and brimstone got served up each mealtime instead of Baked Alaskas and fine Oriental and French cuisine, I might have felt cheerful at the sight of the intruder. But the Green house had never been a religious house, not since the days dashing Grandpa had struck water from the mountains and sluiced it toward the city, which made him rich and daring and uncaring of whatever gods that be. The only religion I ever got was a dose now and then of a hymn from yellow-faced Lee Sing, of the kind with which he'd bade us *bon voyage*.

So, strange boy that I was, I never did learn to hate life enough to want to lose it. The sight of the snake set my heart palpitating like that of a race-horse after a brisk run. I lost control of my bladder and a voice within me said, Oh, ship-talk, Jack, you gone and done it now!

It was then that I heard the raw, rough, crotchety roar from the woods behind me.

"Don't move, young 'un!"

I wanted to turn but didn't dare take my eyes off my adversary—if it was going to strike I wanted to see it coming. And so when its head disappeared in a cloud of scales and dust, I witnessed this miracle in mesmeric fervor as the boom of the rifle echoed through the green and a fountain of blood spurted up from the slender neck of the headless serpent, spurted up, and then died down quickly, as though some housemaid in the bowels of its coils had turned off a spigot. The snake collapsed onto itself after a few involuntary twitches.

My friends came stumbling out of the river, their eyes saucer-wide, shouts on their lips. Ignoring me, they gathered round the dead viper, waving their arms and chattering like magpies while Hairball sniffed and nipped at the large pool of blood and meaty shards that lay scattered in a small area before us.

That was how he found us—Cooney Washington the Fourth, who sauntered up out of the trees at the park's border, his long rifle still smoking. He was dressed all in buckskin except for his hat, which appeared to be made of finest beaver, and his lined and weathered face could have been made out of buckskin too. For a short man he took long strides and, given my friends' nakedness and my own still somewhat uncontrollable state of upset, he loomed larger in that clearing than a man twice his size.

"You saved my life," I said, offering him a trembling hand.

"Naw," he said with a squint, "I think he would've hit the dog before he bit you, sonny. What's that little varmit's name?"

"Hairball," Cliff said, covering his walnuts with his hands.

"Name sounds right," the woodsman said, surveying us with the eye of a hunter or a scout and never giving any sign that it was out of the ordinary for three naked boys, and another with wet pants, to be standing about in a clearing with the blood and stringy ruins of a dead snake at their feet.

"Now which one of you fellers is Jack?"

That's how we met him, our guide for the rest of the journey. He had already saved my life, or Hairball's. My father had divined how much we'd need him and asked Cooney Washington, a life-time resident of the Green forest lands whom my father had known before I was born, to meet us at our first port of call and help us row—or pole, as it turned out—to our destination farther upriver.

The afternoon passed for us in a haze of heat and work and story-telling, since Cooney could not seem to let five minutes go by without explaining to us the origin of some particular marked tree on the river bank or the meaning of the configuration of some cloud or the reason for an odd bird cry or the secret behind a rock or bee. Since he claimed a kinship with the first President on his father's side and also that his mother's aunt was named Sacagawea, he was no doubt the most original American that I had ever met—and if wily old Cooney the woodsman was making up his life the way I sometimes made up my adventures, then at least he carried himself as though it were so. Who cared about the reason why he possessed such keen-eyed aim—whether from his ancient tribal blood or instinct mixed with practice—if he could blast away the head of a poisonous serpent from all the way across the glade? or show us how to knot the sail in place so that it adjusted to the wind? or how to call otters to the waterside? or spear salmon with a forked stick? or sing lyrics about the marriage of earth and sky in Russian, Spanish, French, and three forest languages?

But for all his lore and tricks, I liked him best for the way he spoke about my father. With one hand on the tiller and the other on Hairball's shaggy little head, he balanced himself on a rough-clad knee and described their first meeting.

"It was Christmas, back in '81 or '82, sonny, 'n I'd just come off the mountain where I'd made my home. There I was, walking a familiar trail to the beach, a few days journey on foot, it was, when all of a hoot and sudden I see this wire fence stretched right across the path! Well old Eagle Feathers here, that is, me, myself, was mighty surprised at finding a fence! Imagine you and your pals are walking to school one day, and you're heading down your usual way, and suddenly you come right smack up against a wall! You couldn't think it any more strange than I did, finding a gate some city fool built right up in the middle of the woods laying direck-ly in my path! A fence! I says to myself. Once I saw a bear in a cage, and how it was dying from the confines of it all! I climbed over that fence and kept on walking until I came to a place where the trees, like that bear, was dying of the imprisonment of it all. And a river ran through it, dying from the same. It had turned all a strange color, like nothing I'd seen before. And the birds that nested along the banks, they had a funny look about them. From being fenced in? I asked myself. Or was there something else? And this mind you, boys, was not today, but years back, in what to you is olden times. Not today when there's men to fight off these folk who capture forests and rivers and fence them in and do with them what they will...."

It was a long story; he told it well, but we had made our evening's stopover by the time he got to the middle of it—this part had sawmills and foremen and guards with guns and outriders and Indians enslaved to a mill owner—and we had set up camp for the night and started cooking our evening meal, and the sky dimmed from sea blue to Roman purple to octopus-ink black before he made his first mention of my father and his role in all this.

"All because I don't believe in fences, boys," the shaggy woodsman said. By this time we had eaten and cleaned up the encampment and were sitting around the fire, listening to what we figured had to be the last part of his story, and the night birds and ornery growling cats on the prowl in the dark. "It was summer, by the time we had a lot of this settled...." And before we heard the last of it, we had crept into the blanket-bags that Cooney had helped us fold and made our good-nights and slept.

I awakened once in the night and thought for a moment that I heard the old woodsman still talking, but after a while I could make out his snoring and understood that the other sound was some sort of animal out there that made noises resembling laughter and coughing and whispering, or was it another animal that whispered back to the first? The stars floated as thick as the rose blossoms on the pond in Grandma's prize garden. I wanted to reach up and stir them with my hand. A small shape crawled toward me out of the dark and nuzzled against my face.

"Oh, Hairball," I whispered into his doggy ear, "I'm so glad to be alive! I just hope when I get old I remember all the things I learned today!"

The holiday itself dawned gently, in stages that succeeded each other each time I blinked, like the procession of images in a stereopticon, each stage brighter than the last, but before there was light, there was sound—bird-song and barking and cock-crow, too, because for all of our imagining, we never meandered too far from settlements, and also the faint chunk-thud, chunk-thud of someone applying an axe to a tree or a hammer to a nail so if you never opened your eyes you could tell by the increase in the chatter and the stutter of the world that a change of time was coming, and soon.

The boys knew it. The pup knew it. Even the river seemed to sense the arrival of day, churning faster and faster while the eastern sky turned up pink and then gold and then whitely white, as though the same hand that had snuffed out the stars and touched a torch to the sun had stirred the waters upstream.

We were eating breakfast cooked by Cooney in his woodsy way, the eggs flavored with freshly picked sage and the coffee brewed up right in the pot over the fire, when we saw the first logs come down, sliding in a rush of froth and wave, like otters off the cliffs at the coast.

"We'll drag that raft on shore just to be sure it don't get stoved," he said, setting down his cup and motioning for us to follow him to the water's edge.

"Isn't that dangerous?" Cliff asked as we hauled our craft onto the beach. Logs sailed past in midstream.

"Sure is, up this far," said Cooney, wiping egg from his leathery chin. "Narrower the river, rougher the flow. Law of life, that might be." He chuckled in a way that reminded me of Lee Sing, who hardly ever laughed. "Out in these parts when I was your age, that was just about the only law there was! And a man kind of got used to living by his own rights and lights. Course that meant a lot of downright mean folk got to do things their way 's well as the better people. Guess that's how's it's a good thing that somebody like old C. J. Reed come out here and try to set things a bit orderly. Even if it means butting a few heads belonging to his own crowd."

He patted me on the head the way I'd seen him pat little Hairball and led us back up to the camp. I wasn't quite sure what he was saying about my father except that it made me proud. Perhaps the great wave of excitement that burst upon me that morning had its source in that feeling of pride. But whatever its cause—and it could just have been the glorious morn that had unfurled above us like an umbrella of oyster-shell white light, no cloud, and only a slight breeze from the west—I threw myself into the day.

Once the log flow had subsided, we put "Settlers' Shores" behind us and, with Cooney at the helm, headed farther upriver. Aside from a few women doing their wash at the waterside, we saw no other living beings until we rounded a bend some miles south of our campsite and came upon a raft four times the size of our own heading downstream almost directly in our path.

The dress of its crew made our own costumes pale by comparison. At the rudder stood a black man thick as a sequoia wearing nothing but leggings and a white kerchief about his right arm, while two other loggers, both of them as big around as the dark-skinned man but meaner looking, waved pistols in the air and now and then let off a shot that boomed through the tree-tops, scaring birds from their perches.

"Hunker down, laddies," Cooney ordered us and you could hear the edge of warning in his voice.

"Who's that?" asked Sox, already lowered as far down as he could without making it impossible for him to work his oar.

"Pirates," Bates whispered, hugging Hairball to his side.

"Drunken sots is who they are," said Cooney, himself standing tall—perhaps taller—at the rudder. He moved not a limb, not a hair, staring around at the onrushing raft and its boisterous inhabitants like a sailor lashed to his mast, daring them by his very stillness and the poise of his stature to try to have a whack at him.

"Hoo-there!" one of the white men called as they skimmed toward us. His upraised pistol appeared larger than his arm from elbow to wrist, and where his teeth should have been gaped a black hole.

"Hoo, yourself!" Cooney answered back, moving slightly to adjust our path.

"Popper! You swimming upstream like salmon with your little babes?"

As though in mental tune with the tree-thick nigger at the helm, their raft went into a turn.

"See who 'tis," the toothless gunman said to his white-skinned partner. "It's that breed Cooney, loony Cooney! What you going to do with those fresh young kids once you get them upriver? Cook 'em and eat 'em like tender dogs?"

He raised his pistol and fired into the air.

"Keep at it, boys," Cooney said through teeth as tightly clenched as a lion's on its prey. "Don't lose the rhythm!"

I faltered a moment, but then caught it again, as did Sox at my opposite, and we churned forward, though slightly off the path of the other raft.

"City boys you got there? Eh, breed Cooney?" The toothless logger leered at us across the space of water which had not widened though we pulled as hard as we could. The power of their night-skinned poleman was such that he flicked their craft from side to side and forward and back as though it were a toy. "P'raps we'd like to be the ones eat the city boys for dinner!" He fired off another shot, making the trees and me and my pals shake as though a great wind had rushed down the narrowing corridor of river shared by our crafts.

"They're playing, ain't they, Jack?" Sox pleaded.

"S-sure," Bates stuttered from where he crouched hugging little Hairball, "Jack's p-pa paid them loggers to play-act with us. Kind of make an adventure, huh, J-jack?"

I glanced up at Cooney, as if expecting some assurance from him. But he kept his eyes straight on our neighbors, and he was wary enough not to blink. If it was acting, then it was better acting than I had ever seen. But inspired by him, I got over my fright. It was almost as though I were tired of living scared, and I tightened my own lip and said, "Boys, I think they're out to get us for real!"

I'd no more said the words when a rush of wind nearly tore away my headdress—and a retort followed immediately after with a monstrous blast from Cooney's rifle which all the while he'd been holding slung along his arm. When I looked over at our rival raft, I saw the tree-thick pole-man holding two pieces of stick upraised to chest height—a good height, too, that was—as though offering the broken instrument to some god who might reach up out of the current and claim the damaged prize. The two white-skinned loggers danced up and down in anger.

"Put down the dog and take the rudder," Cooney broke his silence. And quick, before he knew it, Bates had hold of the stick while the woodsman quickly reloaded his rifle. In a moment he stood again to full height to keep his aim upon the raucous travelers.

Twice now in our trip that rifle of his had spoken to protect us from harm. As we watched the other raft spin lazily out of control and drift toward the near shore behind us, I dreamed of perhaps becoming a great marksman myself one day, like this wonderful man of the woods whom my father, in his wisdom, had sent along as our guide.

"Down!" Cooney said sharply.

We flattened ourselves against the rough wet deck as something whizzed by us and thudded into the water. Once again our shaggy guide answered with his rifle, a thundering blast that nearly turned our craft about in the water. I peeled myself off the deck to peer downstream in time to see the loggers' raft recede into the distance, each of its three crewmen holding at least one hand above his head, as though they were performing some strange and wonderful dance that only rivers brought out in them.

We boys whooped and hollered at our victory, shaking the very timbers of the raft with our merriment.

"What a man he is, huh, Jack?" Cliff patted me on the back as though Cooney himself were my father.

"A very picture of a man," Bates said, as though reciting something he had learned out of a book.

"A very picture," Sox said, not wanting to get his own bid left out of things.

And this same very picture of a man pointed out just then our sorrowful news.

"Stop your yammering, boys, and look to that cheerful little Hairball. One of you lads stuff him under your shirts?"

A howl went up from the four of us, one great shriek of pain.

We doubled back, spending perhaps an hour in search of Cliff's little pup who had become a friend to us all—and we were about to give up when Cooney who had been wading chest deep in the current on the farther shore gave a holler. He found our poor beast tangled amidst the weeds in an eddy beneath a large overhanging rock. We rowed across and picked up man and dripping dog's body and rowed to a place upstream where the shore lay level and got to work digging a doggy grave.

Poor sport, little Hairball lay all limp in the hole we scooped out for him in the rooty earth a few yards into the woods, like a broken doll my brother Harry might have dragged into the trees and left.

"Shall I say some words?" asked Cooney. "I'll say some words," he said in reply to his own question. So choked were we, none of the rest of us could muster much to say.

He coughed and sang something in a language I'd never heard, coughed again and chanted something in what could have been yet another tongue—and then made some passes with his hands, fingers moving lithely, over the top of the hole. Out of his fringed pocket he pulled a little bit of something I couldn't clearly see—too small for a piece of food or leather, too large to be nothing at all, and scattered it from his fingertips above the grave and immediately knelt down and started spreading leaves on top of Hairball. The rest of us knelt and did the same so that in a minute or two we'd covered him completely.

It was a ceremony my grandparents would have been proud of, though as we pushed off upstream again I could hear, in my mind, the complaints my mother might have made.

I looked up at Cooney, who kept his eye on the current, on the shore, on the sky, the clouds, the sun. I fixed mine high up where he paused to fix his—a hunting hawk was circling, circling the near shore upstream, and in the few minutes that I watched, I discovered that as we moved near him he seemed to recede toward the river's source in the big trees on the hills some miles beyond.

We put in to shore and dragged our raft onto the bank. "The Rocks," our map said of this spot, the farthest point upriver that we'd travel. After we'd made our camp just up the slope from the river, I stripped down to my altogether for the first time on the trip and prepared to dive in ahead of my friends from one of the large rocks that lined the shore. I wasn't going to stay behind and rest and put myself in jeopardy of some snake to crawl nearby and kiss me while I slept. Not this time! I rushed to the edge and looked across the trees on the other shore—hoo-coo! hoo-coo! some bird called to me across that airy space beneath which the rustling river twinkled in the sun and flowed deep enough for diving—and then I yelled back at my friends to bring up the rear.

"Your walnuts!" one of the boys shouted at my back as I skidded over the edge and I grabbed for them and twisted about and hit the water—splat!—with the force of a beaver's tail, my hands crossed like fig leaves at the fork of me—and though I protected that part something seemed to spring loose below my ribs where I'd angled into the water.

"You all right, Big Jack?"

Cliff was leading me by the hand back to shore from where I'd drifted, half in darkness half in light in the moments that followed my fall, like some barge in tow come in to Portland harbor.

"Nothing ordinary about this trip, boys," Cooney said, wading out to greet us. He made me lie flat on my back on the surface of the stream until he checked me over with light and careful hands.

"Hurt you?" he asked, touching here and there and here.

The pain had drawn into itself, like those smaller and smaller circles sketched in the noon sky by that hunting bird, and I could feel where like a stone rolling downhill it had stopped and would move no more.

"A little," I said, enjoying the pleasure of taking a breath after his fingers lifted from the place where he last pressed.

"Think you can get up?" I answered him by rising from the water and walking unaided to the shore. I took a few steps downstream and spurted forth in momentary pain a gush of pinkish flow. It frightened me when it happened but the ache and the fear faded. And for the rest of the afternoon, while the boys splashed their time away again, I took my chances against whatever snakes might encircle me or other wild things that could creep upon me while I lay by the waterside. Good Luck—I'd brought the complete and new edition of the long poem about King Arthur and his court by Tennyson that my father, on a trip back East, had brought home for me.

Take me.. And cast me away!

I'd read the part about the gift of Excalibur many times that spring and devised oaths of knighthood-errant for me and my close friends and sang the song sung by Elaine when Lancelot came to her mind.

But of the many parts I read, it came to me to dwell, this day, on the end, on the last tournament and the last days of a time that seemed so distant to me and yet so close that when I read of it I fell into a waking dream. Suppose I died of this wound of mine, I asked myself? Suppose my friends had to place me on the raft and set me down the river to my folks and home?

> *Then murmurr'd Arthur, 'Place me in the barge.'*
> *So to the barge they came. There those three queens*
> *Put forth their hands, and took the King, and wept.*
> *But she that rose the tallest of them all*
> *And fairest laid his head upon her lap,*
> *And loosed the shatter'd casque, and chafed his hands,*
> *And call'd him by his name, complaining loud,*
> *And dropping bitter tears against a brow*
> *Striped with dark blood; for all his face was white*
> *And colorless, and like the whither'd moon*
> *Smote by the fresh beam of the springing east....*

"'Smote by the fresh beam of the springing east....'" I said again, bathing my tongue and lips in the cream of that poetry. My friends climbed out of the water and dressed and went off with Cooney on a hunt for some small meat for supper. That afternoon I read further, and as the heat of the day wore on and the heat of the poetry inspired me to my feet, I roved about our little clearing acting out the parts and saying the lines to my other selves.

> *Then loudly cried the bold Sir Bedivere:*
> *'Ah! my Lord Arthur, whither shall I go?*
> *Where shall I hide my forehead and my eyes?*
> *For now I see the true old times are dead,*
> *When every morning brought a noble chance,*
> *And every chance brought out a noble knight....*

I stuttered as I spoke, my eyes filling up with tears and the very Oregon woods blurring in the sunlight.

> *'But now the whole Round Table is dissolved*
> *Which was an image of the mighty world;*
> *And I, the last, go forth companionless,*
> *And the days darken round me, and the years,*
> *Among new men, strange faces, other minds.'*

And I lay back down upon the ground, holding the book to one side of me so that my last good knight could clearly see my face.

> *'The old order changeth, yielding place to new,*
> *And God fulfills himself in many ways,*
> *Lest one good custom should corrupt the world. . . .'*

And off I sailed with him to that distant place, beyond the beyond, where such heroes as he and I lived on. And I lay the book aside and made up the journey, of Arthur and me, and how the raft that was our barge floated back downriver past the settlements and the towns and the city and into the harbor where the Willamette joined forces with the older, mightier stream and westward, ever westward to Astoria, past river boats and keel boats and fishing boats and steamers, and westward across the current into the great bowl of the Pacific and westward, ever westward until sighted by some slant-eyed fisherman and his crew, who cooed and cawed at one another, they having been born under the shadow of a Great Wall, never having thought of any sight more wonderful, of a royal barge breaking through the mists from the east, and their whole picture of the real and the world getting jumbled up as they told stories to their wives and children upon their return.

Something soft and furry tickled at my ear and I called out "Hairball!" and grabbed for it, and the boys laughed in spite of themselves, dangling the dead rabbit into my nose.

"Up, big Jack," said Cliff. "While you been sleeping we caught us two of these and, what's more, a squirrel."

"We'll cook a stew for when your folks arrive," Bates said, holding up that Indian knife, all sharpened, and preparing for Cooney to instruct him in the dressing of the kill.

"Sounds good to me," I said, jumping up and smartly saluting my friends. My side felt better. "I'll make the fire."

The boys cleaned their prey and, on my fire, under the leathery woodsman's direction, prepared a stew fit for us, if not kings. While it cooked, they took their leisure, reading such things to each other as passages from *Deadwood Dick, the Prince of the Road* and *The Adventures of Buffalo Bill* which they had carried in their packs as I had carried *The Idylls of the King* in mine. And we began reciting sentimental poems and singing certain patriotic songs.

After eating we broke camp, beached the raft for good, and set out through the forest for the Oregon City trail. Here we came upon the blackened lands that Cooney had mentioned earlier, acre after acre of fire-pitched soil in which only the smallest shrubs and tallest grasses had grown back after the inferno that had engulfed trees almost all the way to the western horizon.

"How did it happen?" I asked Cooney as the other boys scouted about amidst the blackened stumps while there was still light enough in the sky to inspect them.

"Lightning perchance," he said. "Or a careless logger with a drunken torch. Or a spark from a logging train. Or the flash from a flint-lock rifle? All natural, all unnatural, it never makes a difference how it starts, the ruin remains the same."

It was here on this blackened field that we would celebrate our time. The fire had come to the edge of the road on the far side of the voided acreage, and after about twenty minutes of treading our way over ash and the new grass that sprouted from it as if between the footprints of some age-old giant that had crushed the land where he had trod, we could make out in the distance the motion of some other creatures like ourselves—a wagon actually, though from afar it might have been a herd of cattle or a whale of the kind that approaches close to the coastal rocks in season—and I was glad because I had grown tired of breathing the ashy air, and was thirsty too, besides.

"Hallooo!" I called.

Hallooo, came the cry across the space.

And I took off across the field, toward the road and the lantern, dangling at the wagon-side, that my father had set up for a signal. "Come on, boys, run for it!" I called back to them, inspiring, I hoped, some heroic scene in them such as the one I conjured up, of me leading troops to victory rather than char-black defeat, or settlers meeting the land, or bathers to the edge of the salt-inspired sea toward which they'd traveled oh-so-many months across a desert that had once itself been a sea.

"There you are," my father said to me when I came into his view. And he waved his arm and with the gesture of a ringmaster or stage-manager or a gardener having just

finished the shaping of a masterly garden of exotic design
bade me notice my entire family seated upon the wagon:
mother and young Harry and Grandmother Green herself,
their faces seeming luminescent almost in the thickening
dark; and Lee Sing seated behind my father smiling the same
smile he'd bestowed upon us when we'd pushed off into the
river the day before.

The other boys came running up and heard my father clap
his hands twice sharply at which sound Lee Sing leaped
down from the trap and struck a flame out of nowhere. As
truly as if he had baked the entire earth, he bowed and
dipped to ignite the candles they had set upon it to celebrate
the country's birthday, rushing from site to site along the
road and into the near places of the barren woods. For the
next few minutes the world flashed and boomed, like the
greatest   battle   or   the   first   best   festival   of   peace
and   light
       drifted
   down
upon us   LIGHT
almost to anoint us   but never to
            burn LIGHT
          light light light light light
          light light light light
        light light light
        light light
      light light light light
    light light LIGHT   light
    light light light   light
            LIGHT
   when a boy looked up to see a Chalice in the sky.

Part Two

RECOLLECTIONS
OF A LONG-LOST ALBUM

Commencement

Up I bob out of the water and bark a command at Seeger then sling him a pass that he bobbles just long enough for an opposing player to snatch it from his slippery hands. As he shouts in disgust, I surge after the thief, but he has already heaved the stolen ball down pool. Suddenly I'm yanked into a knot by a terrible cramp in my belly, and I sink like the sun into the Pacific.

Later, I describe for Seeger the images that pass before my eyes as I go down: the ocean's surge, green banks of the Willamette, our doctor's furrowed brow as he bends over my stomach, Grandma's tiny face drying up like a peach in the sun.

"Phantasmagorical!" Seeger exclaims. He never speaks without exclaiming. "If I could just nearly die and bring back such beautiful sights myself!"

"I'd never felt that way before," I explained. "As though no time had passed. I jumped into the river back home, and when I came up I was in the pool in the middle of the polo match. Though it had been months."

"Don't pass off your lyric mentality as philosophy," comes from the mouth of bespectacled Walter Lippmann—*Voltaire Leapman* we call him. He lives down the hall, our middle-aged boy in residence, the voice of reason, an emblem of all that we do not wish to become.

Seeger peers down at me where I'm stretched out on the elegant sofa that sometimes serves as a bed for guests who come to drink and stay to sleep it off.

"Jack," he says, "Hang on to your spontaneity! That's what makes poetry!"

"Chaos is spontaneous too," Lippmann offers, not even looking up from the pages that he turns. "Is chaos poetry? Now that you've stepped out from among the tall trees and come East, Reed, you'll discover that we use analysis here—"

"No!" shouts Seeger, swooping down on the seated Lippmann like a bear charging a woodsman caught unawares. He sweeps up the book—if only he stole passes in the pool with as much alacrity—and holds it up to the window.

"Hey!" Lippmann protests, sitting upright, annoyed.

"To hell with it!" Seeger forces up the sash and holds the book out over the Yard.

"Reed?" Lippmann appeals to me.

"Oh, Christ, Seeger, give him the book."

Seeger pretends he doesn't hear me.

"What kind of writer do you want to be, Reed?" Lippmann speaks in even tones, as though his history is not fluttering in the breeze above the pavement, "a poet like Swinburne or a scribbler like Thucydides?"

"I don't know," I say, feeling foolish because my honesty gets me into such trouble. "I haven't read either."

Seeger moans so terribly that you'd think he has just been shot in the back. He stumbles back from the window and returns the book as though he is giving up the ghost.

So I begin this notebook/album, somewhere west of analysis, somewhere east of beauty.

First Autumn in Cambridge

And suddenly, without any more warning than the sight of several townies in the square glancing up at the darkening sky to the west, the temperature drops thirty degrees overnight. You think it is merely evening coming on. The locals detect the end of Indian Summer. I should return to the room where my friends have already settled down with their books or their verses, but instead I wander, a small knot of sorrow nestled in my gut.

I find myself looking in through the window of a bookstore at a new volume of O. Henry.

"He twists life," a voice says behind me. I turn to see a sparsely bearded gentleman my father's age or older dressed in an evening coat and glistening top hat.

"Sir?"

"O. Henry. He twists life at the end, turns the raw stuff into little bon-bons."

"Actually, I haven't read him, sir. Is he good?"

"Is he?" The man toys with his mustache, as though waiting for me to tell him more.

So I plunge ahead, since he seems friendly enough. I'm nearly a head taller than he is and can knock him down if he tries for my wallet (though it's empty). "I'm reading for my courses and trying to catch up with Thucydides and Swinburne at the same time."

"Quite a pair they make," the bearded man says. "But don't you read any American authors? such as...." He points to a book by Twain. "Or this?" Now he nods toward a volume called *The Wings of the Dove*. "He's got a rather thick style. I suppose we ought to prefer the other, don't you think? It's more transparently native."

"I do native things. I've traveled on a raft up the Willamette."

"Where is that river?" the man asks, "Idaho? Montana?" He pronounces the names of these states as though they lay in India or south of the Amazon.

"Oregon, sir."

"Oregon!" He gives home the same intonation he gave the other places. "I've been there once, a wild and woolly place."

"Yes, sir," I smile, "and a great place."

He nods in return. "But you're here now. Freshman?"

"Yes, sir. Are you an instructor?"

"Lord, no!" The man coughs gently into his sleeve. "I'm what you might call the...uh...village philosopher. I lecture here and about from time to time."

As we talk, the lights go out in the bookstore. A man departs, shutting and locking the door behind him. James and Twain rest together in the dark window. I feel suddenly naked, talking to a gent with a voice such as this without having read Thucydides all the way through and only a few of Swinburne's verses. He suggests that I dine with him. Does he want more than my wallet?

My stomach churns. My solitude burns. I'm ready for whatever life offers me, including a delicious dinner. Even last year at Morristown Prep, I'd never felt as homesick as this.

"Is the life of a freshman still as harried as it was in my day?" the man asks as we put the Square behind us.

"Harried, sir?" I reply. "Well, speaking personally, I've had a hard time settling down." Images of life on Stout Street flash through my mind as though I were drowning while walking along the darkening, tree-lined road. "My school back home wasn't much. And my prep school last year in Morristown wasn't all that hard to excel in."

"Morristown?" He speaks with interest, as though each new foreign bit of knowledge might provide a clue to a puzzle. Is he a detective of some kind? I wonder.

"In New Jersey, sir. Dreary place. Tiny stunted trees compared to home. And beaches without real waves. I'd been East once before to visit my father's family in New York State—in Batavia, a little farm town near Buffalo, funny place, no buffalo in sight, my little brother and I were all ready to hunt them if we found them...." I catch my breath, feeling more words welling up in me than I've used in weeks. "We spent a few days in Washington, and I swam in the Potomac while my father talked with some people in the government."

"Ahah!"

I miss his point. "Swimming is my favorite sport. I have a bad left kidney, why, they can't say, but my grandmother's hawthorn tea fixes it up as good as any modern medicine. You know hawthorn's a member of the rose family, and it fixed me up so I was back in the river in no time, and I swam in the Pacific and in the Potomac when we visited there. That's when we looked up my prep school, Papa wanting me to go to Harvard, you see, and my school at home...."

We pass houses and churches, our feet clopping on the pavement like hooves. I pull up my coat collar against the growing chill, wondering how much farther we have to walk when the man points down a side street and nods me in that direction.

"Your father's in the government then?"

"He just recently was appointed U.S. Marshal in Portland."

"Impressive," the man says with another nod, pleasing me no end.

"I think so." I swallow, hurry onward. "Grandma had her trees, or used to, you see."

"Trees?"

"Trees. They belonged to her father, my great-grandfather, he owned large tracts of forest, then they sold most of it off, and the men who bought it began to cut it all down posthaste without any regard to what was happening to the drainage..."

"Drainage!" the man declares, as though having just tasted a new dessert. "Go on!"

I talk to him of forests and timber barons, Papa's beliefs, Grandma's gardens, Mama's father's water system, my little brother Harry, the plays we put on together in the attic in Cedar Hill, moving to Stout Street after Papa's appointment. My life tumbles out of my mouth, and I don't stop talking until after I enter a large house at the end of the street, hand my hat to the maid, sit down at the dining room table, and spoon soup to my lips.

Ah, my appetite's still there! I bury my sadness under a plateful of meat and potatoes. After dinner we retire to a long, deep comfortable room lined with thousands of books where, under the influence of Cuban cigars and French brandy, we talk about truth, the world, cabbages, and kings. I don't know what makes me dizzier, the ideas that we puff out like smoke or the smoke itself.

Midnight finds us on the steps of the house, finishing a discussion of comic operas. He confesses to a fondness for Eddie Foy and Richard Carle, both of whom I think are real swagger types. We don't know each others' names, but this upstanding person has made me feel much less an orphan. He pats me on the shoulder in good fellowship and bids me a hearty goodnight. I make my farewell.

Returning through the dark streets to the dormitory, I feel my longing for home renewed with triple force. The cigar smoke! Laughter! My confessions about life and time! The wind whirrs through the branches above me, picks a few choice yellow and vermillion leaves and deposits them on my shoulder. The season's changing: home is a place too far away to run to.

Balls

I lose myself. High-ceilinged dance halls attract my gaze. By Christmas, have sipped tea under several heavenly cupolas, but I declare that in a mansion on Commonwealth Avenue exists the finest. The young lady at my elbow. Her name is Lillian Lovell—listen to her laugh!—icicles turn to gushets in bright winter sunlight!—and she comes from an old and golden family. Her eyes sparkle and the lace at her throat chokes my breathing. After my third cup of punch, one of my house chums nods toward the door. It's out into the snow to go slumming at the usual places. But I linger longer at the lacy throat of this old familied young ivory. Her face must be polished each morning at nine. She thinks I'm a bumpkin from the woolly west. And it's true that I have never seen the likes of her before.

Christmas, '06

Already? Christ! My first trip to Manhattan, the Hudson flows whiskey. Before I pass out, I wire greetings home, awake to find that I've vomited on a two-hundred-year-old rug—my host's voice dimly chanting in the background: years, measurements, value. Can't wait for the new term to begin.

Sport

Out of the pool and into entrepreneurship. I haven't finished reading Greek history or English poetry, but spring finds me discovering how to try to get ahead.

Management

Carl Binger, a Jew who never made the water-polo team, runs up to me in the Yard.

"I've done it, Jack, I've done it. Give me another batch of paper and I'll sign up ten more!"

We are selling subscriptions for the varsity crew and at day's end find ourselves well along the way toward gathering enough to make me assistant manager. Bing has been a great help to me. By six, I am ready to treat him to a big dinner at the Cellar.

"Better yet, let's go to town."

"Champagne for this enterprising young fellow and me," I order.

The waiter doesn't blink. He is accustomed to all this fancy food and wine. Not me. Bing hails from Manhattan. He wants to study medicine. He tells me the story of his father's pact with the New York Fire Department.

"They come right into his factory with their hands sticking out in front of them like their bones had grown that way. And so he slaps a big bill into each palm and they leave. About a month later, they show up at another of his factories and do the same thing. For a while, all's quiet. Then comes another delegation." He pauses, sips from his champagne glass. "By the way, here's to your victory."

"I'll drink to that. What happened next?"

"He gives another contribution to the 'Firemen's Ball.' And they leave. Again, it's quiet. For a week. And then—the fire."

"That must have been a real terrible time," I venture. I'm a bit dizzy with our triumph, and my brain seems steeped in the fizzy stuff.

"Picture the flames leaping from the factory roof to the night sky."

"I'm picturing it." I thoroughly enjoy the way Bing speaks. His eastern rhythms intrigue me. When I listen to him, I'm halfway to Europe.

"Hear the shouts of the worried workers? Will the Fire Department ladders reach their perch on the window ledges? Will the mother who secretly brought her nursing infant to work that day find a way out with her baby? Will the foreman save the collection of special dresses that will sell the whole shop's output for the next year?

"No. The firemen arrive late and the factory burns to the ground. Two workers go up in smoke with it, one of them the mother of the little baby. The newspapers go wild! Filthy lie-mongers, all of a sudden they have such a sad and wonderful story to tell! Oh, my father gave them all the details. How he had the Fire Department called and how they were all so drunk they couldn't get their ladders there on time. And how he and my uncles, his partners, rushed in and out of the building trying to help the workers down the stairs, until finally the smoke got so thick they couldn't go in anymore. And how the heroic foreman saved the baby and the next year's styles."

"Two women were killed?"

"It could have been much worse. But with the money from the insurance from the building, my father makes a payment to their families. And he decides he'll manufacture baby clothes in the new building in honor of the orphaned child. That's how he pays my tuition. He wants me to become a doctor. He wants me to help my fellow man."

"My father helps fellow trees."

Bing looks at me, nearly cross-eyed in curiosity.

"Fire's your father's friend," I say. "It's my father's enemy."

"It takes all kinds," says Bing, nodding furiously. "Doesn't it, Jack?"

"In the forests out West," I say, feeling the words heating up my tongue, "we fight fire with fire."

"So it takes all kinds, you see, Jack, doesn't it?"

"Fighting fire pays my tuition."

"I didn't know this, Jack." Bing's eyes bulge out like a stage nigger's. "Is your father a fire chief? Have I insulted him? I'm very very sorry."

"He's a man," I say. "A man of the forests, a crude, rude rough-and-tumble marshal from the old west."

Bing laughs uncomfortably. "He sounds different from my father—a lot different."

"He's different from all the rest of them."

"You admire him a lot?"

"I love him!" I wipe my eyes with my fist.

Bing becomes embarrassed at my show of emotion when all the while I thought that he was the more feeling of the two of us, him being the Jew. He calls for more to drink.

"Tomorrow," he toasts, "tomorrow, Jack, you enter the ranks of the saintly few, the managers!"

The next morning I wake with my head all awhirl. I dress painfully and make my way slowly to the crew office. The subscription list burns a hole in my hand.

The air in the Yard seems to explode. The sound of my breathing makes my brain ache. I stumble onward, daunted somewhat by the effect of the victory celebration. If this is victory, never show me defeat!

"You're Reed?" asks the bored young fellow in the office. The look on his face has always been in fashion in these parts. He's wearing a green suit, the latest thing, and the first straw boater of the season. What is the difference between this fellow and me? We both part our hair in the middle and drink bad gin. He doesn't give me his name until I ask.

"Ray Belmont." That's all he says.

The manager strides in. "Belmont, how do you?" He sticks out a hand toward my green-suited rival for manager, one of New York City's richest college lads. They confer a moment, now and then recognizing my presence by a sharp and intelligently placed glance. A subdued laugh or two punctuates their conversation's end, and the manager bids Belmont farewell. He then turns to me and in a voice that turns my bowels to ice says, "And what do we have here?"

Prose

I pass all my courses though I spend the last month of the term in my room reading and writing.

Strangely quiet it was beneath the great trees, a dusky, drowsy quiet, with hushed noises stealing about in the dark, and the subtle swish of passing dreams...

Seeger has been slipping copies of his verses under my bedsheets all year, so I hand my story to him, pretending to use the bathroom while on the other side of the door he reads, snorts, exclaims, yowls. After a long while, silence. I wait a few seconds more and then steal outside. The room is littered with shreds of paper, as though my story has snowed on the place. Seeger has fled.

I throw open the hall door and race after him.

"You bastard!" I shout down the stairwell.

"It was awful!" he shouts back, slamming the front door behind him.

Back in the room I sit on the floor, pick up a piece of a torn page.

> *Far off somewhere...*

And another.

> *...a few creepers reared their broken ends through a tangle of vines—evidently very ancient ruins.*

He hasn't done a very good job. I pick up a few more pieces and try to fit them together. I might just as well try to put my year back together again.

Summer, '07

A girl whose name I won't be able to remember ten years from now; a night whose sky might have been the one that convinced the Ionian philosopher that fierce fire burned behind the pinpricks in heaven. I walk the beach at Astoria, bare feet grabbing at the sand, hand in hand with the future, lost in thoughts of the past. Wave upon wave breaks the silence that hangs between me and Miss Mysteriously Lost. Will we kiss? Won't we? Will we kiss? Won't we? No Hamlet me! I take her in my arms, but it is by then September, and she fades like the fog into the tidal flux of autumn.

As I board the train, I feel a sharp pang of remorse. Papa tips his hat in farewell, Mama weeps into her handkerchief. I never did the talking to my father that I wanted to do. The train departs, carrying me eastward across the Plains. And I imagine Lippmann tossing aside yet another volume, his hundredth of the summer. And Seeger has just added the final period to his latest sonnet. The train whistle moans. Despite the humid clinging air of buffalo territory in autumn, I shiver with despair. Once I crossed these flatlands shooting imaginary buffalo with an imaginary rifle. Yippee! Whoopee! Crack-em Jack, best shot in the Badlands! Load the darned rifle, Harry, or the beasts will get away! Now I swoon, Swinburnedly mooning after time well lost, thankful that I have days yet to go before I have to meet my school friends again. As America passes westward beneath the wheels of the train, I prepare my face for autumn.

Society

In sophomore year, the Institute of 1770 selects one hundred men from the class, presumably fit social material, who thereafter regard themselves as the socially elect. The waiting clubs, which are final to one another (that is to say, a man can belong only to one waiting club) elect a few more, and further refine from the original hundred. This group, of what is supposed to be the best men in the class, composes the material with which the final clubs fill their ranks in the junior and senior years.

But one of us, Seeger, I think, says we select our own society from here on in.

The Boston Globe

TENDER-MINDED OR TOUGH-MINDED WHICH MAN SHALL YOU BE?

Local Philosopher Asks Hard Questions
of Audience at Lowell Institute Lectures

Cambridge, Nov. 11, 1907. Is your mental type that of the tough-minded or the tender-minded school? No one shifted his seat from one side of the hall to the other when local philosopher William James put this question to his audience last night at the first of a series of lectures at the Lowell Institute on the "pragmatic movement" in philosophy. But there was a nearly audible shifting of mental chairs as he painted the portraits of these two types of thinking, as distinct from each other as Bostonian tourists from Rocky Mountain toughs. Here is the list of traits which separate the two types as we received them from Professor James himself after the Lecture:

The Tender-Minded	**The Tough-Minded**
Rationalistic (follower of "principles")	Empiricist (follower of "facts")
Intellectualistic	Sensationalistic
Idealistic	Materialistic
Optimistic	Pessimistic
Religious	Irreligious
Free-Willist	Fatalistic
Monistic	Pluralistic
Dogmatic	Sceptical

"I know that man," I say to Lippmann after the lecture. "He invited me to his house for dinner last year."

"Keep personalities out of your mind," he says. "Consider the ideas only. Personalities muddy the issues."

"Damn, personalities may *be* the issues," I say remembering how I felt that night last autumn. I'm stronger now, more independent. I worry less tonight that my friends will discover the fear that lurks in the heart of me. I read so much in so short a time that this term I scarcely find the room to fret and brood about my shortcomings. And often the face I put on for society—sometimes Galahad, sometimes Percival, tender and tough minded in one—not only saves the day but *is* the day.

Christmas, '07

Whirl-a-gig city! I'm learning to appreciate New York as well as love her! The country's all flat, various—she with her geometric designs, her arches within circles, and avenues leading south and north to infinity! Home is as young and frivolous as I am: this island's a mature woman, leading me onward, ever on!

Poetry

> *The spring is coming. God! Must we endure*
> *Another flood of that impassioned verse*
> *That burbles from the Monthly so demure,*
> *Or Advocate, so infinitely worse?*
> *Must we sit silent under Lampy's slams*
> *About uncharted oceans in the Yard,*
> *And must we flunk again those damned exams*
> *And slyly dodge the office postal card?*

(The poet is overcome and forcibly removed)

I'm a published writer!

But secretly, my verse makes me sick! I seek out the one doctor on campus people say can help the patient effect his own cure. Professor Copeland—Copey.

I have to stop my knees from quaking as I knock on the door of his apartment.

"Come in if you dare!"

I enter to find him dressed in a morning coat while eating breakfast at his writing table.

"Don't tell me who you are," he says without looking up. "I know who you are. You are a stranger. Only someone I don't know would come here at this hour. Therefore you are someone I don't know, and don't want to know. Good day."

"Please, sir," I say, "my name is Jack—"

"Reed!" Now he stares at me over the brim of his bowl of unidentifiable liquid. "You sent me that ludicrously punctuated note asking me to give you a place in my class. Goodbye."

"Sir! D-does that mean . . . ." My voice fades away. This little man turns me to powder.

"Out!" He looks down at his bowl. I don't know what to do but leave. Then comes a knock at the door.

"Hush now," he whispers in a hiss like a snake's.

Again the knock.

He waggles his spoon, cautioning me to keep silent.

Again the knock. Then, silence.

"I didn't know you could keep quiet for that long a time," he says. "I heard you had one of the biggest mouths in the Yard."

"Sir, I don't know what you've heard," I plead, "but I do want to take your course."

"How can I admit you? You're a troublemaker, talented, but a rowdy nonetheless. Isn't it true that you pasted your calling card on every tombstone in Mt. Auburn Cemetery?"

"S-sir—"

"Is it true?"

"Yes, sir."

"Including the grave of the History Chairman's grandmother?"

"I d-didn't know th-that, sir . . . ."

"And that you attended a Quaker prayer meeting in your water polo costume?"

"In my b-bath robe, yes, sir."

"And that you were apprehended on the Common by the Boston constabulary while urinating at the base of the Saint-Gaudens bronze to the Union dead?"

I feebly nod.

"And that you placed a sheep's head—God knows where you found one—on your English instructor's desk with an anonymous note attached telling him to 'ram it, ecetera'?"

His face is contorted with cruelty. I feel like weeping. I start for the door.

"Wait. And is it true that you poured honey down the dress of the sister of the president of Hasty Pudding while several dozen of the city's finest citizens watched in horror?"

I feel a cold wind blowing in from the hall, as though it flows directly from the Charles to the room.

"Please, sir, I promise I won't cut up. I promise, sir."

"Beg."

"I beg you, sir."

"You Western lout, this is your life, not just some rum college prank. Beg."

"I beg you, sir. I won't make any trouble. And I'll work very hard sir, I write well, sir—"

"I've read your writing in the *Monthly*, Reed. It's your living that concerns me at the moment. Go away. I'll send you a note about whether or not you've been admitted."

I tell Seeger and he assures me about the course. But he also warns me to keep my word. And sure enough the note arrives on the back of one of C's cards: "You may attend the class. I expect a great deal of you. Don't disappoint me."

A Translation from Horace

Now, comrades, drink and let us dance
And tread the earth with joyous feet
Come deck the couches of the gods
With Salian dainties, as is mete
Quaff deep. . . .

Prose

I pass all of my courses though I spend the last month of the term in my room reading and writing. This year I show the pages to no one, and tear them up myself.

Summer, '08

Mornings in Papa's office in the Federal Courthouse. I help him draft briefs about the theft of timber rights, and sift through documents pertaining to the ownership of trees, water, and certain minerals on Indian lands to the south and east. Once a week we have lunch with the judges and prosecutors. There is a fog bank of cigar smoke, and a lot of beer. After one of these meals, Papa seems strangely silent. On the walk back through the courthouse square, he slumps forward, tugs at his waistcoat.

"Papa?"

"It's a tough battle, son," he says, forcing a smile.

"What's that?" I know no battle here, only the canopy of lovely green trees, cool summer sunlight, our full bellies, the good company.

"All of it," he says, then straightens up, and picks up the pace.

Several weeks go by. Our apartment hums with the preparations for my brother Harry's departure along with me to begin his freshman year. A few blocks away at Cedar Hill, Grandma, shrunken like an old cricket, sits in her wicker chair amidst her roses while my Uncle Raymond, returned from the wars, hobbles about on a cane, keeping his mongrel dog, souvenir from the Philippines, from digging up the flowers. Mama seems to spend most of her time over at our apartment directing Lee Sing with the packing. Summer burns off like the morning fog.

Then one night after I've settled into bed with a copy of Byron (while Harry, utterly changed from the babe I once knew, is out on yet one more end-of-high-school celebration with friends), Papa appears in the doorway.

"Can I come in?"

"Sure, Papa, will you tuck me in?"

We laugh together.

"It hasn't been that long ago." He sits on the edge of the bed, and I resettle myself in response to his weight.

"Studying?" I show him the spine of the volume.

He nods approvingly.

"Are we going to see a book of poems by Jack Reed one of these days?"

This makes me blush.

"Poetry comes easy for me, Papa. Like swimming. You just dive in and start kicking."

"I wish I could face my own work with as much enthusiasm," Papa says.

"That's what's been on your mind?"

"You've noticed?"

"Not a joke out of you in three or four weeks. I might have noticed."

"It's hard to laugh when you see your friends turning into your enemies and your enemies turning into your friends."

"Your friends in the Club, you mean?"

"Yes. They've asked me to resign. Seems they got wind of the fact that we're going to try for an indictment of two members in good standing."

"Good for you, Papa."

"Good and bad, son. That rough-rider in Washington, the fellow who shook the Spanish tree and took a bite out of the Cuban apple? I received a letter from him commending me on my good work as marshal."

"I'm proud of you, Papa." I picture myself parading about the Yard with a letter from the President.

He shakes his head distractedly. "I must be doing something wrong."

"Could it be T.R. has changed his mind about the world, Papa?"

"I doubt it. He'd much sooner change the world. But then..." He looks tired, as though he should sleep, not I. I close my book, sit up, touch his shoulder.

"Now I know what you meant a while back when you told me what a tough battle you were fighting."

"Yes, like the canal down in Panama we're trying to dig. They blast one day, and the mud slides down into the ditch and fills it up again the next."

"They're making progress, Papa."

"But at what cost, Jack?" He suddenly sags forward and covers his face with his hands.

"Papa?" I reach out to him.

"Just tired, son, is all." He doesn't uncover his face. I sit up, encircle his shoulders with my arms.

"Which is your favorite over all the rest?" he asks.

"Favorite what?"

"Byron," he says. "Read it to me." He uncovers his face, smiles, sits back, and props himself against the wall. The air is thick with the cries of bandits, the clink of sabres, and the snap-snap-snap of pistols when Harry returns home for the night.

Society

The selection of a properly qualified father and mother is an operation which demands a tact and finesse seldom possessed by children as young as Harvard men. Punctuation too is important. Hyphens are of immense value—remember that anyone will always be glad to lend money to an Endicott-Sears-Cabot, a Wendell-Wendell, or a Trumbull-Peabody...If the child is too late to corral a Back Bay Brahmin for a progenitor, let him seize upon a self-made man who has made a good job of it. Money will finally land anyone among the Captains of Society.

I Decide to Get Tough-Minded

"On the one hand, you talk about making a better life for the millions—you take a utilitarian line. On the other, you smile broadly when you're in the company of the boys who will become the men who rob the millions. You cheer them on. You belong to the Cosmo, you're in Dramatic and

President of Western. But when I invite you to our Socialist club, you make excuses about your time. How do you account for that?"

"Are you calling me a hypocrite, Lippmann? Because if you are, I'm going to—"

"You're not a hypocrite, Reed, you're simply confused."

"Lippmann, take a skate up a wall! Your problem is you don't get any of life's juices, all you get is the bone, dry bone. What I do with my spare time is to write, write, write! And that's what feels good for me and that's what is good for me."

"Jack, you won't have much of anything to write about for very long if you have no thoughtful basis to your activity."

"Oh, *Leapman*, were you sent by the Gods to plague me? I already have one conscience and that's quite sufficient for a Western lad like me."

"Reed. I like you. I do indeed. It's just that you might—"

"Halt! Hold the presses! The man expresseth an emotion! He likes me! He LIKES me! DID YOU HEAR THAT? GENTLEMEN, THE MAN FEELS. PRICK HIM; DOES HE NOT BLEED?"

"For Christ's sake, Reed, sit down."

"AS POET LARIAT AND PRESIDENT OF THE WESTERN CLUB, I TAKE GREAT PLEASURE IN INTRODUCING TO YOU, FRIENDS AND FELLOW COWHUNKS, THE NEXT PRESIDENT OF THE UNITED STATES, MISTER VOLTAIRE LEAPMAN!"

"Reed, sit the hell down, you're spilling beer all over us!"

Mills

A disciplinary problem. We're exiled for the rest of the term to Lexington. Night after night I endite the dark away.

A note from Lippmann arrives saying that a few gents from the Socialist Club plan a trip to inspect the textile mills at Lawrence. I sign on.

The drive begins rather pleasantly. We talk about the world situation, the problems in Spain, Cuba's quietudes, T.R.'s strength as compared to Taft. Lippmann expresses his admiration for Roosevelt's manipulation of the smaller nations.

"He's a master," he declares, never looking at us while he speaks. He appears to be counting the trees alongside the road, but I think he wants us to believe that he has become a visionary of some sort or other.

"And how is your father's little crusade against the timber barons?" he asks. "I hear he may have gone too far against certain influential members of his own party."

I hadn't heard this news he asks about, and to hide my ignorance I protest that the reports are quite false. Papa has recently written to tell me that he is thinking of running for office with the support of his party. Shouldn't that be proof enough, I assert, that the party majority supports his crusade against the timber interests.

"You don't put a couple of mayors and a United States Senator behind bars, Reed, without making a few enemies," Lippmann says.

Is that what he's done? I say to myself. My modest Papa, why didn't you tell me? I leap out to him in my heart as we rumble along the roadway through the Massachusetts night.

Lippmann suddenly pretends he's bored, counts more trees. Then he begins nimbly discoursing again on the necessity for socialist legislation. We're nearly in Lawrence. The driver joins in on the subject of the working conditions at the mills. The picture he paints is that of a cross between a medieval dungeon and the inside of a locomotive. The filth, the bad air, harsh orders given by foreman, no time for bodily necessities, the low pay, the long hours . . . .

"How did you find out about all this?" I ask, "is your father a worker there?"

Leapman looks around at me, a ferret-like smile on his round little face: "His father owns the mill," he says, obviously pleased at my own surprised expression.

Prose

I spend the last part of the stay in Lexington writing essays. When asked, I tell friends that I'm working on a novel and a book of poems, a play, and an operetta. The cat in our boarding house gives birth to a litter in the shelf underneath the cash drawer. I try a description of that event, but it doesn't turn out well.

"You want to make them see," Copey says when we gather for a group discussion of our writing. "Not make them see-sick!"

"Above all else not that!" Seeger exclaims.

Bob Hallowell, an artist friend, nods his head gravely. "Too much blood, not enough of the animal's emotions."

Dour Tom Eliot at the edge of the group murmurs something about parody.

Home Again

Spring yields to summer, the Charles flows into the Willamette. Once again, I seem to splash about in one stream, surface in another. Cloudy mornings; afternoons muggy, faint sunlight. Bates, just up from the university in Eugene, wants to hike. Seven days down the coast we go, seven days back. Every night under the high ocean sky we strip and strut naked, new pagans, braving the surf with the benefit of our fabulous futures only! Star-seekers to the bottoms of our souls!

But it's not all idyll worship for me this time. Papa has become a figure in town. One morning as we walk down to the courthouse, some men greet us with respect but coldness, others in sycophantic tones that I have heard freshmen use in the Yard when addressing older classmen. I want to hurry along, but Papa does not break his even pace, nodding to the right and left as the occasion demands, balancing himself like a tightrope dancer with the cedar walking stick he has carved with his own knife.

I keep up with him, and shoulder to shoulder we approach the courthouse steps.

"Marshal!"

We turn to see a swarthy fellow in a cowpuncher's outfit huffing and puffing his way after us. Papa climbs.

"Marshal Reed! You forgot this!" the man calls out. Again Papa ignores him.

"Papa?"

"Ignore him, Jack."

A few men in tall hats and long coats regard us coolly as we mount the stairs. A policeman walks down as if to meet us and when I see his eyes fixed on someone behind us I turn and look.

"Marshal, you forgot this here little envelope Mr.—" (and here he names on the biggest of the lumber company bosses, one whose trial is only a few months away) "—wanted you to take along with you from your breakfast meeting."

The policeman moves past us down the steps.

"Awright, cowboy, that's enough of that!" He speaks in a tired voice as though he's been through all this many times before.

Papa releases breath I was unaware he held in.

"I hate this part of it," he says with teeth clenched.

"It sure is harder work than my history class," I say, trying to cheer him a bit.

"Marshal!" The cowboy breaks away from the policeman, charging up the steps with alacrity his bulk would seem to deny.

"Sir!" Papa shouts.

"Your cash!" the man shouts.

"Away!" Papa declares, raising his walking stick and shoving it in a single smooth motion against the man's chest.

I'm trembling. Papa's trembling! The rest of the day becomes a blur. Papa feels ill, returns home early. The doctor calls later that night. By morning, Papa is ready to return to Court again. I've written this down. Summer ends.

Autumn in Cambridge

Freshmen parade through the Yard. Their attempts to appear calm and knowledgeable merely emphasize their nervous postures and unnatural movements. They recall to me the impertinence of my own early start: stacks of books, hundreds of verses, reams of essays, examinations, nights of drunkenness; naiveté, sophomores, junioritis ad infinitum trail behind me. Now I sit contemplatively with fellow seniors on the steps of the library enjoying my fourth Indian summer.

Long hours in the library, short days to live between. Time zones mingle in my mind: the first year's solitude, the second year's climbing; my palpable achievements ("I'm published! I'm published!"); this year, who knows? Each stage punctuated by a train trip west and then east. By a pretty new face whose hands seemed too cold for her heart's expressiveness. I've worn overalls; I've worn soup and fish; composed poetry; written papers for the richest boy in the class (to earn him a believable pass but no more); I've leapt into the gap between what is and what ought to be. Socialite or socialist, that is the question. Whether 'tis nobler...

April

Bird-notes in a gust of rain
Silver trumpets shivering
Spring's steel armament again—
Hear the world's blood mount and sing
Sweetly on the flowery plain!

April!
Withers all the grass and dies,
Here the flowers dull and fade—
How shall cities know her guise?
See this new-met man and maid
Tremble at each other's eyes!

Midnight Ride

"Do gentlemen do this sort of thing?" I ask Bob Hallowell as he turns the car off the Lexington road and slows down to survey the landscape.

"Gentlemen don't do this sort of thing in town," He suggests. "And what the hell do you know about what gentlemen do, you lumberjack bastard?"

"Jus' cause you're drunk doesn't mean you can insult me! You'll have my challenge!"

"Dare you!"

"Stop the car!"

"I can't, I'll never get it started again."

A wave of remorse breaks over me. I fall back against the seat. Bobby slows the vehicle to a crawl. Outside, a few farm houses glimmer in the nightwind. Be more tough-minded, not tender. It has to happen sometime, I tell myself, it might as well be tonight. It just couldn't work with Lillian who wears steel corsets. Oh, Byron, stand me in this hour in good stead! How can I graduate a virgin?

"It's over there!" yells Bobby. "By the lights!"

"There's actually a red light hanging out there?"

I perk up again, overcoming my hesitancy.

"There sure as hell is," says Bobby, turning sharply up a dirt road to the right. A small row of yellowish, reddish lanterns sit atop a fence. Beyond them lies a flat patch of snow-dusted corn field and a farmhouse, a gray shape against the darkness.

"I can't say I'm not scared," I tell him. "But I can't say I'm not amused either. There's everything but a dollar sign painted on the side of the barn."

"That's love in America for you, Jack. You pay cash on the barrelhead."

"Maidenhead," I correct him.

"If that's what you're looking for, don't go any farther," says a familiar voice, a fellow from the football squad who is also a member of the Institute. We meet him, and a friend from his club, in the large front room of the farmhouse. I repeat my joke nervously while waiting for the husky Portuguese woman in the flouncy robe to return from another room.

"How dee-do, fellesh," she crows. "Looks like all Harvard Square has tumbled in tonight." Four young girls follow after her like chicks behind a hen.

"Ladies, meet the fellesh."

Bobby steps forward and bows, as though this were a church social. I hang back, hands crushed into my pockets, fussing with my fingernails. One of the four girls looks at me as though we've met before. This of course turns out to be untrue, but by the time I admit this to myself, it is too late.

She is slender, with wispy curls of dull brown hair that caress her neck and a complexion whiter than I imagined on a Portuguese girl. In her plain brown bathrobe she looks quite forlorn, as though she has just been awakened from a sleep she had been coveting all day. We repair to a small bedroom in the back of the house. I sit uncomfortably on the narrow bed. She undresses as quickly as a small boy at the riverside on a hot summer's afternoon. Her breasts are pendulous, but her hips are slender.

"You want a dance?" She raises her arms, clasps her hands behind her head, and moves her feet without wiggling her hips. Her voice is flat, unappealing. I attempt to picture Lillian ungirdled, but all I can think of, as we proceed, is the cat giving birth beneath the cash drawer in my old Lexington boarding house.

The walls of the farmhouse are as thin as spring ice. The football player shouts exuberantly, as though he's scored a goal.

The girl and I dress in silence.

"How'd you like her?" Bobby asks me on our way out the door. His face is flushed and I presume mine is as well.

"I didn't get to know her well enough to know whether I like her or not," I say. "But I liked me pretty well through it all, and that was the main thing I was worried about."

"Did you think you'd be...reluctant?"

"Bobby, you have such a fine sense of it all. That's exactly what I feared."

"Sure, I did too, or I couldn't have thought of it, Jack." His face turns a deeper shade of red. I feel a sudden fraternal bond with him. But on the ride back to school I remember that Lippmann has probably read an entire book in the time that it has taken me to lose my virginity. And I'm suddenly very sad.

Politics

I meet the same fellows again the next day in the Yard. At first they want to drink beer and again compare the anatomies of the girls. But after an hour or so, one of them suggests to us that we ought to attend a meeting of the fellows who are making up the slate for senior officers. After some disappointing years, I feel truly a part of things, being in on the decision of who'll do the honors at commencement.

"Good night, fellesh," I say as we leave them on the Square. Bobby can't afford to live on Mt. Auburn Street where a number of us from our class have taken up lodgings. He tells me that, while he himself is not involved, he's heard that some of the boys who remained in the Yard are going to put up a slate of candidates to challenge our ticket.

"If I run with Mt. Auburn Street, you'd support me against the Yard boys, wouldn't you? By the oath we've sworn together, the packet of Lexington farms?"

"I'll vote for you, Jack, though I didn't know you were thinking of running until you said it."

"Neither did I. I'll admit to you, I'd like to be the Ivy Orator. I can make a good speech. 'Forefathers and cuntry-boys, lend me your wares. I have come to worry Caesar, not to trade 'im. When in the foreskin of our counterparts, the detritus of—'"

"I say I'll vote for you, Jack. But I can't say what the other fellows—"

"Fellesh—"

"What the other fellesh in the Yard will do. They're somewhat contemptuous of the clubby boys. You know...."

"I do indeed. I've often felt that way myself...."

I can't go on to explain my exact position toward all this. How can I say aloud that the suggestion that I might run as a candidate for Senior Class Orator excites me more than the charms of a Portuguese prostitute.

Show

Elected to a club because they need someone to write their senior show. Up all night composing. Swaggering through the Yard full of lyrics, pride. Pass a familiar face without a name. "Hey, Jack!" "How're you?" Boomer...Bugger... Binger! Binger, the fiery Jew from New York! He wants to talk but I've got my goals to meet! On!

> *And*
> *at*
> *the*
> *Somerset*
> *Things were rather wet*
> *Big exclusive affair—*
> *From the lack of heat*
> *All of Beacon Street*
> *Surely must have been there....*

Prose

My writing goes public, in lyrics for the show, in poems, in essays. All of it strikes me upon rereading as the work of a silly young madman. In a private album of clippings and prose, I try to reconstruct and comprehend my public ways. I'm passing all my courses. Life looms ahead. I rush toward her, with open arms!

For Lillian

Now in the east pale sleeping fairies weave
From dreams, the wan grey gossamer of dawn
And lay it on your hair; so fair, so fair
you sleep—and yet, the shadowy dancers leave,
The swaying phantoms one by one are gone,
The deathless music fades in breathless air.

Steffens

"Hail, fellow!"

Even before I fall in love with the glint in his eyes and the tender way he smiles, I succumb to the sweetness of his speech. As we clench hands heartily, I inhale the breath that flows from his lips, my nose swimming luxuriously in the almost ambrosial stream.

"You look so much like your father I'll wager that goes for your insides as well as facade. Hail, fellow!"

Never have I met an adult whose demeanor soothes me as much as Steff's. If our talk hadn't filled up with sparks and flames, I could have basked lazily forever in the balmy good will, good spirit, good feelings, good light given off by the eyes of this dapper, pointy-bearded California gentleman, who just happens to be the most famous journalist of his day.

"Your father, in fact, sends his best greetings and says to inform you that if you've made up your mind to graduate, he's made up his mind to come east and watch you commence."

We repair to a local saloon, waiting for the arrival of Lippmann and a few other fellows whom Steffens has come to interview. I put to him in frankness questions I have been saving about my father's situation.

"It's true," says Steffens, in that tone as golden as the foamy beer brimming in the mugs between us. "He's got the lumber barons so speedily on the run they can't see the road for all the dust they raise as they travel. He's a good in-fighter, old C.J., and a lot of folks are hoping he's going to win that seat he's running for so he can do even more. I'm hoping that you're truly made of the same stuff as he, Jack, because I know a few new magazines in New York City can use talents right now. Which is why I'm here in Cambridge...to recruit you fellows in the war against capitalism. Ready to join up?" His flinty eyes score the question in my brain.

Show

Just insist that your aunt was a Cabot
And your grandmother's real name was Weld
Try hard to make rudeness a habit
And be care-ful
with whom
you're
be-held!

Plans

Harry and I meet for a discussion of the letter and a walk.

"I liked the musical a lot, Jack," he says as we leave the Yard.

Skinny kid. Looks so much like Mama I want to kiss him. An independent sophomore, much more so than I was. He abjures the Clubs without a wrinkle on his brow. And I know him too well to imagine that inside—like me—he feels regrets for his actions.

"And your poetry," he adds as we cross the Square, "it's getting real good."

We're heading for the river, but in my mind I'm back home, in sick-bed, with little Harry fetching books for me by the hour.

The Charles, the Willamette....

"Hare, I hope you don't think I've been avoiding you."

"Jack, aw, no!" he protests, but I can hear the opposite answer in his tone.

"It was just I thought you ought to get a start here on your own. The worst things about this place grow out of family ties. What's a college for if it doesn't teach you to make your own way?"

We stray along the river bank, our eyes on boats, on birds, clouds that scud across the light blue sky. A letter from home with bad news and good.

"It must have been drink, don't you agree?"

"Mama took such care in keeping him dry and Christian," I say.

"But when we moved out of Cedar Hill no one really paid much attention to him anymore when he wasn't working. It's my impression that he'd sneak down to the waterfront on his time off and booze it up with the sailors."

"You're convincing." My little brother speaks more like a lawyer or a physician than the kid who cried out while I slew worms. "So the verdict is death by drink."

"But we musn't tell Mama," he nods. "Let her think TB just the way she wrote to us."

"What if it was, poor man. Born under the Great Wall. He might have caught it in China as a child, or while he shipped east in the hold of a freighter."

"Sure," Hare says, "home is too healthy a place for him to catch TB."

"You catch it right here in Cambridge," I say. "There's a black man going to graduate with my class if he doesn't die of the thing first."

"Sad," says Hare.

"Old Lee Sing," I say. "Passed over."

There's a commotion down the path at Harvard Bridge. Gulls rise on the heat, like paper swaying fitfully on a geyser of hot steam. We're walking in that direction, looking at each other, at the water, at the birds. And does Hare think what I think, that we've grown so quickly that we can't believe it, that the years have flipped past us like pages in an album?

"Will you make the folks' reservations?" he asks, deferring to big brother.

"I think you might be capable yourself."

"Of course."

I like the way he says that. I tap his shoulder, returning his earlier touch in kind.

"Mama says that Papa's going to lose the election if he comes east."

"I hadn't heard any of that."

"She says that the party people don't want him to leave."

"But he's coming anyway."

"Mama says he says he wouldn't miss your commencement for anything."

"I'm going to send him a wire."

"It won't do any good. You know Papa when he makes up his mind."

We boot it on down toward the bridge. There's something in the water, an overturned sailboat or scull, some swimmers. They're diving beneath the bridge.

"Someone else has passed over." Hare says, shaking his head.

I grab him by the shoulder. "Aren't you glad we're good swimmers and couldn't drown ourselves if we tried?"

We walk swiftly toward the spectacle, break into a trot. The Charles, the Willamette...the living, the drowned, I'm thinking about Lee Sing, crinkly faced, ginger-smelling fellow, gone now like the boy we see bob up beneath the bridge, in tow behind a diver, like somebody's little pup reluctant to come ashore.

Graduate

I know the route so well by now that each morning I awake and picture the train rolling eastward, ever eastward, through forests, mountain passes, over the plains, past wheat fields, racing rivers, horses. Barking dogs announce the outskirts of cities that command a view of a hundred miles of nothing, then Chicago—imitation Manhattan!—cattle barns, dwarf forests, finger lakes, and suddenly I smell oily steam, hear the hissing of brakes, the screech of great metallic wheels, and I turn away from the progress of several young girls parading through the station in gauzy summer dresses to see the majestic engine rolling slowly toward the line's end.

Mama's face—at first I think it's Grandma's—appears in the window, and then Papa moves slowly into view at the top of the platform, a conductor assisting him as he takes each step as though it were a rope stretched above an abyss. Mama follows, and after we embrace, she hands Papa a cane.

"Shocked?" His eyes still light up as he speaks. His body seems wilted, like a delicate plant kept too long in the sun.

"Why should he be shocked?" Mama asks, pecking me on the cheek. "I wrote to him about the kind of schedule you've had to keep up."

"Maybe you wrote that to Hare, Mama." I return her kiss.

She smiles, "I can't keep track of what I write to which of you. But Harry is a much more faithful correspondent than you, Jack. You're supposed to be a writer! You don't write home much."

"He's sent his clippings," Papa defends me.

"That he does." Mama makes a mouth at me as though I were back at the dinner table at Cedar Hill. I can easily translate her meaning: you'd rather write for your friends and the public than for your own mother.

"I hope the trip was comfortable," I say as we walk slowly into the station followed by a wagonload of baggage. Though my impulse is to help Papa, I decide to take Mama's arm instead.

"I've forgotten it already," says Papa, looking about the station.

"Where's Harry?" Mama asks.

"Fetching a car for us," I reply.

"At least we have *him* for another two years," Mama says. Nervously, purposefully, we pass through the station.

The visit goes surprisingly well. We're a family again, missing only Grandma and a few aunts and uncles. There's a new gardener back home, a black man named Dumas has replaced our dear late Lee Sing. (Harry shoots me a sharp glance to remind me of our pact about keeping quiet on the cause of death.) Uncle Raymond has returned home from a job as a manager in the wheat fields of Patagonia.

"My brother just can't stay home and grow plain old American wheat," Mama says over supper.

"Patagonia is America," Papa says. "It's North America stood on its head."

"'Or that there were such men whose heads stood in their breasts?' Shakespeare," I say. "Gonzalo's speech, 'The Tempest,' Act Three, Scene Three, oft thought to signify European notions of what the earliest Americans looked like."

"Show-off," Harry says.

"He's educated," Papa nods.

Mama stares into my eyes.

Papa stands, picks up his cane. It seems always a part of him now, as though he never walked without it. "Where're these campus politicians you wanted me to meet, Jack? Steffens wrote me that you're right in the swim of politics here."

"C.J.," Mama interrupts, "you promised me that if we came east that you would take it easy."

"This is a heck of a lot easier than I've taken it in months, my dear." He stabs the air with his stick. "Jack, I'm sure you've been wanting to show me off to some of these slick fellows you've told us about. So show."

I show him off, beaming throughout our interviews with Lippmann and the fellows from the Institute. But when we return to the hotel I want to try out my speech on him. He tells me to go ahead; he's asleep before I'm halfway through it. Though Lippmann had insisted earlier, and Papa did not dispute it, that politics rejuvenated its practitioners, his new profession seems to have aged Papa twice as fast as any other.

I attempt to talk with Mama about his health, but she will not discuss it. Shoos me and Harry off to our rooms and bed. All these years and still only somewhere east of childhood and someplace west of my true mission in life.

Passport

Age	22
Height	5' 11½"
Forehead	High
Eyes	Brown
Nose	Small
Mouth	Small
Chin	Prominent
Hair	Dark Brown
Complexion	Light
Face	Long

"The Day in Bohemia"

I would embalm in deathless rhyme
The great souls of our little time:
Inglorious Miltons by the score—
Mute Wagners—Rembrandts, ten or more—

And Rodins, one to every floor.
In short, those unknown men of genius
Who dwell in third floor-rears gangreneous,
Reft of their rightful heritage
By a commercial, soulless age.
Unwept, I might add—and unsung,
Insolvent, but entirely young. . . .

The American at Work (Briefly)

A warm spring afternoon in 1911, and I am rapidly losing my job.

"Ten years!" the tipsy editor of the *American* calls after me, as though he wished he'd hurled a brick instead. "You'll come crawling back to my desk in ten years, Harvard boy!"

"In five you'll wish you'd published me today!" I toss back in farewell, slamming the door behind me. "I won't be censored by any man!"

I stride ferociously down the hall, pausing at the top of the long flight of stairs. A touch of vertigo assails me. Swift and bold as lightning in a western thunderstorm, my mind flashes back to the moment on the courthouse steps when Papa sent that bad actor tumbling down into the street. Since he entrained for home after commencement, Papa has lost the election, lost his vigor, and now writes me letters in a script as uncertain as Grandma Green's. With Harry himself commencing in June and planning to return to Portland, I have no worries that the folks will feel neglected. But it saddens me to know that I will have to write and say that I have just walked out—nearly been pushed—from my first full-fledged editorial position. The *American* has been thoroughly American but not American enough for the likes of me.

Forty-Two Washington Square

In winter the water is frigid
In summer the water is hot;
And we're forming a club for controlling the tub
For there's only one bath to the lot.
You shave in unlathering Croton,
If there's water at all, which is rare—
but the life isn't bad for a talented lad
At Forty-two Washington Square!

Lower East

I've become more a follower than a leader, a reader more than a writer. And one of the men I follow (and one whose writings I read as though they are sacred script) is Steffens. He not only found me my first job and kept on the lookout for free-lance work for me but moved into 42, where the boys and I have set up housekeeping in a florid, unkempt style. His territory is by now our entire nation of corrupt cities; he has taken it upon himself to follow in his own footsteps, just as he has followed in the trail of Jacob Riis.

He leads me on a merry race through political clubs, gambling shops, sweat shops, brothels, crime factories, the beggars' union hall, introducing me to hundreds of people, thousands of new sights. He initiates me into the pace and passions of the city's rhythms, and there comes a night when I read "Crossing Brooklyn Ferry," picturing Steffens at the deck-rail along with old Whitman and me.

Steffens once confessed that my father had charged him to show me the world. Now Steffens guides me to the front lines of life. For reasons of his own, beyond my father's plea, Steffens reveals to me the source of all poetry and art: the people themselves.

Those are in fact his words, spoken to me one hot summer afternoon as we walk under the shadow of the El, the Village a steamy shape of heat-quavering buildings far behind us.

"Now that you're writing for the *Masses*, Jack, I thought it was time that you saw the thing itself."

"That's fine with me, Steff," I reply. "Only it's the smell itself that may do me in." A wave of cooking odors and horse dung rolls up from the region of darkest Jewry to the south and east.

"I thought you'd put your Harvard Yard snobbism behind you!" he snaps at me. Crossing Delancy Street, Steffens launches into a panegyric on the glories and surprises of the Lower East Side. The wails, the shouts, the scents, the dash, the visions, the language of other times, other realms...I understand then the meaning of his Semitophilism.

We are approaching Rutgers Street, and the people of the ghetto swirl up around us like dust in a Kansas wind storm: hawkers, peddlers, fish bellies, bells ring, girls shriek, men shout, children flash by, long gowns and sideburns, women in dark dresses, their hair hidden under kerchiefs, their faces masked as much by lines of sadness as actual veils; and suddenly the whorl turns as sensuous as its odors, the mystery of its depths giving off an effusiveness, a sensation as powerful as that which moved through the forests of home. Life! It calls out to me, Life is Here! And damned is he who dares to tamper with even a hair!

Stepping around a pile of malformed human turds, Steffens claps his hands in gleeful contemplation of the scene before him. We travel as far east as a man can walk in New York City without needing to walk on water, and the spectacle around us conjures up the Orient, the exotic tents of Araby, places I've never seen though I have already traveled Europe. Women glide by, reeking of the Casbah, and despite Steff's warning against taking a Jewess as a lover—or because of it?—I allow myself to wander with them in extravagant imaginary copulations only a fellow such as I, still wet with the Charles behind my ears, can imagine. Weird and un-New Yorkly undulations emanate from the buildings around us, bricky edifices dark with soot crowded closer and closer together, knitting up the spaces where blue autumn sky still tries to color as we turn down an alleyway, putting the crowded street and my fantasies behind us.

"If you'd like to meet some emancipated women, I'll introduce you to five or six," Steff suddenly interjects as if, all along, he has been listening to my inner dialogue of desire.

"I would, yes," I reply. "I'm always available to the next experience." I pause with him in front of a filthy black doorway near the end of the garbage-heaped alley.

"You ought to try new kinds of writing, Jack," he says

quietly, studying the place in search of a handle, though none seems to exist. "Women just lead you to one lyric poem after another. You need some adventures that will knock you over into prose. That's the material of our age, not your lyrics. What we want is an epic, if we can get one of our own to put it together..."

He lapses into silence, touching his beard as though it might be the handle which would open a way into this dilapidated building which seems to be our destination. I look about nervously, listening to the life-shouts from the vital crowded places looming over us. He is discoursing on poetry and the age, on our society's wants and lacks, in a dead-end alley in the city's depths, where the detritus of the new mechanical age is swept.

"Pliss."

I turn at the voice.

"Pliss to gif me all dollars," says the bearded man, torso swaddled in musty rags. In one hand he holds a small, black pistol.

"Dollars," he repeats.

"Give him all he wants," says Steff, his voice trembling slightly.

"We don't have much, friend," I say.

His eyes turn blank, as though egg-white had been smeared across his retinas.

"Pliss," he repeats, jamming the pistol sharply into my stomach. With a trembling hand, I fumble in my coat for my billfold.

"Here it is, friend," I say, handing over the entire billfold.

"No friend to you, goy," says the gunman, slipping the prize inside his flowing, ragged wrappings. "Gif," he says, nodding at Steffens.

"I'd like to give you more than money," my elderly friend tells him. "I'd like to give you—"

"Uh!" He jams the gun hard into my gut. "Steff," I grunt, "no lectures. Give him your cash."

"I don't have any. I never walk about the city with any on my person."

"Gif now!"

"Uh!" I try to catch my breath. "*Steff*, he's getting angry."

Steffens emits a bunch of rapid foreign noises.

"What's you—uh!—say?" I ask.

"I told him in polite yiddish that I don't have any cash."

"Vatch," says the gunman.

"What?" Steff's Yiddish fails him.

"Your *watch*! He wants your *watch*!" My voice sticks in my throat. I can't tell if Steff has heard me.

"Goniff!" A sharp outcry echoes through the alley. The gunman sinks to his knees, his weapon clanking onto the alley floor. In front of me now stands an enormous fellow with a large black beard, holding a large black hammer. The smile on his face expresses my own great pleasure.

"Misteer Lincoln?"

"That's me," says Steff, peeling himself away from the wall and straightening his coat. "Are you Judah Mack?"

"He's upstess." The man nods toward a small door in the side of the wall out of which he stepped to wield his hammer in swift justice against the thief. He looks inquiringly at me. "You vant your wallet?"

"Oh, yes, of course," I reply, about to retrieve it when the hammerer himself stoops and yanks it out of the silent huddle of rags, skin, and blood heaped at my feet. "Thanks. But will he be all right?"

The bearded hammer-wielder shrugs carelessly. "For coming in our territory, he gets what he deserfs!" But as if to assure me that he has not murdered anyone on my account—he knows by the look of chagrin on my face—he kicks the fallen figure, and the man moans like a loon.

"You come in?" asks our savior, and he stands back to allow first Steff and then me to enter the narrow passageway in the wall. He pulls shut the door behind us, plunging us into darkness. "Straight front, chentlemen," he says with a chuckle. I follow closely behind Steffens while behind me I hear the tap of the hammer against palm and the breathing of our guide.

"Why, hello!" Steff's hearty greeting suddenly swells the obscure passageway. Light blooms around a turn in the hall, and as I approach it, I see his silhouette in the frame of another door. A man stands behind him, drawing him into the light.

"Jack," says Steff, "I'd like you to meet Mr. Leader...."

I shake the rough hand of the little fellow in front of me. Although he is dressed much the same as our assailant was, his grin offers me some assurance that he looks at the world in a slightly different way.

"Not my real name of course," he says in colorless English. "Names are not as important as deeds. What does it matter what I call myself?"

I remain silent, intrigued by both the certainty and the mysterious meaning behind our encounter.

"Mr. Steffens, I know, of course," the man continues. "But I don't think I know your identity, Sonny. You a journalist also?"

"He writes for the *Masses*," Steff explains. "A jolly good writer he is, a bully magazine."

"Ah, yes, the boyish revolutionaries."

"Leader has his opinions," Steff says.

"I have my deeds," says Leader. "Come with me." he motions to Steff and me.

We walk single-file through a narrow hall to another door. First Leader, then Steff, and then I pass through it into the semi-darkness of a stairwell and I hear him shut the door behind us. A small light flickers some distance below, but around us the darkness muffles my vision. Strange odors float up out of the abyss.

"We're pledged to secrecy, by the way," Steff whispers to

me as he takes my arm and helps me descend toward the source of the illumination. "Remember how hard that hammer strikes?"

"Do they keep white slaves here, Steff? They don't look like the types."

"They hope they're making all slaves free," whispers Steff again, helping me keep my balance during our stroll in the dark.

We reach the bottom. A door slams shut above us. Light floods the space around us. As my eyes become accustomed to it, I discover that we are standing in the middle of a large group of stoves on which pots and tins of various sizes and shapes are cooking. Some give off mere steam, others flourish noxious looking fumes, the odd scents and seasonings I sniffed from the top of the stairs. On tables nearby sit boxes of different shapes and colors. I peek inside the nearest box and spy a fine, yellowish powder all in a heap.

"Feel this, " Leader says to me. And he shoves my hand into the next box.

"Gunpowder?" I ask, fingering the grainy mixture.

"The powder of a hundred guns, a thousand guns." A new and distinctive odor floats up to my nostrils. It seems familiar and yet I cannot place it. I try to recollect where I have smelled it when a curious noise echoes over the bubbling of the pots. I listen closely but it fades. Then it rises again, and behind it still another sound embroidered on the steamy air. Steff is listening, too.

"What is that?" I ask.

"Don't be distracted," says Leader. "This is just our neighbors. The walls here are thin, my friend, unlike the walls in castles of precious stones where the likes of you live."

I listen more intently now and make out the wail of an infant, the sounds of adult voices raised in argument, the whining of middle-sized children, the clanking of dishes, and from a great distance the sweetly rasping meow of a violin.

"Isn't it dangerous...?" I nod toward the concoction in the largest tin on the nearest stove.

"To make our 'Haymarket Stew' with all these people living in the same building? Sure it is, my friend. And it's even more dangerous for them to live in this building without us. We can only blow them up. Without us, they would live lives worse than death." He motions toward a part of the room where a thin hanging curtain masks some makeshift beds and clothes hampers. "We all share the dangers together."

"And the pleasures," comes a voice from one of the beds. "Vich is vhat I'm having now so you'll please excuse and make your voices quiet. The light I don't mind so much, I'm used to. But the voices, this is too far to ignore."

"Excuse us, please do, Morton," says the Leader, moving toward the lamps. I understand now that not all the noises I hear come from behind the wall. The whine that I take to be the petulant voice of a demanding child drifts over to me from the curtained-off space. The curtain flutters, a slender white hand catches it before it falls back, and a round, pale face, all wide-eyed, like a doe in the instant before flight, peers out at me.

"Sorry, please excuse, Morton and Malka, my darlings." Leader's voice turns soft and apologetic, a note he has not struck before this. As he douses the lights, my memory of the wide-eyed girl remains imprinted on the ensuing darkness. From somewhere behind the wall, the violin squeaks, the quarrel continues, a real child raises its voice in anger or hunger. I recall the name of the familiar odor, the smell of my own, dripping sweat.

Scraps

Uncle Sam starring John Barrymore
Kismet starring Otis Skinner

Riders to the Sea
Green Stockings
The Witness for the Defense

Masses Motto

"...to everlastingly attack old systems, old morals, old prejudices—the whole weight of outworn thought that dead men have saddled upon us, and to set up many new ones in their places...."

The World of Letters

Dear Bobby,

I'm very happy to hear the news about your teaching post at M.I.T. Of all of us, I don't know any better one to show young men how to care about the books that meant so much to us and how to put their innermost secrets into prose...

I've often wondered during the past few years about my own possibilities for teaching. The prospect of influencing so many minds each year is a tempting one; standing at the door to civilization and admitting those who measure up to your standards is tempting also. After due consideration, I can declare that I don't have the style for it, or the voice control, the histrionic abilities, the fundamental faith in one's own allegiance to the great art of balancing Homer against Dante against Shakespeare (not to mention the man who made the Wife of Bath)! It seems lost to me forever.

Now this journalistic work is another kind of art, and one that I'm not entirely ungifted in ....

Dear Jack,

Papa, Harry, and I were so proud to read your latest article! We both wish though that you wouldn't give all your time to that rowdy magazine and would write more often for the more refined places. The very title of that magazine makes me shudder. Your father would have said something...His health....

Dear Mister Reed,
  We will be pleased to publish....

Dearest Mother,
  I would certainly love above all else to visit this summer. But my job obligations here seem to mount up by the day. I've promised so many articles that I don't know that I'll be able to take....

Dear Jack,
  ...for your letter. That variety of life sounds swell. But the work does not make sense entirely. Haven't you thought that now, with a volume of verse under your name, it's high time you diverted your way from becoming the nation's most published journalist and emitted a novel or something?...

Dearest Jack,
  I miss you so much and you have not stopped by the store in a week now. Papa still bothers me about last week....

Dear Mister Reed,
  Your article makes a great deal of sense to us. We will be pleased....

Dearest Jack,
  Now that summer is near, we're about to plan a little trip and wish you could be along with us. Mother....

Dear Steff,
  How quiet the city is without you! You mount up for points westward and all the streets of New York turn into last year's lakes, now all cracked and drying in the light of a sun without any benevolent rays whatsoever....
  I had to borrow ten dollars from of all people....

No, I've stopped seeing Malka since she has gone back to the arms of her Leader. Two men made her feel quite anarchistic indeed but three confused her. I will miss her, but not the crab lice she bestowed upon me in honor of my dishonorable intentions....

...doldrums of the year, doldrums of my life. I feel so entirely useful that I don't know what to do with myself. And a bit too self-satisfied to imagine that this is the blissful state I imagined. So too the cave man who dragged his lunch behind him on a trailing bed of sticks, I don't know that there is a wheel in my future....

...Roosevelt or his antagonists ....

...every good prospect of a pleasurable existence ....

Dear Jack,

...for your letter. It must be grand to find oneself initiate into all the city's great mysteries. I long for the time to return when I will find myself capable of engaging myself in that fashion again ....

Dear Copey,

A friend of mine brought the new Conrad back from England and I spent the last day and a half, when not banging out a story about the latest unethics of a large American industrial chieftan for a new rag called *Trend*, immersing myself in the prose of the masterful Pole. No other writer I know fulfills so well the expectations which you put before us as new writers, and no writer, except perhaps Jack London, gives us so much of the active part of life without ever expending the slightest droplet of the contemplative or the inner life. The sorriest thing I know is that Conrad did not come to the United States but became an English citizen. Can you imagine what he might have done in the way of storytelling if he had had some of our best Eastern coastal settings and western scenes to use as backdrops for his tales? But that seems unfair to him, doesn't it? His backgrounds form the substance of his novels rather than the mere setting.

The sea, the south Sea Islands that give off such sparks of vital effluence while his characters never seem to do more than roam about and moon upon their interior gloomities....

Give me a story where the outer setting and the inner feelings are one!

...But he does do what you have always demanded of us, he makes us see. And may we never know a time when we will become, as readers, see-sick....

But you asked what I am writing and not what I am reading....

Dearest Mother,

Your last letter made me quite the happiest son you have living in New York City! The situation sounds....

Dear Lampoonists (ers?) (ites),

Thank you for sending me the the issue with the story of the birth of the cheer-leading team. It was, I am delighted to say, inaccurate in every damned detail!

Safe

The last light of a warm afternoon loiters on the window ledge as I work over yet again the galleys for a new issue.

"Jack?" Eastman's voice drifts in from the other room.

"Not finished," I reply, reaching up to switch on the work lamp. "Just a few minutes more."

"The printer's not going to like this. He sneaks us in between runs so we get it on the cheap. You bloody perfectionist! All we want is the truth, not the beauty! If we miss his deadline, he's got to charge us extra."

"The truth, not the beauty," I mutter to myself as I race my eyes along the type. "There's no distinction, no distinction."

"The facts are all that matter!"

Eastman, the athlete, a bawdy, dashing figure out of moving picture romance, plants himself in the doorway like a runner poised for flight. I glance up from my work, feeling his eyes bearing down on me as I press ahead on the proofing of my article. How can an American appear to be as noble as Eastman? It amazes me! He's a George Washington figure, so handsome that I sometimes want to pinch him in order to see if he is made of flesh. No surprise that women worship at his temple. He always looks so healthy; perhaps his Ma and Pa, both of them ministers upstate, fed him calves' flesh and goat cheese and other nourishing foods from birth...He exudes confidence Steffens only hints at.

I complete my job. The light fades from the window. Lamps blink on along the avenue.

"That's going to cost us, I know," he mutters as he leads the way out the door.

"I don't give a fig for that." I turn back toward the corner of the room.

"What are you doing?" he complains as I wrap my arms around the small safe which houses our current receipts.

"Showing you that I put myself completely into my ideas." I grunt, hug the safe and...lift it off the floor.

"Jack, put that down!" Eastman growls at me as I move toward the door.

"Leave it!" he shouts as I force him out of the doorway and head toward the staircase.

"No," I say when I finally deposit my burden on the sidewalk, "I'm throwing out the ready cash. I don't give a fig about being safe."

At which I dust off my coat, bid goodnight, and stroll away toward MacDougal Street. But I can't help turning back once or twice, and laughing, as I watch him in the thickening dusky shades, straining to lift the thing, push it, shove it back toward the entrance to the building. My back aches and my right testicle feels as though it has dribbled down my leg. Yet the joke keeps me happy, beyond all the powers of whiskey and beer chasers at Polly's restaurant, through the rest of the evening and into the next day.

"The Day in Bohemia"

And in the last an-al-y-sis
He says it narrows down to this:
A fig for the favors that the high gods gave!
Excepting the Belly and the Phallus and the Grave—
If you have drunk Life to the lees
You may console yourself with these:
For me there are some things that I do not crave
Among them the Belly and the Phallus and the Grave—
What ho! the Belly and the Phallus and the Grave
The Belly and the Phallus
And the ballad very gallus
And the Grave!

Evaluation

I have now lived in the city long enough to know its east, west, north, south. I climb the Heights of Brooklyn, of Washington, of Harlem, and sail past the Battery, etcetera, etcetera...I spend a night sleeping off a drunk in a basket of squid on Fulton Street. When my friends disbelieve me, I show them the cleaning bill, offer testimony from the owner of the establishment. Sleeping with a squid, I explain, is like making a night of it with the oldest prostitute in Billings, Montana, after she's had all the boys in the big cattle drive up from Texas.

I write some pieces that people in the know have to read. I produce insights into matters which to others before me had seemed unknowable, and I perform this with a prose that has an edge, a bite, a heft, a life, and an insouciance which belies a certainty almost ingrained in my growing soul. My optimism knows no bounds! The world is my oyster and I fairly well swagger!

Confound it, I am a happy fellow, a whirlwind, a tornado, a west wind racing across the land! Some of my friends admit to miseries so profound and unnerving that they have taken up a new treatment called psychoanalysis administered by Dr. A. A. Brill with whom I sometimes drink beer at the Liberal Club. I myself prefer, in summer at least, to sweat my hurts out while swimming in the muddy Hudson near Croton with my pal—the-minister's-son-turned-philological-neohearty-socialist—Max Eastman. (Together so far we have swum a hundred miles, loved dozens of girls.)

I have been to Europe, nearly married a French peasant girl; poem after poem, hymns to the city, pour from my pen. I want to drink more, I want to stop drinking (it sometimes tickles my ornery kidney), I want to visit China. On hearing my poems, members of the Liberal Club buy me more beer, cheer me on. When I talk of writing about the real things in life, they cough and huff and shuffle their chairs, pick their noses, riffle their lapels (those that have them).

Yet I still long for the comforts of college life. Hyp Havel announces one night before ducking out to cook a meal for everyone at Polly's restaurant next door, that I am trying to turn the rest of the world into Harvard Square.

"Max!" I shout across the gurgling waters, bucking freshets of icy flow which announce that summer has not yet fully settled in upstate. "Max, I want to fly! I want to float! What does it all mean, Max? Sometimes I feel five years old, sometimes five hundred! What does it all mean!" And Max replies by laughing like a duck and showing his bare ass to the heavens, blue skies above Croton, in summer almost always dramatically blue.

Clipping

Among the readers of this volume will be some with whom the late Professor William James was at one time or another in correspondence, but of whose identity or whereabouts no record has been found among his papers. His letters are currently being prepared for publication and I would appreciate any notice from parties who belong to this category.

H. James, Sr.
95 Irving Street
Cambridge, Massachusetts

Real

I am sitting in a chair by the window which overlooks the Mews behind our building, the latest volume of E. A. Robinson spine up in my lap. My feet are bare, my chest bared as well, my trousers stained with coffee which I spilled on myself while furiously finishing an article for *Smart Set* earlier this morning (furious the pace, furious my temperament since I hate to find myself reduced to producing such pap for the masses when I should be writing serious matter for the *Masses*).

In the other room, Bob Hallowell suffers with similar agonies.

"How much? Much as I want, goddamn it! Soul of the artiste, bloody hole of a soul! Can you put a price tag on it? Goddamn the bloody Belial beast!..."

Muttering out loud as he produces a cover painting for the *Metropolitan*...

Above us, a telephone rings and someone in Steffens's apartment clumps across the ceiling to answer it. A pigeon floats past the window. An old red-haired woman peers at the bird and me from a vantage point behind a parapet on the rooftop across the Mews. A fire horn blares in the distance, a horse whinnies, the bird disappears behind the edge of the building beyond. Sweat runs down my temples, tickles my chest.

"Goddamn soul of the artiste—etcetera, etcetera."
Hallowell curses from the other room.

I turn the volume over and read glancingly a poem I know,
a poem I think I ought to know.

> Miniver mourned the ripe renown
> That made so many a name so fragrant;
> He mourned Romance, now on the town,
> And Art, a vagrant...

"Goddamn soul, etcetera, etcetera."

I work my toes into the underside of the small rug at my
feet, wondering, at the sound of the door slamming
overhead, if Steffens is going out. I didn't even know that
he'd returned to the city, not having kept track of him (nor
had he of me) for many months. My stomach rumbles. Shall I
read further? Or walk through the sluggish muggy air to the
Liberal Club for beer and a chat?

> Miniver scorned the gold he sought
> But sore annoyed was he without it...

I've thought and thought and thought about that afternoon. The stillness of the air, distant voices, the intense lack
of motion precluding all activity but negative thought. Steffens...hungry, yes?...pretty girl sometimes comes to the
window wearing nothing but her bodice...this poetry good?
pigeon flies again, the same pigeon? my poetry . . . .

"Goddamn soul of the artiste, etcetera, etcetera."

It is then that I hear someone bounding swiftly up the stairs
from the street. A smart knock shakes the door. I slide lazily
from my perch, marking my place in the volume to which I
will return...*Miniver coughed, and called it fate....*

"Telegram...!"

I open the door to discover a neatly uniformed young
messenger.

"Telegram for Mister John Reed!"

"That's me."

I haven't received a wire since commencement. Hastily I tear open the envelope, breath coming hard, kidney kicking as if in anticipation...it is already too late....

In Memoriam

Clouds sail over the prairie, stately proud ships of fleece. I conjure up King Arthur's funeral and then return to the present. Hyperbole will not help. The train clacks westward. I doze, it seems, for days, looking out now and then upon a desolate prairie, longing for a vision of boys swimming amidst the wavy buffalo grass but seeing nothing except skeletal crosses marking the graves of pioneers.

In Memoriam, C.J. Reed
Died July 1, 1912

Calm he lies there,
In the brave armor he alone could bear,
With a proud shield of Honor at his side,
And a keen sword of wit. And when the tide
Mysterious—when the swift, exultant Spring
Thrills all this hillside with awakening,
Wild-flowers will know and love him, blossoming.

Part Three

PAGEANT

I was trying desperately to hide my grief in the composition of a poem that had been plaguing me for weeks when there came a knock at the door.

"Busy!"

"Not so busy you can't let me in!" came the reply through the barrier.

It was Steffens! I rushed to let him in.

"You're supposed to be in Pittsburgh," I said, embracing him.

"Oof! You're strong as a python, Jack! Let me loose!"

He strode over to the desk where I had been working. "Mabel Dodge is holding a gathering tonight, and I wonder if you'd like to attend."

"I'm too busy with this Dionysian labor to stand about watching daring dames puff on their cigarettes."

"You've been there before?"

"No." Steff seemed to be studying me in a curious way. I fiddled with the old gold watch, once my father's, now, sadly, mine. "Don't get me wrong, I like dangerous dames. If I ever find one volatile enough for me, I'll light her fuse. You can bet on that."

"Next to Emma, there's no one more volatile I know than Mabel Dodge," Steff said. "Are you sure that you don't want to accompany me? There's going to be some interesting political talk tonight. Bill Haywood is supposed to be there, among others."

I pushed away from my desk with a determination and effort that I had not put out since the time, years gone by, I pushed the raft into the beckoning river and set off up the Willamette to adventures beyond imagining. But tonight, I was on my own, no father to meet me at the last bend of the river, fireworks, family, and all.

"I'll go," I said.

The Dodge apartment, as it turned out, was no more than a few blocks from our building. All I had time to say was, "I'm awfully glad you happened by," and all he had time to say was, "I had been missing you, chum," before we found ourselves standing at the large wooden door to her apartment. In silence, I contemplated the large brass knocker whose ornate designs seemed to glow with an inner light. It was divided into four separate scenes, all of them contained within an outer rim of another design. The first quarter showed a sun rising over rolling countryside, with a slim moon barely visible in the upper right hand corner. Tiny figures stood on the hillsides, gazing out, as if toward some unseen ocean beyond the rolling land. The second section held a bizarre quartet of objects, a caduceus, a tree not unlike a cactus, a pistol with wings, a fluted pastry. The third quadrant gave the illusion that it was something other than fixed and hard—silvery females, moon maidens, flowed back and forth, in and out of the steely girdle that bound them, in reality, to a single space and posture. The fourth and final quarter expounded in a tiny sequence the history of it all, from the explosion of the godhead to the discovery of America and flying machines. It made my eye and mind work overtime, all this, the most portentous doorway in all New York!

I hadn't realized how caught up in its images I had been until it swung away from view. I heard Steff cough behind me as I looked up into the eyes of a stalk-like creature with frizzed-up hair wearing a nurse's uniform.

"I thought someone was here," said the woman in white.

"Nurse Galvin," Steff said, "Jack Reed. Jack, this is the lady who takes care of Mrs. Dodge's little boy John."

"Diddle, diddle, dumpling, my son John," the nurse sang into my ear as she led us over the threshold. Tunk-tunk! The heavy door clanged shut behind us. I didn't have much time to wonder about this. No sooner had I stepped down the hall than a fluttering cloud of white enveloped me in its folds.

"Good evening," came a shimmery voice. The sheer girth of its owner impressed me at once, for I met her broad, heavy breasts all wrapped in brocade and the outstretched arms before seeing that she had a head. "Good evening." She was standing on a foot-stool before the hallway mirror asssuming the posture of a figurehead on a Yankee clipper. I offered my hand. She stepped regally down from her pedestal. Her perfume rolled over me like sea-fog. Her body remained Nike-like, while her hair in all its coils and rings, loops, and traceries, resembled the coiffure of a modern Medusa.

"And what does he do, Steffens?" she asked, clenching my fingers quite tightly as she spoke.

"Jack Reed writes for the *Masses*, among other things," Steffens told her, as though he were accustomed to behaving like my keeper. "He's a doer, most of all, and probably becoming a socialist these days. He hates the things we hate, loves the things we love..." Steffens said a few more words that I did not quite catch. It seemed of a sudden that Mabel Dodge had a grip not just on my hand but on a personal part of me.

"You're a very interesting man," she said into my ear. My brain swirled helplessly, sucked into the powerful whirl of her perfume. She released my hand and gave me a little pat on the rear. "You'll be happy to meet some of my other guests tonight. Bill Haywood's here to talk about the strike he's leading in Paterson and he's brought several of his compatriots with him. And now that you're here, we'll have a socialistic evening indeed! That seems to be the great thing for Americans these days. How glad I am that so many of my good friends are tending in this direction!" And then, as though she were a mother bird and Steffens and I two of her ducklings, she led us purposefully down the hall.

Rumors had reached me about the great surge and mix of the grand lady's salons, but no words about it from either Hyp or Max or Lippmann prepared me for the carnival atmosphere of the dining room. From single-taxers to Fourierists, Fabians and Steffens-ites and many readers of our *Masses* as well as some of our writers, the inhabitants of the large room shouted and declaimed to each other, through each other, about each other, for each other, with a fervor that joined the passion of the French Revolution to the hysteria of the Second Coming.

There were other subjects besides socialism, of course. In one corner of the room, I saw Dr. Brill discoursing on the new psychoanalysis, which many of Mabel's devoted friends and acquaintances had taken up; in another was a make-shift university seminar on the new poetry of the age which, after listening to it for a time, I found somewhat unsatisfying. And what other subjects? Women's powers, and the need to show them fully to the world. The discussion was led, I gathered, by a feisty young woman named Margaret and some English dame who had once struck a bobby with a golf club during a demonstration for equal rights. And with the talk of women's public rights, came words about freedom in women's private lives, signaled by the dense clouds of smoke emanating from another room. And the shy fashion in which several of the women in the room touched each other, held each other, nuzzled, and, once, much to the chagrin of even the undemanding masculines in the discussion, embraced.

The room was packed with smoke-eyed women, gaunt anarchists, several artists who frequented the Liberal Club, one black man dressed in a shiny, worn suit, some swarthy boys in gadabout rags, and bespectacled and bejeweled ladies who may have stepped down from the upper reaches of Fifth Avenue to see how the rest of us lived.

Steff took a seat on the sofa next to a tall, rangy fellow whose western shirt and boots singled him out as a man separate even from the working types who clustered near him. On the other side of him sat Lippmann, his eyebrows moving as fast as his mouth. I was about to join them when I felt a strong hand on my arm.

"Don't wonder about my forgetting you, Jack Reed," said my hostess close to my ear, her warm, now wine-steeped breath making me shiver in spite of myself.

What does a young fellow say in a situation such as this?

"I couldn't be sure you noticed me with all this mob."

"You underestimate your charm."

"I don't usually," I threw back.

"Then it's a new aspect of your charm that you did just now," she replied.

"I'll have to try it again if it brings me such success."

"You must."

"I will."

"Do you promise, Jack?"

"I do, Mrs. Dodge."

"Mabel."

"I do, Mabel."

"Has she gotten you to accept her proposal already?" A smiling Steffens popped up out of the crowd. "She's always on the lookout for a new Mister Mabel, Jack, so watch yourself."

She slowly turned her curls toward him.

"Steffens, when I require your assistance, I shall ask for it. You'll recollect that you failed to perform the last favor I asked of you, failed miserably."

"Oh, Mabel," Steff groaned, stroking his neat white chin-beard, "how was I going to get the boss of New York's underworld to come in and talk to your houseguests about the pleasures of being a thief? There's no Big Boss, only lots of little ones."

"I wanted a Fagin and you brought me a pickpocket. So much for your powers among the underside, Mister Muckraker."

"Steff has shown me a thing or two about life in New York's tunnels and caves," I broke in, glancing about the room and catching a glimpse of another familiar face. I nudged Steffens in the ribs. "Why there's a man right here in this very room who could blow the building sky high if he cared to!"

"Don't say that," Mabel hushed me, her hands aflutter about her broad chest. "I don't mean to sound like an alarmist. But we have had police spies before, and with Mr. Haywood here tonight, we just ought not to talk about making bombs. Everyone who enters through these portals leaves whatever secret or illegal matters they care about outside the room. They can talk about them, however, which is why we're all here. I decided in France a long while ago, Jack, that what our country lacked was a sense of intellectual congress, a place where one might investigate the living ideas of another mind, and when I returned to live here again I pledged myself to the establishment of just such a place where ideas—"

"Oh, Mabel," Steff interrupted, "you know that you wanted a sitting room filled with interesting people. France and Germany, that's one thing—but Americans don't have ideas, they experience them."

"Steffens, I disagree. But what a marvelous thing to say!"

"Christopher Columbus was the first person to say it," Steffens offered. "And he probably heard it from a red man on the beach. Mabel, if you'll let me be frivolous for a moment in your palace of seriousness, I must say that I find myself charmed by your ability to decorate a room with all the right varieties of idealogue. You've got the perfect touch.

With the exception of my young friend Jack here. He's no idea man whatsoever. He's a real American through and through. He does things rather than think about doing them. Even those bomb-throwers over in the far corner of the room have to think a little bit about the religion of anarchy. Jack shows you what he thinks by what he does!"

My face was turning quickly scarlet. Between Steffens's words and Dodge's Olympian physique, my head was spitting sparks. I tried to change the subject to the President's latest frolic, but my hostess wouldn't let the matter drop.

"I've read what Jack has written hereabouts and yonder," she said, "but I'm not quite sure what you mean about what he does."

Steffens declared without a ripple in his chin-beard, "He makes poetry out of his life and his life into poetry. Mabel, with all your talk about Europeans setting the standards for us here, you're looking our country's new young Byron right straight in the eye and you don't even recognize him."

"Steff," I said, finding my voice at last, "I can take care of my own tub-thumping, thank you."

"Bravo, Jack," said Mabel, planting a large, wet, heavily perfumed kiss on my cheek. And as if it belonged to another, some being employed to make things clear where there might be the slimmest chance of misunderstanding, the back of her hand brushed across my trouser front, a movement hidden from Steff because of her enveloping, rippling, white draped (one-armed) embrace.

"But now you must come," she said, a bit of glitter in her magnetic eye. "Come and see the special center of the evening..."

Leading me by the wrist toward the far end of the room, Mabel drew the glances of the room's men as she flowed past. My head wobbled with the rising noises of the salon.

"Electric magnetism...the answer to it all...."

"—whether true or not, I wanted it to be—"

"—in his colors rather than his features—"

"—and his lines? What of his lines, dearie? Did you ever see such ragged, jagged, incomparable, monstrous—"

"—who is?"

"—What?"

"Crimea is the place to go for color. I have never seen such blues!"

"You goddamned Victorian . . . ."

Hyp's head bobbed up out of the smoke. He smiled at me, then sank down out of sight behind two pigeon-breasted women smokers.

"—so I say to the Mayor, 'What must I do to impress—'"

"—or your ego, darling, sometimes you confuse the two."

The wrangler's eyes lighted up as we approached, and he pushed himself up from his comfortable place on the sofa, rising and rising as though he wouldn't stop until the top of his head hit the ceiling. His face, scarred and streaked as the side of one of your western mountains, made you feel as though you were in the presence of one of God's works of art. This rabble-rouser, who extended toward me a red-knuckled hand big as a shovel, smiled like a man who knew that most of the hundreds of folks he met each wanted to be known as his brother. His eyes swept over me like a great searchlight's beam off a stormy coast.

"I'm Bill," he said, pumping my hand. "Who're you, friend?"

"Jack Reed," I said, discovering as only a fairly tall fellow such as I can, what it's like to look up to someone for the first time in his adult life.

"Jack," Mabel offered, "writes for the *Masses*."

"Then he writes for me," Bill said and hugely guffawed.

"But I won't anymore," I said.

"What!" exclaimed Mabel.

"What?" Voices nearby echoed her excitement. We were surrounded suddenly by Big Bill's bodyguard and the bodies of a half dozen or more guests. I caught a glimpse of Lippmann's dour visage behind a lady's bare shoulder. He moved away, noticed me, shifted back to Big Bill's right.

"Why's that?" said Bill.

"Because you're crushing my fingers!"

"Boy!" he shouted, flinging my hand back to me as though it were a hunk of wood, "I like you!"

"And I like you, Bill," I said, rubbing my hands together. Some people around us applauded, pleased, I suppose, that they weren't watching the brawl that they thought for a moment they might get a look at. Suddenly all the world was a stage; we'd become the center of attention.

Bill Haywood shook his large head and said to Mabel, "Hey, you going to give me a chance to talk tonight the way you promised?"

"I certainly am," Mabel replied, turning already to herd the guests back to their seats.

"Let's talk later," Bill said to me by way of farewell.

I nodded, drifted away across the room to watch Morton, the Jewish bombmaker, in the window seat eat an *hors-d'oeuvre*. (But where was wide-eyed Malka tonight?)

"Friends, comrades, welcome!" Mabel's voice rang through the room, overpowering the chatter of her guests. On the street outside, several large black vans cruised by. A milkman, of all people, halted his horse and cart across Fifth Avenue, and I glanced at my wristwatch, compelled by the occasion to mark the odd time of night for such a delivery. The bombmaker's chewing noises subsided. For the next half hour, I stood and listened to the wrangler's narrative of events in the mill town across the Hudson. My head soon swelled with images of workers, pickets, factory wheels, wagons, guns, searchlights, police guards, bosses, bullets.

"Paterson is only a train ride away from where you sit, folks," Haywood thundered in conclusion. "You can't pretend any longer that it's on the planet Mars!"

Mars! Strikes! War!

"I'll be going then, Jack..."

Steffens's voice reached me as though through a coastal fog.

"Good night," I watched him push through the crowd toward the door, thankful that he'd brought me here but also strangely thankful that he was departing. A thick cloud of smoke billowed up from the ladies who swarmed about Bill Haywood. The attentive Lippmann stood next to him, nodding, noting, punctuating big Bill's words with his mousy grin. I trembled and wasn't sure why. White-gowned Mabel hovered near them, pure and oceanic in her billowing robes.

Suddenly someone yanked my arm and yelled. A woman shrieked! The bomber brushed past me, spitting bits of food as he bumped people aside.

Blam! something crashed behind me. Blue helmets bobbed through the foyer.

"Awright, don't nobody move!"

No one moved, but people still shrieked, shouted, and blustered about as policemen waded into the room.

"There's a law against this—" Mabel's voice protested loudly over the din.

Flash! Flash! Treble high shrieks! People fell to the floor in fear. Flat against the floor myself, I peeked at the encroaching boots of the police. Mars! Strikes! The war's begun!

"Awright, let's stop the screaming! Calm down, everybody!" A copper shouted on! But a pistol reported! "Come on, folks, it's only a couple of newsboys wants to take pictures of you fiends."

"No three of us look as fiendish as any one of you!" Mabel stood defiantly before the reporters, a great curtain of white. Slowly, foolishly, those of us who had thrown ourselves onto the thick carpet picked ourselves up. Here and there a person wept.

"It all happened so quickly, darling," one uptown lady said, lighting a cigarette to puff her fears away.

"Hold that pose, madam!"

A photographer fumbled with his large camera; the lady's eyes opened wider and wider—FLASH!

"Thank you, madam,"

"What ever for? Oh, oh, where is he going? Darling, he's going to show me off!"

I caught a reporter by his coat sleeve and kept him standing with me a moment while men in blue and other fiendish reporters mingled with the crowd.

"What's all this about?"

"I don't know," the newsman told me, "the cops said they were coming over here and asked us did we want some stories about the zoo this Lodge lady keeps over here. What they're supposed to be doing I don't know. There's some kind of an agitator hiding out in these parts. You know, one of those *anarchals*...I don't think I've seen you around. When did you join our outfit?"

"I'm with the zoo, a dangerous *anarchal*," I replied.

"I thought you didn't look fam—" He couldn't finish his words.

"Ladies and Gentlemen," Big Bill called out over the buzzing of the crowd, "I thank you kindly for your attentions this evening. These fine uniformed officers have graciously volunteered to escort me back across the river and as you can see—"

"Awright, shut up!" the officer in charge shouted.

"—I have willingly accepted their generous offer. I hope that you'll—"

"Let's go!" shouted the cop.

"—come and see us out at the Paterson picket line."

"I said move along!" The cop shook his stick at Haywood. He was about to reach for his arm when Big Bill gave him a glance that said I'd-die-as-much-for-a-dime-as-a-dollar and the policeman shrugged.

"As I was saying, we'd appreciate any kind of assistance you can give us, from your face out there cheering us to your voice out there talking for us wherever you can!"

"We support you, Bill!" Other guests joined in, more sprightly now, showing their contempt for the police. "We're with you! With you all the way!"

"Come on out to Paterson! Come, come join us!"

Haywood kept up his patter as he moved slowly along with the policemen flanking him like palace guards all the way across the room. As he passed me, he looked me straight in the eye and said, "We need you out there with us, Jack Reed. We need your voice!"

The last sound I heard before the door slammed behind them was the booming baritone of Big Bill Haywood, crooning, "Officer McNeill, how are you? I'm trying to catch the midnight train. Can I get a ride in your milk van?"

In the room meanwhile, chaos returned to its normal level. Steffens had inexplicably returned and was holding court on the subject of the raid.

"Capitalist police defend capitalist property," he was saying, "and if a man or, worse, a group of men, dare to speak out against that property, why, you saw it this evening, ladies and gentlemen, they haul him away like garbage!"

"Will they publish my photograph?" one of the smoking women interrupted.

"Do you want them to?" asked her husband.

"I don't know," she said.

"They will whether you like it or not," said Steffens. "so you had better like it. That is another example of the way in which the capitalist forces manipulate the news system..."

He lectured on to a diminishing audience of men, who were worrying that they had not stood up strongly enough to the police, and women, who wondered if they wanted their freedom to be bruited about in the next day's daily editions.

Throughout this uproar, Mabel strutted and flourished her foldy gown at the doorway, bidding guests goodnight. "Steffens," she said, when all but the two of us had departed, "when we first met I was a naive young woman who had just fled a marriage, and I thought that the world was all askew.

You were the heroic muckraker in seven-league boots. But as the years pass, you become ridiculous and I become cynical. I thought that I invited Haywood here to help his striking mill workers, not to give you the chance to take to the pulpit."

"I wasn't implying that you had intended to do that, my dear," said Steffens, huffing himself up to size. "But that seems to be the result. What's going to come of this night's palaver if someone doesn't act on what he's heard?"

"I'm going to," I said quietly, hearing my low voice gather resonance in the now empty hallway.

"Jack! Of course!" Steff started back, surveying me like some old prospector out of his California youth.

"What will you do, Jack?" asked Mabel, gathering me in familiarly with her eyes.

"I'm going to Paterson," I said. "Perhaps tonight. Tomorrow, for certain."

Steff appeared to be pleased. But an odd note entered his voice when he spoke again.

"We'd better go home then, Jack, and get some sleep. I've found that a man needs a great deal of intense gathering of perception when covering a story the likes of the Paterson strike. You need your rest."

"I was planning to head down McSorley's way," I said. "Come with us, Mabel, and we'll make you the first woman to set foot on their sacred masculine bar rail!"

"Oh, let's leave such petty issues to the petty types," said Mabel. "Why not stay and drink with me here? I'd love to have you stay."

"I'm going to lasso my sleep right now," Steffens said, nodding toward our hostess. "And I suggest, Jack, that if you're going to prowl around Paterson tomorrow you do the same." He sounded almost peevish as he pulled open the heavy door.

"Damn it all, Steff," I burst out in a voice that surprised me most of the three of us, "my father's dead. I'll be the father of myself from now on! If I want to stay up all night, then I'll stay up!"

"Perhaps I will stroll with you gentlemen, at least part

way," Mabel said. "Just wait until I get my parasol. It seems to be drizzling."

"Those poor pickets, walking the line on a night like this!" Mabel fussed and clucked as we made our way down the steps to the pavement.

Steff drew apart from us as we reached the curb.

"I'm going to walk the line, Mabel, Jack, if you'll excuse me."

"Are you going to Paterson now?" Mabel looked astonished. "Jack goes in the morning. Why don't you wait and go with him?"

"Jack will do just fine for both of us," Steff said. "I'm going home now to sleep. I had a hard trip back from Pittsburgh."

"If you must," said Mabel, bestowing a polite kiss on Steffens's cheek. Then in a low voice, as though they were fellow conspirators, she said: "Thank you for bringing Jack to me tonight."

In those days, all the city was our stage. Steff walked out of the pool of light from the streetlamp, fading away toward Washington Square. Mabel and I were left to recite our lines alone.

"We will love each other," she said, "by loving the toiling workers."

Part Four

CROSSINGS

STRIKE STRIKE STRIKE STRIKE STRIKE

Ten times a minute these bold words blinked out from the Madison Square Garden marquee, drenching the terrified faces of the mounted policeman and the dull eyes of their horses in pure banker's-debit red.

STRIKE STRIKE STRIKE STRIKE STRIKE

Direct from Paterson, where I crossed a street to talk to the pickets and landed in jail for four days. Nothing better for me or them could have happened. Some of the kindest immigrants ever to ship over taught me folk songs in their native tongues, and I taught them Harvard yells in return. Their story sang in my newly stirred blood, a tale much too ferocious to be left to newsprint alone. And so we sketched out the pageant that would amaze and outrage a New York crowd accustomed only to theater that was politely removed from life. We made a script, built a platform, and rehearsed the mothers and brothers and fathers and children of everyone who sat in jail; we turned Madison Square Garden into an arena for aggrieved and grieving workers.

I sang at the top of my voice with the best of them, pranced and mourned for days on end, living off nothing but buckets of beer and slices of sausage. By the time we left the Garden at the end of the last performance, I was trembling with hunger of one sort or another.

STRIKE STRIKE STRIKE STRIKE STRIKE

One last glance back at the sign, and then I sank into Mabel's ample breast.

"You were marvelous, Jack. As daring and dashing and

heroic as any of the strikers themselves! What an artist you are! I love you, dear boy. I really do!"

I trembled, as though suddenly splashed with icy ocean water. I wept on her bosom. Was I in love with her? The car spun on toward the Village. But we stopped at the apartment only to pick up the waiting Nurse Galvin, Son John, and hand luggage. Mabel produced tickets for an Atlantic voyage. Bobby Rogers met us at the docks with the rest of our baggage. Who knows what would have happened had I remained in New York the rest of that week? Once before I'd sailed for France, on a cattle boat with schoolmate Waldo Pierce, a big big fellow, but not half as brash as I. We made big pranks, and I'd fallen in love with a French farm girl before sailing home again. Now, on board this ship, I collapsed, like a punctured balloon.

All the way to Le Havre, Mabel and Galvin nursed me as though I were their mutual child. Was Son John drinking milk at the bar all the while? Perhaps he played checkers with Bobby Rogers. And Big Bill and all the strikers? How could we have left them so suddenly after we had made them a part of our daily existence for a few tense weeks? Where was my conscience? A thousand windows blinked the answer back at me from the coast at Le Havre. At dawn, pigeons soared up in vortices of gold. Le Havre to Paris, my worries bounced up with each bump of the train. Green forests flashed past me. Paris, all a grillwork of streets, gushed rushing pedestrians. Entrained again for the border and Mabel's Italian retreat at Arcetri. *Questa la gubbai? Festa la border?* They carried me off the train.

It took me more than a month to put myself back together again, and I don't know but that our surroundings hurt as much as helped. I ate copiously, drank lavishly, and meandered about the grounds. The carefully tended gardens carried me back to the Green mansion where, behind the music room, Grandma grew her prize Portland roses. Such thoughts of home pricked and stung like thorns. Mama sitting in solitude in the Stout Street apartment, attended only now and then by loyal Harry. My Uncle Ray in an old folks' hotel by now, victim of endless falls and tumbles which crumbled his bones and brain. The workers striving through grease and muck to find bread for their tables. Children squalling. Brutal snarling police, the dogs! Their smiling bosses. The news had come that the strike had been broken. A pageant of misery lurched through my head while around me Italy, a Renaissance painting, gilded itself with each new summer day's sunrise.

And what did I do to make the world better once I grew better myself? I wrote poems to Mabel who had, after directing Galvin to bathe Son John and tuck him into bed, arrived in my room each evening, followed by a servant with small logs for my fireplace, carrying a copy of *The Divine Comedy*. I pawed her. She slapped my hands aside and continued reading. I attempted to loosen her garments. She huffed and puffed herself up to story-book size and shriveled me with a glance. Was this what true love was like? I didn't think so, but couldn't be sure.

Calm prevailed for awhile. I built my new self from the scraps of the old. Mabel encouraged me to write more verse. I became, once again, a tough-minded man.

Important visitors arrived from France. I couldn't remain in the presence of these large, lordly ladies for more than a few minutes without again feeling physically ill. I wanted to talk to Miss Stein. She had interesting theories about writing. But we hadn't gotten very far in conversation before I had to excuse myself. There I stood, doubled over, under the intense Italian starscape, vomiting into the shrubbery.

Mabel presumed that it had something to do with the abstinence she had forced on me. She came to me one night far too late for our customary reading, dressed in filmy garments, nervous as an actress.

"Tonight, dear boy," she declaimed, as though announcing a concert or a dance, "we must cross the threshold! Are you ready, my darling, for the travail?"

Mabel was much broader beneath her gauzy gown than I had imagined. She leaped onto my couch, knocking aside the volumes of Byron and Marx which I had taken for my own late-night bedtime reading.

"Sorry, sorry, dear boy," she crooned, laving my face with her winy breath. She reached over and grasped my head in her large, firm hands. As she did so, her gown fell open, revealing an inner garment of shot-silk that shimmered and flickered in the fading light from my fireplace. My heart thumped like a bass drum in a small-town Fourth of July parade. The couch creaked as Mabel, still holding me by the head, leaned back and away from me in such a fashion as to allow herself to stretch her rather short legs beneath me—I had to scramble like a crab in order to accommodate her in this—and drew my face into the valley between her jutting breasts.

"Ah, Jack, Jack," she chanted, "I don't know that either of us is ready for this, but we must plunge on. Don't we both know the way? We're not infants, and the world must be ready to accept the results. From the moment you walked into my parlor and I saw the light sparkling about your beautiful head, I knew this kind of power would pass between us. It is power, isn't it, Jack? The kind of energy that drives machines and messages across the tundra! Oh, Jack, dear boy, can't you feel it pulsating even now?"

Suddenly Mabel's mood shifted, like a sea in transition between two weathers. Her voice turned peevish, ornery. With a flick of her wrist, she veiled herself to me.

"You must have had so many other women before this."

"Girls, not women, darling," I said, "and not as many as you think."

"Is that the truth, dear boy?"

"I swear it."

"On what do you swear?"

"On this Bible."

I picked up a book.

"*Don Juan?* Swear on *Don Juan?*"

Laughter crossed Mabel's teary face.

"Oh, Jack, Oh, my darling," and she unveiled herself to me. A little while later, I opened my eyes to discover ourselves in darkness.

"The fire's dead."

"Not mine, dear boy," she whispered.

"Did you cross the threshold, darling?" I inquired.

"I'm there," she said. "Are *you* feeling better?"

"Yes, my darling." I stroked her cheek. "Enormously better. You knew the medicine I needed."

"Oho, perhaps you'd like Miss Galvin to administer it to you each night before bed?" She reached for my head again, as she had when she first came into the room "Eh? John, son John?"

This annoyed me a little, and I wanted to break away.

"I wrote a poem for you today, dear Mabel. Would you like to hear?"

Gently, she released me and lay back against the couch, her body a pale continent against the oceanic darkness of the room. I took a breath, sat forward, then began.

"'Through the halls of the Medici, queenlier far than they,/Walks she I love, half peasant, half courtesan—/In her right hand a man's death, in her left the life of a man—/Beware which you choose, for she changes them day by day;/Sun and wind in the room of her soul, all the beasts that prey!'"

"Jack..." She was weeping. "It's a bronze. A piece of...of...eternity!"

I fell back upon the couch and closed my eyes. The next thing I knew golden Renaissance sunlight spilled over all the objects in my room. The air itself burst with birdsong. A knock at the door.

"Darling?" I called, "please come in!"

A servant entered, bearing a letter on a silver tray. Seeing the return address, I nervously tore it open and devoured Lippmann's sparse prose. Telling me in no uncertain terms that I had betrayed the workers' movement, that I was an airy dreamer if not a fully ripe hypocrite. My guts lurched inside of me, as though I were back on board ship.

"Bastard!" I shouted into the beautiful air. "Jew bastard!" I crumpled the letter into a ball and tossed it into the gardens below my window.

Mabel arrived again shortly thereafter.

"Darling's upset?" she crooned. "Does he think it's time for his Medici? Later, sweetness, because Mabel's invited two Italian anarchists for lunch. We can't play doctor all the time, my pet."

And I couldn't play sick. On a lark, after a dream about old Lee Sing, I wrote to Carl Hovey, editor at the *Metropolitan* asking him to send me to China. I agreed to travel with Mabel to Paris. But that trip was disastrous. Mabel noticed me admiring one of the mannequins who frequented the studios of a Spanish painter whose work Gertrude Stein told her to buy, and for days thereafter she pawed me like an old lion.

"You don't love me anymore!" She screamed loud enough to wake the people in the next suite. "Isn't that true? Isn't that true?"

I tried to make love to her to dissuade her, but some Western part of me, long buried, roused up a vigilante mob in my brain, and instead of giving myself over to pleasing Mabel (and myself) I wondered about what Stein did to Toklas and Toklas to her. Mabel calmed down. But when we returned to Italy, I felt ready to crack again. Then a letter arrived from Hovey telling me that once I returned to New York he would seriously consider assigning me to China. I discovered myself dancing up and down the terrace chanting football yells! So did Mabel.

"It's this, isn't it?" she asked, holding out a piece of crumpl-ed paper in her palm. It was the letter from Lippmann that I had thrown away before our trip to Paris.

"Where did you find that?"

"I crawled about on my hands and knees in the rose bushes for you, dear boy," she said in a voice I hardly recognized as hers. "One of the servants saw me. I told him that I had lost a stone from my ring." Mabel's eyes flashed wetly in the glorious light of the sun. Her body quaked, but she made no sounds of weeping.

"Please, lovey, don't cry."

I wrapped my arms about her, as though sheltering her from a pelting rain. That didn't help. With the same stealth she had put into the planning of our original departure from New York, Mabel bought us tickets for a steamship heading west.

And we kept on going.

On the evening of our arrival in El Paso, I sat insomniac at the window that overlooked the Rio Grande, waiting for the new day to arrive. I soon forgot about Mabel's heavy breathing and the occasional creak and tick of the bed behind me. Barking dogs and barking pistols punctuated the darkness, yanking me from my chair. Snippets of antique music, accordion and harmonica, drifted up out of the border night, with here and there a clear stretch of voices raised in foreign song. Cries of children, a tooting trumpet, the asthmatic braying and wheezing of courting donkeys, how different the voice of this evening from our own! No whining sirens pierced the air, no roar and rumble of subterranean trains, and the stars were as clearly visible as on the high seas.

Up from the streets, the pattering of smooth-bottomed san-dals and bare soles soothed and massaged my aching mind. That shuffling and stirring of peasants already slogging toward the day announced to me, even before the outcry of the cock, that the night was already on the wane. A glimmer of light too close to earth for starlight settled on the southern blackness. Mabel stirred but did not wake. The very texture of the air had changed. Smooth darkness turned grainy gray. Something shifted in the southlands in countermotion to the already fading starblink. Was it the river emerging out of the absence of space? Cock crow! Another and another! I gurgled along with them, wondering if this were false dawn or real. It was still too dark in the room around me for me to see the dial on my father's gold watch. Then, as if a dozen stagehands had yanked upwards on the handles of God's dimmers, dawn breathed out of the sky. The ribbony border sparkled between two dark shores. The world took on noise again, as a ship takes on ballast. Whispers, children crying, clang of pots, sounds of cocks, more cocks, burros, hens, dogs, horses, these wafted up to my window, along with the first bright smells of cooking. The stars had gone. The winding silver of the river twinkled and glimmered in the approach of the sun. That morning, after breakfast with a rather sullen lady, I crossed over.

I've written elsewhere about how wildly I lived on the far side of that border—how I rode with "La Tropa," that swaggering, thundering band of gunmen on horseback; drank cactus whiskey straight from the wormy cask; ate the raw flesh of a freshly slaughtered calf; slept while rattlesnakes crawled past my bedroll; heard the tune of bullets whistling past my ear; and saw the people put up an army onto the land. How wildly I lived! I've written also about how close I came to having to give up my father's gold watch at gunpoint, about my sadness upon hearing of the death of my new found soldier friends, about my happiness at witnessing the simple, moving pageant of these impoverished thousands struggling for their own piece of desert soil. Mexico, that piercing nation, where you live, as they say, on the edge of the knife! It seemed only a few breaths ago that I had returned to Manhattan in search of an assignment to the Orient, and gotten diverted here to the southern desert with no one for company but a band of ragged soldiers with whom I could barely converse. My own troubles faded into the furor of the battles and the bitter beauty of the terrain.

The last days of Villa's siege of Torreon, the last major federal garrison between the northern army and Mexico City: our artillery had commenced the deadly business of laying waste to the outlying districts of Gomez Palacio, the smaller town that guarded the approach to the larger city. With several friends who were scouts for Villa, I spent hours reconnoitering the Federal lines. Though we dodged bullets now and then, it was worth it all to gaze, without the aid of field glasses, upon the faces of the enemy soldiers manning the few remaining rooftops that stood between us and the center of town.

The workers' struggle had been mere theory to me before my sojourn in Paterson, and war had been a myth until this New Year's. Words, no more than words. I knew my Tolstoy, my Stephen Crane. But not even their vivid battlefields had prepared me for the electric shivers that coursed through me as we crawled along trenches drenched in blood, or for the high, nose-choking stink that hovered over the no-man's land between our lines and the outlying buildings of Gomez Palacio.

The soldiers joked with me whenever my face turned pale.

"Juan, Juanito, don't you like the Mexican sun?"

"Juanito misses the north, the land of ice and snow."

"Juanito, Juan, move along before the bullet bites you in the tail!"

Their teasing voices soothed me in the midst of the furor of battle. Shells burst nearby; a machine gun rattled somewhere off to the left. When a dog leaped into the ditch, I nearly jumped out into the line of fire.

"Juan does not like what the dog eats," said one of the troopers.

"What can he do, poor doggie," said another. "Life is hard and food is scarce."

The dog meanwhile chewed on a human hand.

"Give me your pistol," I said to the unshaven trooper nearest me.

"You going to kill the poor dog?" He laughed. "Is this a Federal dog? Or one of ours? We must inquire of it. Well, dog?"

The filthy, red-skinned beast went on mauling its grisly find, oblivious to our voices, oblivious to the noise of the guns.

"It's clear," said another trooper. "He is a Federal dog because he doesn't listen to our questions. Juanito must execute him."

I stared a moment at the drooling, dark-fanged beast that worked its jaws up and down, up and down, on the bleeding knuckles. The dark-cheeked soldier handed me his weapon. I shook my head. I asked him to lead me into the trench closest to the enemy.

"Now give me your gun," I said when we reached the point of the line. We were nearly within the shadows of the few hulks of two-story buildings that marked the outskirts of the nearly demolished town. Aside from a group of snipers atop a water tower that commanded the main road, only a few riflemen here and there prevented the entrance of the army into Gomez. Villa, I had learned upon awakening, was giving his men some rest before marching through this town so that they would be ready for any major resistance that might possibly await them down the road in Torreon. Weapon in hand, I watched for the shadows of gunmen along the plaster eaves. Soon enough, one of the Federal snipers spied us crouching in the trench and commenced firing. I fired back, watching my shot spit wildly into the side of the building while his tore uncomfortably close to our position.

"You aim with care," said the owner of my pistol, motioning for his comrades to hold off firing their own weapons. The duel between me and the rifleman went on for several minutes. Bullets kicked up dust on the rim of the trench. I fired back, my aim improving. Twice my comrade helped me to reload. One of the other men cried out as he was hit in the shoulder.

"Juanito, please hurry," said the owner of my gun.

The blue braided cap I had used as my target appeared again around the turret of the roof. I breathed in, out, aimed, squeezed the trigger. The rifle fire ceased.

"Did I get him?" I asked.

"What did you say?" The soldier helped his wounded comrade back along the trench. I had spoken in English.

" ¿Lo Mate?"

The man nodded. I handed him his gun.

"Better him than the hungry dog."

I was scarcely able to crawl back toward our lines. Another border lay behind me. After years of jabber, jail in Paterson, the failure of the strike, my collapse like a punctured balloon, I had performed in a way that meant no turning back. I had picked up a weapon, aimed, fired, hit the mark. A Federal rifleman lay wounded or dying on the other side of the trenches, and I had done it. I kept this little secret close to my chest as I returned to the encampment.

I had plans for my return. I had an article to write for the *Metropolitan* about the destruction of the snipers on the water tower, and I wanted to write letters to Mother and Harry, telling them that I was all right, to Max (laughing to myself as I thought of how hairy bear-chested Eastman might fare out here on the murderous plain), and, of course, to Mabel who, when I had put her on the train at El Paso, looked for all the world, in her light brown leather shirt, vest, and chaps, like the Queen of the Cattle Range in the latest picture show about the Wild West. My bowels had other things in store for me.

Feeling a pitchy motion in my nether regions and a certain fine pain up my alley, I waved farewell to my companions and headed for the peace and privacy of a thick-boled Joshua tree and the shade of its spiny arms. Squatting, I squinted up at the sun. My stink assured me I was still alive! In need of a wash, I followed the path to the muddy stream that meandered through our lines. It was deserted. The other troopers and the few women who dared to come out during lulls in the fighting to do their wash were kept away, I supposed, by the terrible midday sun.

I undressed at the edge of the sluggish brown stream, careful to hang my clothing over the limb of a cactus in order to avoid inviting scorpions or snakes. Stepping gingerly over the rocks and pebbles, I dipped myself into the ankle-deep water. Bathing in the warm, gritty wash was a bit like laving oneself with the best Little Italy minestrone. Bits and pieces of cloth, inky paper, straw, feathers, and other matter floated past me. Someone had drawn a sign and pinned it to the low bushes on the other side of the stream, but now it hung soddenly in the wash, indecipherable. I splashed myself with the soupy water, kneeling now and then to sip. How calm it was in the center of that muddy trickle now. The guns had taken a siesta. The only noise to be heard aside from my splashing was the chirring of beetles at the waterside.

Death and I were becoming more than passing acquaintances, I said to myself. I pretended to soap myself when all I had to cleanse my body with were pebbly handfuls of stream bottom. The morning's madness faded away into the awesome stillness of a desert noon. If I were an eagle I'd swoop by me overhead, noticing the tall, burly, brown-haired human specimen singing old college songs and revolutionary jingles in a language he only half-understood, and I'd say to myself, this country is getting overcrowded. Why doesn't that lunk simmer down? He'll scare the best-tasting lizards into their holes! That bird couldn't read my soul, though. He couldn't know that I had overcome my terror. I had loved a large, lively woman and lived! I had shot at a man in battle and survived!

"Down with artists! Up with revolution!"

The desert sopped up my shouts with its silence.

"Yip!yip!yip!hoo-ray-y-y-y!"

I kicked my way a bit upstream, shouting at the air, the sun, the mountains, and any birds of prey that might be swooping there. Naked as a new born child, I baptized myself in the name of Max Eastman, *The Masses*, and the Holy Grail, and lapped another drink from my own cupped hands.

It was then that I noticed the dog. It was lying belly up on the far bank of the wash, its ugly maw contorted in the agony of death. A number of insects had already begun their work. I got just close enough to catch a whiff of the awful perfume that led them there, before I turned away in disgust.

"Poor foul beast," I muttered, discouraged that someone had taken up my aborted mission and killed the sickly scavenger. When I reached my cactus clothes hanger, I stood a moment in silence, letting the sun dry me while I mused on the death of a dog. Then I shook out my garments and dressed.

The guns kept their peace long enough for me to try the article for Hovey. I was about to begin a second draft when a faint rumbling made me sit up and peer around the flap of my tent. A smart stab of pain in my stomach assured me that the rumbling came from within rather than without. I wrote a few pages before a jab of pain made me sit up straight. A cold wind whistled through my belly. I took my cue and stood up, lurched toward the tent flap, and unloaded everything in my stomach across my shoes.

The guns started up at that moment, bringing shouts from the soldiers in the camp. A few rushed past me, glancing curiously at the pool of bile, then hurried on toward the line. I staggered out behind the tent. The pain I felt upon squatting was twice as cold and wrenching as before. Yanking up my trousers, I stumbled toward the center of the camp. My mouth felt as dry as a cattle skull in the sun. More soldiers rushed past me, some turning to smile at the staggering gringo, *borracho* so early in the day. My goal now was to reach the rail line where the hospital car stood. They knew how to cure these things, I told myself, collapsing into a hip-high patch of weed.

When I awoke, men were singing some of the same songs I had chanted to myself while bathing in the stream. The smell of iodine mingled with the odor of my own vomit. A man wrapped in bandages sat across from me. When I looked up, I saw Villa standing alongside my cot.

"How do you feel?" he asked me, touching a stubby finger to my shoulder.

"You are lucky, friend, that your intestines did not fall out your backside or blow up like a bomb. You are a journalist, are you not?"

I nodded weakly, rather mystified by his presence.

"I could not read until last year, my friend the journalist, but I can see a sign that says 'poison.' We even draw a picture of a skeleton on the sign for those that cannot yet read. But you drink the water."

"The dog—"

"What dog?"

"It couldn't read the sign either. It died in the stream just before I arrived."

"Well, the Federals almost kill you with their poison. Perhaps they wanted you in exchange for the man you shot this morning. That would be unfortunate because you write good articles about us. This is what my friends who read English tell me."

My eyes felt suddenly heavy. I wanted to sleep. But Villa rarely made such appearances outside his headquarters except in battle, and I wanted to keep him talking.

"You heard that I shot a man?"

"Sí. He was your first?"

"Sí, General Villa."

"That is difficult. But if you stay with us it will become easier. Like the fucking. That was hard too the first time, was it not?"

Villa patted me affectionately on the head, as though I were his brother (or his child or his puppy), and then waded past his entourage to the door of the car, leaving me on my cot to mend awhile.

Washington in summer is a dripping, windless city. As I strode briskly up the path toward the White House, I had one of those curious moments of objectivity that comes to us now and then, in which I saw my burly self all spotted with sweat, pinching up my nose at the whiff of the colorful Potomac, wondering how the picturesque odor made its way this far from the banks. I had come (again on assignment from Hovey) to ask President Wilson some questions, about Mexico among other things, and it amused me to notice by the smell of things that Washington, after all, did not seem all that far away from the state of Chihuahua.

Joe Tumulty greeted me at the door.

"You'll want a cool drink, Mister Reed," he said after finding me a place to sit down. A black waiter appeared bearing a silver tray and a single glass of lemonade.

I sipped my way through the drink while Tumulty gracefully lectured me on the rules of interviewing the Chief of State. The odd habit he had of curling up the right side of his mouth at the edges while trying to sound honest kept me amused while he spoke. After dryly pointing out to me the kinds of statements I could attribute to the President and the kinds I could not, he suddenly reached into his pocket and took out a copy of the *Metropolitan* with my byline.

"You should know that the President has read your writing, Reed. And he likes the style of it. Not the international workers stuff, of course, but the descriptions of Mexico. You give a man a real picture of the landscape, that's what he told me. If he likes the way you interview him, he might even consider you as someone who could write *for* us rather than just *about* us."

With that insidious bit of flattery to ponder, I was ushered into the waiting room just outside the President's office. While I rushed through the questions I wanted to put to

Wilson, Tumulty went on about the kinds of benefits a writer might gain from working in the White House. Feeling a bit oppressed by the pomp and circumstance surrounding me—black servants, white guards—I refrained from telling him that all in all I preferred the way Villa's lieutenants worked, which was to shoot you or embrace you, depending upon their true feelings.

A buzzer buzzed. A door opened.

Gauze curtains billowed out from the window, framing the dour man's presence in an unreal white glow. Dabbing rivulets of sweat from his wattled underchin, the President bade me be seated.

"Tell me all about the Mexican business, Mister Reed." His voice was a gentle murmur, almost drowned by the whirr of nearby electric fans and the clatter of garden tools from the lawn below. "And your General Villa."

"We must stop seeing the revolution in terms of personalities, Mister President," I said. "Villa is only one man. But he has an army of people behind him. You might say that he's merely the foam on the wave of revolution. Zapata as well, from what I learned about him." I felt like a school boy reporting to the principal. "They're both men who began their lives as poor, illiterate peasants, Mister President, and both pulled themselves up by their own bootstraps. Or sandal straps, I ought to say." I watched for his response. "They're almost democrats, sir, and I think that you ought to consider their fight the extension of our own."

"Mister Reed, I don't know what they call it at Harvard, but in New Jersey we call what you're doing chopping logic. A moment ago you insisted that we ought not to pay too much attention to these individuals and concentrate on the people instead. Now you try to compare them to our Founding Fathers...."

We laughed quietly at my being caught in my game.

"But tell me," he said, leading me into the next figure of our encounter as though he were a dancing master at court, "when you talk of the Mexican 'people,' are you talking about them in light of German philosophy?"

"Excuse me, Mister President, but I think I read a book about a fellow named Dionysus once and if it was written by a German then I've read German philosophy. But when I mention the Mexican people I'm not talking about any concept in philosophy, I'm talking about the actual, live mule-riding baby-making bean-eating folks who happen to be settled down that way!" I was sweating profusely, ready for another glass of lemonade.

"Not the volk but the folks, that's cute, Mister Reed. I had been told that you were quite an idealist, but you seem like a most practical man to me."

"You can't be an idealist and write well, Mister President," I wiped my brow with my shirt sleeve, feeling quite pleased at having done so. "At least you won't write well enough to be read by a lot of folks."

"I don't know about the number of your readers, Mister Reed. But I do have some friends who have commented to me about the effectiveness of your work."

"Thank you, Mister President," I said. "And may I ask who these people are?"

"Some...industrialists...." He looked coyly over the rim of his spectacles, rather plainly enjoying the way the compliments worked on me. I steeled myself against any further ploys such as these, but he had already detected the smile I was struggling to control. "Now this is not for publication, you understand me, but John Rockefeller himself was deeply affected by that story you wrote. And I emphasize the word story, because from everything that he told me, a great deal of what you said simply did not occur."

"Mister President, he didn't tell you that the miners decided to commit suicide by burning themselves and their families alive?"

Wilson pursed his lips, giving himself the look of a tormented owl.

"I'm your President as well as John Rockefeller's, Mister Reed. You needn't subject me to the kind of irony that one expects you to heap upon others. I'm trying quite hard as a matter of fact to remember that when I accepted your invitation to interview me I thought that it would give me a good opportunity to hear the other side of the Mexican story."

"Story, Mister President? It's reality, it's history, the same as the article I wrote about how Rockefeller's men massacred innocent women and children in the coal fields in Ludlow."

Wilson leaned to one side and reached under his desk. A buzzer sounded in the next room. I was still cursing myself for going too far before saying my piece on behalf of Villa when the same black servant glided into the room bearing a tray of lemonade.

"Tumulty tells me that you're writing a book about your impression of Mexico. Give me a preview of it, Mister Reed. Tell me all you know. And no more of this fencing match between us, you hear. Take off your coat and start talking."

When I left the office, I was exhausted. But at least I had accomplished my mission and I *hadn't* been offered a job.

Mabel had planned everything in advance. The apartment was empty. No salons on the calendar. Son John and Nurse Galvin safely ensconced in a summer house in Provincetown on Cape Cod. The telephone lay off the hook, the doorbell was disconnected. It was a lover's scene of the highest order created by a passionate woman who loved to create great scenes.

Yet a different rhythm seemed to have commenced for us now that I was back from my travels. At lonely times during the desert war, while shells burst around me, while wounded horses coughed up blood and peasants died on the sand, I longed to be here in bed with Mabel. In Washington, while the highest flunkies in government directed my steps through hallowed national shrines, my thoughts fled to Mabel and her bountiful affections. Viewing smoking pits and mounds of rubble filled with charred mementoes of families no longer intact, surveying the burned out miners' camp under the indifferent tourmaline shell of a cloudless Colorado sky, I pictured myself back in her generous arms.

But now that I had returned, I seemed again to live on the edge of the knife, having become, in spite of myself, two beings, one a person living in the present, the other a creature leaping into the future seeking more adventure, revolution, cataclysm—my destiny! Lounging in Mabel's bed, I felt like a snake.

I had been lying back, flaccid, in a stupor of post-coital fatigue, but her statement made me sit up in the middle of that great white bed.

"While I was away?"

"Yes."

"You've made love to Andy Dasburg? He invited you over to have your portrait painted and you ended up in bed?"

"Oh, how jealous my dearie is," laughed Mabel, brushing the back of her hand across my thighs.

"No joking," I said, pushing her hand aside. "Is that what's happened?" Storm clouds gathered. We had promised each other before I had left that we would be true to each other and I myself had been saint-like in my self-restraint.

"Dasburg would like that," Mabel said, "like to *paint* me, that is, dearest. He's told me that many times. *Portrait d'une grand dame en fleur!*" She went on twitting me like this awhile, posing in odalisque fashion while allowing me to leave the bed, pull on my socks, underclothes, trousers. I was as angry at myself by then as I was at her. I hadn't realized how possessive I was and never suspected I would become this jealous. I wanted no middle-class Midwestern churchgoer's version of medieval chastity to put a brake on the life I loved. And yet I loved Mabel, and so didn't truly want any other woman in earnest. As I buttoned my shirt, I was close to tears.

"I don't care to tease you any longer, my dearest. It's just too painful to watch. No, Jack, I simply mean to tell you that

I'm *enceinte*. Yes, my dear boy. And *you've* done it!"

"That's horrible!"

"You're not happy?"

"No, I'm not happy. Mabel, that's a terrible thing. The world's a mess. I don't want to bring a child into this world."

"We'll make it a better world, darling. I know you can help to do that."

"Mabel, I'm too young to be a father. I want to write our names in fire across the sky! Not wheel a baby buggy up the Avenue!"

"It's the fruit of our affections, dearest Jack. You've told me how much you loved your own childhood. Won't you love to make a lovely childhood for the offspring of our *amour*?"

"Mabel," I said, hearing my voice become uncharacteristically strident, "in good conscience I can't. I couldn't be a good father doing the kind of work I want to do. I'd be away from home too much. I'd be in danger. I could be killed in one of a hundred ways, in a revolution or a strike or a war. Better that we be a loving childless couple than have a child who grows up with half a family."

A rather unhappy time began for us. From the outside, we must have appeared to be quite the sportiest, dashingest couple in our circle. People in the Village had begun to hail me on the street because of my Mexico articles. And Mabel, of course, had had quite a following before I ever took up with her. Our closest friends began to gossip when Mabel was seen one day coming out of Dasburg's studio, but I was the only one who knew that she went to be painted before her belly grew so large that Andy would notice. This shouldn't suggest that she had convinced me to become a father. I urged her to have the problem taken care of. With money and connections, this was not a difficult thing to arrange.

Mabel had stopped reading the newspapers after the end of the silk-workers' strike. Because I was deeply immersed in my Mexico pieces, I had not been keeping up with the headlines as much as usual, and one day in Provincetown, while we were visiting Son John, I was surprised to hear from our friend Floyd Dell, fresh from the city, that the world was in worse turmoil than our private lives. Armies were mobilizing across the face of Europe.

"Perhaps you're right," Mabel said to me over lobster that evening.

"About what is he right?" asked Dell, who, though he advertised his own affairs quite little (yielding, as all of us did, to Eastman when it came to choosing a champion of the bedsprings), never looked away when electricity passed between other couples.

"Yes, about what is he right?" I inquired, pointing a meaty claw at my buxom lover.

"The world is in an awful mess."

"You agree then?"

"Yes."

"About what does she agree?" asked Dell, wanting desperately to be in on our secret.

"That the world is in an awful mess," I repeated. "A hell of a thing, Dell, for you to bring up this European war just when I was getting the hang of writing about Mexico."

"Will you go and write about his one?"

"Of course he will," said Mabel. "He's no stay-at-home. Do you think he's the type to push a buggy up the Avenue when there's a war to write about?"

"I never thought of Jack as the domestic type," said Dell. "Why, you weren't thinking of marrying, you two, were you?"

"Never," said Mabel, pointing a lobster fork at me, "Jack's too young to marry. And I'm too old to marry again."

"What a lovely arrangement you two have," said Dell.

"And now I'm going down to New York to have Andy Dasburg finish my portrait."

"Oh, you are, darling!" I exclaimed. "That's marvelous."

"You allow her to pose for that lecher unchaperoned?"

"We've made provisions for me," said Mabel.

"That's a second mysterious thing you've said tonight, Mabel." Dell again looked inquisitively at us both.

"Armies are mobilizing all across Europe and you're wondering about an innocent remark like that?" I offered Dell a glass of beer. "You ought to write a novel, Floyd," I said. "That way you can make up as much as you like about what people really mean when they pass such innocent remarks across a table."

These days were a strange mixture of sadness and happiness. Mabel returned to New York, accompanied by Dell, and I took charge of caring for Son John.

Armies mobilized across the face of Europe.

I taught Son John how to swim.

I finished the Mexico series, taught Son John how to scan poetry.

Marsden Hartley came up for a visit, accompanying Mabel on her return from the city.

"Well, it's done, Jack Reed," said Mabel that night in bed. "You needn't worry about pushing a baby buggy this year."

I wanted to ask her about the pain, and wanted to comfort her. But she shut me out cold for weeks and weeks. Armies mobilized across the face of Europe.

"I don't believe there'll be a war," Dell said one night over another lobster. His grandfather had served in the Union Army, and he assured himself that this made him quite an expert on military matters.

I hadn't read much about the European situation, and so I could concur with Dell's hopes but still feel quite ignorant.

"I'm going to study up on it," I said.

"The scholar-reporter," said Mabel, staring at her lobster claw.

"Is that bitterness I detect?" Dell looked pleased at the prospect of domestic dispute.

Hartley cracked his lobster shell loudly and sighed.

"I hate war! It's a bad time for painters. Nothing stands still unless it's dead or demolished."

"There's always Goya," said Mabel.

"That's not art, that's illustration," said Hartley, picking at his food. "There's a difference."

"Unfortunately, it's a good time for writers," I said. "We're at our best when things are on the move."

Dell muttered into his plate.

"Something Eastman said to me about you."

"Tell us!" Mabel looked up dramatically from the shards of her own meal.

"Jack's like a whirlwind, only always just passing through."

"Is that a compliment or a criticism?" she asked.

"Dunno," Dell muttered.

"Aha!" Mabel spat out a piece of shell.

"There is bitterness here, isn't there?" Dell asked.

I decided then to visit the folks in Portland. Mabel said she would meet me back in New York. But when I returned from the West, there was a note waiting for me at the register at the Liberal Club. Mabel had sailed for Europe.

The first wounded men from the stalled war hobbled along the boulevards, marring the usual picturesque scenes. In the hotel room where she had sequestered herself since her arrival, Mabel mourned the passing of our idyllic days.

"I'm too old for you," she moaned as soon as we began to make love.

"That's not true, dearest," I soothed her. "You're the ripest fruit, at the height of your powers—"

"I've been unfaithful to you, Jack."

"Name me no names. You're a free spirit and I love you for that."

"We're murderers! I dream of the child we punished for our love."

"Dearest, talk that way and you'll go mad. And I'll go mad with you."

"The world's in flames. I had a dream. What does it matter now? Pont Neuf awaits me, the river, the Seine."

I shook my head.

"I worship you, Mabel. You're the only good thing in the world for me. If you hurt yourself, I *will* go mad."

"And so to protect and preserve the life of your ego, I must desist from doing myself in?"

I fled to the front, thinking foolishly that work might create for me a better mood. A day or two in the trenches soon put a halt to thoughts of change. Machine guns parted the hair of several men each morning. Mortars splashed bodies about like porridge. The only thing worse than waiting around to catch shell-fire or running under the spitting mouths of the machine guns was the killing itself. Boredom ranked alongside terror on the soldiers' list of worries. Men could not charge into the enemy fire at all hours of the day and night. They needed to rest a bit. And the rest was boredom. They played cards, read books, wrote letters, sang songs, joked, talked, wept, even—kissed. I saw two young recruits at this activity way off to the rear of the lines early one morning on my second trip to the front. But nothing could fend off long the horrors of the terrible trough between the waves of killing and dying.

I returned to Paris with hopes of writing about this strange special mood. For the second time in only a few months Mabel had out-flanked me. As suddenly as she had sailed for Europe, she packed her bags and returned to the United States.

"*I need something more than all this!*" her note declared. "*Your love for me splashes splendidly in my cup, and my cup splasheth over in turn. And yet there must be something MORE!*"

I could write nothing for days. I crossed the Channel and found all London in a fit of passionate declaration of its killing powers "for King and Country." I fled back to France and wandered to the front again in time to witness the fiercest hours of a battle on the Marne.

"Try to write down all of the verbs that you think of when you recollect the battle," Stein told me when in a fit of despair I visited her in the painting-bedecked apartment that

Mabel had frequented during her stay. "Verbs are the war. You Harvard boys write with nouns. You must change your style."

"I write what I feel," I said. "And what I feel now is this terrible upset. And the writing comes out all jumbled."

"Feeling and writing are distant cousins," Stein said. "Every now and then they visit, but most of the time they live apart and hardly ever correspond. Write verbs."

But my feelings produced nouns: night, steel, blood, splinters, shellings, trenches, mud, bloody water, animal shit, wounds, looks of despair. . . . This war had nothing to do with what I saw in Mexico. It ground up troops with precision and treated them to boredom before it killed them in forthright ways. No music of guitar and mouth organ, no cheery voices in the ranks raised in tribute to their always present leaders. Soldiers cursed, muttered, rarely laughed. Mostly they moped about, passed poor food through their sickly bodies, ate more, grew bored, then picked up their weapons and went rushing to die. . . . You have some nouns, I said to myself one cloudy autumn afternoon. But not enough verbs. Waiting, dying. But what does that fat critic roosting on her sofa know about war? She and Mabel faded temporarily from my thoughts.

I talked to candle makers, shoemakers, tailors, street cleaners, a bicyclist, students, sons of businessmen, ironmongers, furniture makers, a wireless operator, a chimney sweep, a ditch digger, an automobile worker, all of them as young as or younger than the Mexican troopers I had known. But none of them anywhere near as happy. Why did they fight? The French didn't even bother to mouth what the English pretended cheerlessly to believe. I interviewed a few officers, though I knew what cliches they would offer. Their men, meanwhile, marched into fire, suffered, inflicted suffering and death, and died themselves. Those who returned to the trenches lay bored under the terror of the next day's sunrise.

"Thank God, we'll never get involved in this mess," said Andy Dasburg, when he turned up one night at a Left Bank cafe. He told me that he had come over to enjoy the last flowering of Parisian freedom. The war might soon put an end to all that.

Arthur Lee, a sad-faced sculptor, sat with us, not worrying about the war but about his convalescing common-law wife Freddie. While we drank our wine, she lay at home recovering from a serious internal ailment.

"Did you ever contemplate a portrait of Mabel in the raw?" I asked Andy after we had all drunk quite a bit of wine.

"No," he said. "But I must confess, Jack, we—"

"I've done my wife in metal," Lee interrupted. "Would you like to see the piece?"

"Let's go and visit her," Dasburg said. "She'd enjoy us coming over to take a look." He must have been relieved that I wasn't angry.

"At the metal piece, old boy," I said to him, noticing the reddening about the sculptor's ears at the joke.

"It's not an awfully expensive piece, Jack," Lee said when we reached his apartment. "Dasburg tells me that you know the Stein woman. Perhaps...."

"I believe she buys only French," I said. "But if your wife is a treat, Stein might think of purchasing her."

I was in the best mood in months. Lee's voice thickened.

"I'm not much for jokes these days," he said as he trudged alongside us through the middle of a decaying courtyard. He kept his studio in an old cow barn. The state of art and the war weighed down on him. It was not a cheerful overture to a sick bed, but I looked forward to viewing the sculpture. What else should we care about when the world is filled with uniformed maniacs sending battalions of ordinary working men into the trenches?

"Beautiful!" declared Dasburg, when he saw the wire sculpture that writhed its way up from its base toward the ceiling of the old barn.

I nodded at its simplicity, but my eyes returned at once to the model, a pale woman about my age with a thatch of closely cropped red hair. She lay swathed in robes and surrounded by pillows on an old camp bed at the other side of the large studio amidst metal, canvas, stretchers, paint tubes, paint buckets, a forge, piles of wire, a week's worth of dirty dishes piled in the corner near the water trough, and an overturned wardrobe. Flecks of ghostly hay swirled through the dim, humid air, and the scent of cow piss cut its way through the tang of paint and spoiling food. The sculpture itself seemed like just another bit of clutter. But the model, her eyes still glowing with the heat of her recent illness, was set in this squalor like a precious stone in muck.

"Jack Reed, Frederika, Freddie, my wife...."

"Have we met? At the Liberal Club once...?"

"Probably," Lee shrugged.

"I'm sure," said Freddie Lee. She shivered in the draft from the open barn door, and gave a shrug, the essence of her fragile victory over death. Her voice shivered as well, with its attractive little German lisp.

"What do you think?" Lee asked me.

"I don't know how you've done it! It's a wonder!"

"And the space," Andy added, "I marvel at the space."

"It was hard to keep my mind on it," said Lee, "what with Freddie as sick as she was."

"Artists must overcome such petty afflictions as wars and ailing wives," said Dasburg.

"But you can't leave her here," I said.

"Would that woman want to borrow it, you think? To see how it looks in her house?"

"Lee, I told you Stein buys only French. I meant your *wife*. She can't go on living here in the middle of this drafty place. She'll catch pneumonia."

"I've already recovered from that," said Freddie Lee from the bed.

"Look, Arthur, I have an entire hotel suite to myself, since Mabel went back to the States. And I'm not even going to be there because I'm returning to the front."

"You've just come back," Dasburg said. "And you told me that the French ordered you to keep out of the war zone."

"I'm going to the German front," I said, deciding then and there that I must make the trip. Again I urged Lee to move into my hotel suite immediately. "Perhaps you'll even have a chance to meet Stein," I suggested. That crazy idea, more than anything else, convinced him that he and Freddie ought to take up temporary quarters in my suite.

Dunn—my illustrator—and I hired a car the next day and rode out to the French lines. But before we saw anything more than a thousand soldiers digging a thousand new trenches to replace the lines they had lost, we were stopped by the military police and told to return. So it was somewhat of a surprise to Freddie Lee when I appeared back at her new lodgings only a few hours after I had, with a great show of friendship, departed.

The wiry version of fragile Freddie stood in the main room, its slender limbs pointing toward the corner in the ceiling where I was aiming a bottle of Pouilly-Fuissé.

"You're feeling better?"

"I'm still feeling rather weak, actually. But Arthur's back at the studio working. He's very strong."

"Tell me, how long did you lie there in that barn?"

"A week, two weeks, I don't remember exactly. Arthur doesn't let us keep a clock. He believes that an artist must regulate his day by the sun and the moon. He reads Blake instead of the daily papers."

"Blake?" Spok! The cork shot wildly toward the ceiling.

"An artist who wrote poetry. A romantic. Like Arthur."

"You don't appreciate romantics? Here, have a glass."

"Thank you. Do you think I can? Just how far should my

faith in the artist's integrity be stretched? I'm thinking of my husband now, not you. You rescued me. Cheers!"

"Cheers. That's nice of you to have noticed. But what do we do with you now?"

"Help me convalesce."

"I thought that that's what I was doing."

"I mean *help* me."

Dunn and I made inquiries the next day about the possibility of traveling behind the German lines. We had a wire from Hovey back in New York saying that he was trying to do the same. By the morning before we were to board a train for Switzerland, Frederika Lee and I had fallen deeply in love. In a moment of euphoria, I declared my intention of marrying her, thus giving up forever the seesaw game between man and boy that Mabel had forced on me. I sent Mabel a letter.

Imagining her response when she opened it gave me great pain. I had loved that woman and still embraced her in my mind. As far as Arthur Lee's reaction, I did not have to imagine much. Freddie was his little half-German *Hausfrau* and model. As far as he had ever seen, she had no will of her own and was surely being led astray by yours truly. Lee had not meant to mistreat her by bringing her home to their little cow-barn to recuperate from her illness. He just never thought of doing otherwise. She, a good, dutiful daughter, had never complained. When he returned to the hotel from his studio and found us drinking wine and reading poetry to each other, he accused me of carrying on behind his back.

"Then from now on it will be in front of your face," said Freddie.

"Traitor!" Lee wailed, attacking her.

"Hold off!" I cried, leaping to Freddie's defense. I grabbed Lee by the wrists and wrestled him to the floor, but his superior strength, acquired by years and years of work with metal sculpture, helped him to toss me aside. In a moment, he was punching her again while I kicked at his shins like a harmless floozy in a stage play. If Dunn hadn't walked in just at that moment, Lee might have put Freddie in the hospital for a good long time.

"Stop, you bastard!" shouted Dunn.

"Oh, I am! I am such a bastard!" said Lee, throwing up his hands. Freddie slumped to the floor in a pool of tears as her husband rushed past Dunn and cursed us all as he slammed the door behind him. I attended to my weeping little sweetie whose precious mouth seemed unharmed by her nasty brute of a husband. Dunn was drunk on good French wine, I was drunk again with love!

"Frederika, darling, we'll leave this vile city! We'll go to England, out of the war! We'll sail for America!"

I was skimming along on a great wave of feeling, pleased to see the world below me gaze up and wonder!

"Would you like me to excuse myself?" asked Dunn.

"Stay, stay!" I urged. "You can be the witness to my testament!"

"Are you proposing to me, Jack?" Freddie asked weakly from the sofa.

"I am."

"I think that we should go to Berlin to talk to my family."

"But how can we do that? Dunn and I have been trying—?"

"And succeeded at last," Dunn interrupted. "That's why I came by. We've received our permission to visit the German front."

"Wonderful," Freddie murmured, visions of our wedding already filling her head.

We entrained the next day, without much fuss or packing, for Switzerland. Thus war and love intertwined in my life in a way they never had before; and Berlin, I found, was a wonderful place to celebrate such coincidence. Although it lay as far east as I had then yet traveled, it seemed more western than London or Paris. In fact, it gave me the impression, on account of its gaiety over the feats of the German army, of a cowboy capital like Cheyenne or Denver, and so I felt quite at home.

I wrote about this to Hovey. "Interview the Opposition! Or get to the trenches," he wired back. Since I had not yet received the proper papers for the front, I hunted up Karl Liebknecht, the Socialist leader, and talked for a few hours with him on the nature of the war. He was just as optimistic as I was, about the forces at work to end it, but it seemed that all the workers I interviewed took a different view from his, different from the French workers', and from my own. "Anything for the Kaiser!" was their cry. No order was too impossible to carry out for the Fatherland!

New Year's Eve. A year had gone by since I had crossed the border into Mexico. I drank my champagne, a solitary wine drinker amidst Freddie's beer-drinking family—mama and papa and cousins and aunts and uncles and nephews and nieces, all gathered to celebrate our impending engagement.

"Why don't you cheer up?" asked her father, a textile manager from the Midlands who had emigrated to Germany to advise in the setting up of a mill and had remained to prosper. "It's going to be a quick victory for the German army. I know my English soldier. He's good for fighting wogs, but put him up against his own kind and he becomes rather shy, shows a politeness that prevents him from killing with much passion. I don't know why the two governments don't just cut up the pie right now. What's the purpose of waiting for all the mud to settle on these perfectly fine young lads." As if to demonstrate for me how it should have been done, he sliced me half of a delicious walnut cake baked by Freddie's mother and urged me to devour it.

"Papa, he's all filled up by now, don't force him." Freddie took my hand and led me to a group of chunky female cousins who clucked and giggled over me. Freddie had filled out a bit now that her mother's cooking had replaced the spare cuisine of the Left Bank artist's table. She looked so much like her stout relatives that it made me shudder. Later, back at my hotel, I noticed that we embraced with a predictability that annoyed me.

"You have cured me, Jack," said Freddie, clinging.

"And I feel low," I said. "I have to get to the front."

"Then come," she said, and rolled over to show me what she intended.

"I can't now."

"You're all the time thinking of the war. And you don't even like it!"

Her laughter irritated me.

"Am I supposed to? I'm going to talk to Dunn," I said, getting out of bed.

"It's late, darling."

"I know where to find him."

"Jack, please come back. You can see him in the morning."

I pretended not to hear her and silently slipped into my clothes.

"At least tell me that you love me."

"I do, Freddie, *Liebchen*. But I need to see the front and write about it."

Several more nights passed, adding to my waistline and my suddenly renewed dark feelings. My low mood carried me back to the indolent days at the Villa in Arcetri. Something about old Europe depressed me no end. Drinking with Dunn at the newsmen's bars only increased my unease. We spent the next few days snooping about the War Ministry and the Foreign Office in the hopes that we might stumble on some way for us to do the job we had come to do. It was finally at our own Embassy that we found the means to reach the front, arranging in a few hours what we had spent weeks pounding our skulls about.

Freddie wept when I told her the news. "Don't you love our love anymore?"

"We'll keep the home fires burning for you, old boy," said her father. "Just keep your head down and your eyes open and you may live to write about your trip."

Freddie's Mama wept along with her sisters and her cousins in one of those intense scenes that you know you musn't ruin by your own desire to beat a hasty retreat.

"Perhaps I should return to Paris?" Freddie asked as we reached the station.

"Oh, no, darling, I'll come back here."

"But we won't be married. You don't love me. You love the war, you love going to the war, you love the writing about—"

"Please," I said, taking her by the shoulders, "calm down, Freddie." I tried to kiss her, but she pulled away. "Come, love, we'll do all that we said. Do you have enough money for a ticket to Paris? Are you sure you want to do that long round-about trip by yourself?"

"I'll feel better in Paris," Freddie said.

I thought I knew what she meant, but I did not think about it much at all. I was as euphoric as I had been when I had written the letter to Mabel about my love for Freddie. Dunn and I boarded the train that would carry us westward toward Brussels. Freddie waved disconsolately from the platform. As the cars rolled forward, she ran a little way along the track, but we quickly left her behind. She now seemed spun out of airier wire than her husband might ever employ in his sculpture.

The tracks lay straight ahead, and the engine pulled us forward toward Belgium. Not a twinge of conscience afflicted me while we smoked and drank in the compartments reserved for the party of Senator Albert Beveridge on whose coattails we had climbed in order to gain entry to the tour of the German front.

Beveridge was a hard-faced fellow from Indiana, and his enormous paunch bespoke his rise to power during an era whose signature was the full belly and the empty head. I had heard him discourse on the Senate floor during my last trip to Washington. I had hoped that I might hear him declaim about manifest destiny and the American role of power in the world, his favorite topic, but he had spoken instead on the virtues of a certain bill with respect to the future of the businessman. Still, he had employed a great amount of violent gesticulating and quoted from the Bible, Shakespeare,

Milton, and Mrs. Alcott. He was a big fish of that special variety that swims in our American seas, devouring the minnows and bass, and ranging, certainly, with the biggest whales.

With us "boys," as he called us, he employed fewer quotations and calmer gestures, but portrayed himself quite effectively as a patriot. He saw America as co-manager of a world of imperial governments, such as the kind Germany had formed.

"You can't see us hooking up France's corset, can you now, boys, without first having the pleasures of what's beneath it? All her glories lie behind her—as it were—while Germany is a young power. A hundred years ago you couldn't even find her on the map, let alone watch her armies advance to the very outskirts of Paris! Now, France? She's sitting on her fanny, drinking wine—*uhn poor bwar, sil voo play*? Her troops don't even care enough to stage a formal retreat. They sit all day discussing the finer parts of philosophy or how to make a cow pregnant while a perfectly splendid fighting army like the Kaiser's wastes its ammunition on an already defeated nation! Now don't you think we Americans know which side is which? We always did! We always will! *Uhn poor bwar, sil voo play*?"

We finished the wine in his aide's picnic basket. Before we reached the Belgian border, I asked the Senator a few questions. Did he believe that only business should have the power to design the future of government or could he imagine the possibility of the workers in those establishments having a voice? What, in fact, was his stand on the question of the union of all workers? Did he have an opinion on the view held by some that the war, whose zone we traveled through, was a battle between traders rather than anything else, and the spoils would belong to the trader who sacrificed enough of his workers to win?

He heard me out, and then sat back in his seat and yawned.

"You don't want a pleasant talk, you want a Senate speech,

boys, and I'm not about to give you that." And he emitted a belch that resounded over the noise of the train wheels. "Everything I stand for comes down to that little phrase which I'm so fond of, 'Manifest Destiny.' 'Manifest Destiny.' That's something schoolboys will remember me for. It doesn't mean a tinker's dam that you and I and the trainmen don't know half the time what it means!"

"What do you think we ought to do about the Mexican question?"

"Damn it, boys, can't we just sit here and enjoy this wine? One of the few good things those French do well is squeeze grapes, and you want to go on with politics! Why, when I was your age, I could tell a hawk from a handsaw, but I couldn't spell politics if you bribed me! It's business called by another name is all it is, if you want the truth, and as far as your greasy Mexican question goes, for me there's no question at all. Wilson sent the troops in, and he's going to keep them there until we get a government we want! The same damned thing as Cuba! You got apple trees like Cuba and Mexico in your front yard, and you got to shake them real hard till the ripe fruit falls into your lap. That's all there ever was to it and all there ever will be! Now stop pretending that there's two ways to look at the question. If more existed, I'd ask one of these German soldiers to put one of them up against a barn wall and shoot it. Keep the world simple. That's healthy. It's the sick who die of complications. That's my motto, boys!"

In Brussels, we boarded touring cars provided by the German General Staff and rolled eastward over flat countryside toward Lille. The land itself looked defeated. The fields had been tilled by mortar shells. Few birds flew. No one but corpses slept beneath the trees. I had entered Death's *desmesne*, and though the German side of it seemed a bit more orderly than the French or Mexican, the odor was familiar.

The next night, an officer and Dunn and I found ourselves stumbling along a road in pitch blackness under a steady rain. On our right, splinters of trees smashed by shell fire looked sharply into the hellish illumination of the rockets.

The whistle of bullets over our heads blended into an almost steady sound that lashed tree trunks like whips. Half a mile ahead on the left, three large howitzers smote the air one after another with a deep sound. Footsteps crunched the muddy road. The trenches opened up below us. Leaning against the wall of the front trench, men stood shoulder to shoulder, shielded by thin plates of steel, each pierced with a loophole through which the rifle lay sodden with the drenching rain, their bodies crushing into the oozy mud. They stood thigh-deep in thick brown water and fired their weapons eight hours of the twenty-four. The riflemen paid no attention to us. Through their loopholes, they stared absorbed, alert, into the blackness, waiting until the next rocket should show the least movement.

Up a gentle hill straggled the French trench, a black gash pricked with rifle-flame. Between lay flat ooze, glistening like the slime of a sea-bed uncovered by an earthquake. Only a little way off lay the huddled, blue-coated bodies of the French in three thick, regular rows, just as they had fallen a week and a half ago, for there had been no cessation in the firing.

"Look," cried the lieutenant, "how they have been slowly sinking into the mud! Three days ago you could see more. See that hand, and that foot, sticking up out of the ground! The rest of the bodies have sunk."

We saw them, the hand stiff, five fingers spread wide like a drowning man's.

"No need of graves there—they are burying themselves!"

Far away mighty lightning split the night, and the roaring, accumulated thunder of a bursting big shell attacked our ears and sent us reeling. An artillery duel continued until bloody-fingered dawn stirred in the east.

"Try your luck?" asked one of the officers during a lull in the shelling. He handed me a Mauser. Having lost my battlefield virginity in Mexico, I calmly pointed it through the nearest loophole, squinted out into the reddish dust of dawn, and pulled the trigger. Dunn took his turn and then I tried it again.

"It's like firing at ghosts," I said to the officer. "You can't see anything."

He shrugged, as if my desire for a target were some curious misunderstanding which civilians held about shooting. The big guns took up their chorus just then, almost as if in reply to the puny shots we had fired, and the officer urged us to make our way to the rear of the lines.

"Why? We've stayed all night under the shells. Why must we leave now?"

"Let's go," Dunn urged. "I'm tired and no less frightened than I was twelve hours ago."

We climbed out of the first trench and started back along the way we had come.

"I don't think we should have fired at the French," Dunn said, his voice fading in and out of the boom.

"It was a gesture, that's all," I said. "I'm on both sides and neither. This bloody mess." I slid along a torn up patch of pathway and felt my legs give out. "Don't worry, we didn't hit anything. Those emplacements haven't been moved in weeks. One of the officers told me that earlier."

Farther along the road we caught up with retreating soldiers, straggling along with rifles carried under their arms. They were mute, for the most part, with the silence of desperately weary men. Dunn and I (though not our guide), as if at a signal, lowered our eyes with shame as we passed them. Suddenly, a man on the path just ahead began to scream. We could not see him, but we could hear his moans and unintelligible yells and the scuffling of struggling feet. A moment later we came abreast of him. Someone had forced a gag into his mouth and bound his arms tightly to his sides. Two comrades held him firmly by the elbows, forcing his head forward. His wild, staring eyes snapped like a beast's at the sight of us—he wrenched his muddy shoulders convulsively to and fro.

"Another one," muttered our guide as he led us forward. We walked briskly ahead, leaving behind the last shuffling man. We were alone again, on the road to a farmhouse where we might wash and rest. Neither of us talked much.

Fleeing the front, and Freddie, I found more violence awaiting me in New York.

"Open up, Mabel!" I shouted through her thick apartment door. "Open this goddamned portal!"

Pedestrians gathered to watch at a reasonable distance from the steps. It was a gray, cold day—passion warmed them.

"Open this door or I'll break it down!"

A retired general lived in the apartment on the upper floor. He stuck his head out the front window of his living room.

"Mrs. Dodge is not at home!" he called as though delivering a battlefield communique. "She is, repeat, not at home!"

"Open up!" I shouted, resuming my pounding. Finally, I threw myself against the heavy barrier. My shoulder ached but the wood showed not a dent.

From the corner of a weeping eye, I saw a figure detach himself from the crowd and mount the steps.

"Welcome home, Jack, she's not there."

"Max! Where has she gone?"

Eastman, with his dutiful smile and glorious shock of hair, appeared to me as a delivering angel.

"She's in Croton, Jack." He patted me gently on the shoulder. "If I had known you were back, I would have told you that directly. No need for all this." He swept his arm toward the crowd that had gathered below us.

"We're having a few problems, she and I." I allowed Max to lead me down the street. I wiped my eyes, rubbed my aching shoulder. Although I had felt fairly well numbed on the crossing to New York, a great wave of sensation engulfed me of a sudden. I stumbled at the street corner, Max reaching out and preventing my fall.

"So she told us."

"Us?"

"Mabel gave a party for a rather large number of people. I hadn't realized you had so many friends. The occasion was a...letter you wrote to her from Paris. She and Steffens had an awful brawl over that."

"He defended me?"

"Of course, Jack. He defended you and so did I. But between Mabel and the daily papers, you're getting an awful lot of abuse in friendly school-boy fashion. Welcome home!"

I walked in a trance. I didn't think much about the daily papers until I boarded the train to Croton. Max had accompanied me to the station, offered me the key to his cottage. I declined. He brought me a stack of newspapers that carried columns and editorials attacking me for firing at the French from the German trenches. I hadn't been so foolish as to write about this, but Dunn had mentioned it during an interview he gave. A group of reporters in Paris had roundly condemned me, as had several politicians and a few university presidents. Normally, I would have laughed in the face of such criticism, but that afternoon I crumpled up like an old ball, hugging the arm rest on the seat as the train chugged its way toward Croton.

The day seemed to reflect my worsening mood. It was snowing when the train deposited me at the Croton station, and I hiked up the hill to the front door of the cottage (really a rather large old farmhouse) that Mabel had rented in my absence.

"Private Reed, reporting for duty!" I called through the door. My heart leaped as I caught a glimpse of Mabel through a front window. Her new short haircut, with several curls dangling over her broad, pale forehead, gave her the appearance of a Greek goddess.

"Open up, darling!" I tried to sound as cheery as I could.

Silence.

"Open UP!"

I pounded on the door, shaking off feathery piles of snow that had settled on my arm.

"Or you'll huff—?"

I turned at the sound of a window creaking open.

"—and you'll puff and you'll BLOW my house down?" I raced to catch her, but she slammed the window shut. I watched her pace about on the other side of the pane. She huffed and puffed on a cigarette, giving the impression of an Eastern potentate.

"Woman!" I yelled through the glass, hoping to rouse nurse Galvin or Son John, if, in fact, they were present. In this agony, I might need allies. Mabel disappeared into another room, and I went around to the back door, reaching it just as she clicked the lock shut.

"Open UP!"

She waggled her finger at me from behind the pane in the door.

"I'll break it down! I swear I will!"

She must have noticed by this time the snow falling rather thickly about my shoulders and perhaps didn't want to risk suffering a storm with a broken door or window. So she opened the door a crack without unlocking the chain, so that I could not force myself in.

"Yes, what can I do for you? Are you selling subscriptions to the *Masses*? or *The New Republic*? That's a coming journal of the arts and politics. Get out of my life, Jack Reed! I never want to see you again!"

"Mabel, I've come home to you, I swear—"

"Where's that little half-Kaiser bitch? Did you leave her at the depot while you came to terrorize me? 'The truest love I've found!' Now there's a wonderfully poetic phrase. Or 'With airy limbs the stretch of angel's breadth!' How's that for imagery! You unfeeling beast! Piss-bowl poet! Monster! Two-timer! Liar! Show-off! Cheat! I nursed you through your breakdown. Now I curse the day I ever laid eyes on you! You stride-about double-tongued bastard!" She pushed the door shut in my face and left me huddling aginst the wood.

"Please, darling." Tears spurted from my eyes. "Please..." I tapped feebly at the glass. "Let me explain."

Like a great wild eagle, she shrieked through the pane:
"Coward! Fork-tongued coward!"

And she turned her back to me again. Through the window I could see her kneel on the floor and shake with inaudible sobbing.

"I thought we were free..." I whimpered, blinking at the snow tumbling thickly about my face and shoulders. Retreating to a bench at the front of the house, I counted snowflakes until the air turned white. The first skirmish had gone to Mabel.

"All right, you dumb baby, come in before you freeze!" Mabel called to me from the doorway. Shadows from the fireplace danced in the room behind her.

"Are you c-con-vinced," I sputtered through frosty lips. My eyes seemed nearly frozen shut. It took several minutes for me to stop shaking. My back ached, the fault, no doubt of sitting in one position out in the cold.

"Convinced? Convinced by *you*?" Mabel strode manfully across the room and breathed whiskey into my face as she denounced me. "...lying, unfeeling, *traitorous* son-of-a-BITCH!" She slapped me on the face, sending me reeling back against the stone mantle. My head throbbed. Blood seeped from the corner of my mouth. Mabel ignored these effects, pacing about the room, railing at me in language quite advanced for a woman of her background, age, and class. I attempted a series of apologies, each of which grew more feeble as the intensity of her rage became more apparent.

"Vile strutting fiend! Stealing a woman out of her sick bed! Flattering her with false proposals of marriage and then dragging her across the continent so that you have a sweet-tootsy traveling companion until it's time for you to throw her off!"

"I *was* in love with her, Mabel. I was quite honest in my letter. There's no need for you to look surprised. Hurt, maybe. But not surprised. I *was* in love with her. But now I'm out of love with her!" I shouted over the noise of crashing wood and pottery. "I fell *out* of love with her because she couldn't give me what *you* give me. She couldn't make me feel the things that *you* make me feel. She never had the power to make me—"

"'Her mouth a streak of gaiety across—'"

"I wrote that to *you about* her, not *to* her, dearest—"

"Don't 'dearest' me, you cur!"

"Mabel, that's true, I've been a cur. But now this cur needs to be taken in out of the storm. Is Son John here, dearest? I'd love to see him...."

Squinting at me in the flickering firelight, she became a stranger, a woman out of another epoch. Her anger suddenly subsided.

"I was going to make myself a light supper. You might as well join me."

No sooner did this lull settle upon us than a wave of jealousy swept over me. Pretending to amuse myself while she prepared dinner for two, I searched for evidence that Mabel had had other visitors. But everything I found clearly belonged to her, except perhaps for a questionable volume or two at her bedside. Her scent suffused the air in the small bedroom, enchanting my lungs. I lay down a moment in the dark, listening to the flutter of the wind on the pane; it became the chatter of train wheels in the distance, punctuated by a dog's bark, and then changed back into wind again. Mabel had been faithful! And she had received me in a calmer state than I could have hoped for, and now she was cooking my dinner. My long journey from the front had ended, I thought, ended in peace at last. I loved this woman, her sculptured marble face, her forehead, the stately shape of her breasts that had nursed Son John and would again, tonight, sustain me, her vital core that pulled her to my side when I needed her. Sounds of wind again slurred my thoughts. Her perfume, like a hospital anaesthetic, drowned my mind. The next thing I knew my eyes were closing, I was falling down a slope....

"Dinner—Jack, dinner!"

I sat up to see Mabel in a lovely apron, her cheeks and eyebrows dotted with flour. She beamed down at me as though nothing had ever come between us. Old times!

"You're so adorable," I said as I rose from the bed and tried to embrace her. "Your hair, your curls!" But she side-stepped my grasp.

I lighted candles for the table and found a bottle of wine.

"How long have you been out here alone, darling?" I sank a screw into the cork and worked it free.

"Several weeks now," Mabel said, delivering food to the table.

Pok! I flinched at the sound of the cork, the candles shook, sending our shadows quivering about the walls of the small dining space.

"It must have been lonely. How could you stand it?"

"That," said Mabel, seating herself opposite me, "was the wrong thing to say. It was ghastly at first, but now I've come to rather enjoy my solitude. You should try it sometime. The next time you're arrested, ask to be put in solitary instead of crammed in with all the teeming hundreds."

"That was an unpleasant thing to say."

I served myself some food. Mabel sat awhile, taking nothing for herself.

"I feel most unhappy, really, Jack."

"I'm sorry that I had so much to do with that, darling." I reach for her hand across the table, but she drew it away. "Dearest, I am sorry."

"Perhaps I will eat."

"Do," I said, "it's quite delicious."

"I haven't cooked for myself in such a long time."

"You make a swell meal, Mabel. You ought to do more of it."

"I should say 'thank you.' 'Thank you.'"

"You're quite welcome, lady."

I ate slowly, savoring the taste of meat, wine, and calm.

"How's Son John?"

"That's nice of you to inquire. He's perfectly fine, ensconced in New York in school where he should be."

"And Galvin?"

"With him, of course. And in good spirits."

"She didn't answer the door when I called at the apartment."

"When you...why I can just see you, Jack, like some Victorian beau coming to pay me a call. Did you bring flowers?"

"Please, darling." I swallowed a large bit of food, choked, coughed.

"Did you leave your card? No? Why, how could she have admitted you if you didn't bring the necessary accouterments. Did you bring—"

"Have more wine, Mabel. It will make you feel so much better."

"Thank you, but I've changed my vice." Mocking me with her smile, she ignited a wooden match in the candle flame and applied it to the small pipe she had placed, quite without my noticing, at the side of her plate.

"How long have you been smoking this?" I watched her inhale the creamy white steam. She sat back, her handsome chest expanding like the breast of a great swan.

"Since I left Paris," she said, exhaling an acrid cloud.

"You've been reading quite a bit. I saw Dell's new book in the bedroom. But what's *Sons and Lovers*? And Engels on the family? I should read that. You don't have any magazines. What's that you mentioned? the *New Republic*? Is it the one that Lippmann and his pals down in Washington have started? Have you seen it?"

Mabel sat stoically while I talked on, as though she were watching a stream flow past her.

"Haven't you?" she asked, laying her pipe next to her wine glass.

"Not a sign of it in Europe. Max told me that they had put out an issue or two, but he didn't have any handy. I saw him on the street, and he rode with me on the subway up to the station."

"Didn't he tell you about the piece that Lippmann wrote?"

"No."

Mabel leaned closer to the flame.

"Poor Jack, you so wanted him to like you, didn't you?"

"It's an attack. Because I fired on the French lines! Well, fortunately I've done much worse than that."

"I know you have. You can find a copy of the famous issue when you get back to Manhattan."

"That may be a while. There must be someone in Croton who has a copy. Maybe...I can walk over to Max's cottage and jiggle the door open. He might have left a copy lying about. I'll see if the snow's stopped. Do you have a light out there?"

I got up from the table and opened the front door. The wind whistled in, wafting snowflakes with it. Even with a light, I could not see much more than a few feet beyond the porch.

"It's hellish out here!"

"You'll find your way," Mabel said, draping my coat onto my shoulders. "It's as easy as falling downhill."

"I'll wait until tomorrow, I think," I said.

"You can't."

"It's just an article...." I tried to step back toward the table, but she blocked my passage.

"You'll find one in the city."

"I thought—"

"I know what you thought. But you're not staying here tonight."

"Darling—"

"You must go now!"

I tried to embrace her but she shoved me out into the snow and slammed the door.

"You can't do this!" I yelled at her through the glass.

"But I have done it!" she called back triumphantly from the other side.

"Let me in!"

No! she wildly shook her head.

"I love you! Let me in!"

"No!"

"Let me in! You've tricked me! Let me back!"

"Please..." I shouted to the weather, to the spinning world, to all lovers, cannons, generals, to the workers of the world. I pounded and pounded. Mabel appeared at the window, pointing a polished silver pistol in my direction.

Go *away*, she gestured with the gun.

"Take me back!"

Go *away*.

"How can you—?"

I lunged at the door, heaving my shoulder against it until it shook on its hinges.

Mabel tapped on the window with the nose of the gun.

"You'd shoot me?" I pleaded with my eyes.

She nodded, the faintest smile tugging at her lips.

"You would shoot me, wouldn't you?"

She nodded again, leveling the weapon at me through the glass.

"Then shoot, why don't you?" I shouted as I ripped off my coat and flung it onto the snow. Advancing toward the window, I tore open my shirt front and bared my chest.

"Shoot the only man who's ever loved you! Shoot the one who's gone through hell to come back to you! Shoot the man who's traversed battlefields and oceans to reach your side! Shoot! I command you!"

Reaching the window, I worked feebly to raise it from the outside. Mabel again tapped the weapon on the glass. She motioned for me to come around to the door. The look on her face was exceedingly strange. Before she unlocked the door, I was off and running. Her first shot flashed past me into the trees. The second kicked up snow at my instep.

It was a bad time. Shoot! I ordered stone-faced Mabel in a recurring fantasy that appeared, like the feature at some psychic nickelodeon, around three each morning, shoot! And I flopped backward, stunned, blood running into the cracks in the floor. I resurrected myself each day to find that the street was not indifferent to my fate. Mabel lurked behind every lamppost, on the upper deck of every Fifth Avenue bus. When I began to see her face in every glass and hear her voice inside my room, I knew that I had to leave again for the front—a dangerous but safer place. This meant heading first for the office of the *Metropolitan* and then to Washington. I didn't know that I'd have to battle a roughrider before I made progress in my latest quest.

Hovey had hired him to write a monthly column for the magazine some weeks before, the same T.R. who appointed my father to the Federal marshalcy that gave me and Harry the means to go to Harvard. What a strange mixture of gratitude and anger I felt when I encountered him at the pencil sharpener!

The stocky little man threw his hands into the air and then stepped close to me. "What a way to end my career! Ambushed by the infamous Mr. Reed! How could we have avoided crossing paths until now?"

"It was hard work," I said, standing my ground.

He settled into a relaxed posture, as though he believed he could drop the post of world statesman and become nothing more than an old bully boy and bear hunter, now that the truth was in the air. "I've seen assassins at work," he said, "and you have the look of an assassin about you, Reed. A character—"

"Call me Jack."

He looked annoyed at my interruption. "A character assassin, Reed. There's something about your way of looking at things that strikes me as dangerous."

"But you don't want to hear what I have to say."

"I've heard enough. Even if I'm not in Washington, I still read the papers."

"I don't see myself as doing anything I didn't learn from my father. And you respected him."

"Your father was a splendid man. I was sorry to hear of his death. C. J. Reed worked long and hard on the side of justice. Why are you blackening his name?"

I sucked in breath, stepped toward him.

"Sir?"

"You heard me." He stood his ground and glared, his voice becoming that of an outraged schoolmaster or drill sergeant. "You wrote that guff about the Mexican bandit Villa. You praised that murderer and rapist."

"Well, I don't know what's wrong with that, Colonel Roosevelt. I believe in rape."

"Reed, I'm pleased to find that you believe in something. Shall we add firing at your own allies to the completed bill? Well, I happen to know that you won't find yourself anywhere near the front again, so we won't have to worry about a recurrence of that particular treason."

"What do you know about that?" I demanded. But he had already turned and walked off toward his office.

I snapped in two the pencil I had held in my trembling hand.

Hovey had convinced me to write a letter of apology to the French ambassador in Washington, and I had followed that up with a visit to Washington. The interview had been a disaster. The French minister kept me waiting for hours and then gave me about four seconds to state my request. I got drunk that night and stormed about the grounds of the Washington Monument. I had even humbled myself and talked to Senator Beveridge. And now I had come home to hear from Roosevelt that none of my efforts to return to the front were going to work.

I bullied my way past Hovey's secretary and caught him in an argument over the telephone. "Why can't we go ahead with the project without first getting the approval of the entire Yard? This is other people's America besides Harvard's, Mister Whitney—"

"Are you talking to the publisher about me?" I demanded.

Hovey held the phone away from his lips and blasted me with a look.

"You think that the entire country's talking about nothing but you? I've got a hell of a lot of other problems, so sit down and wait it out. The Colonel's going to be in here in a minute to—yes, Mr. Whitney, but the way I see it...."

I cursed Roosevelt, cursed the cosmos, took a seat on Hovey's sofa and felt as though I were back at Morristown Prep and about to be reprimanded by the headmaster. For a moment the office spun about and I felt myself tipping toward the ceiling. Then my anger saved me and it all became clear.

"I'm not kissing Roosevelt's ass, even if it gets me a visa into heaven!"

"Well, I've already dropped my pants for you, Reed," came the Colonel's harsh voice behind me.

Hovey said something quickly into the telephone and hurried around his desk to stand between me and Roosevelt.

"You called Washington?"

"I did, and I would have told Reed earlier except that, for a man opposed to killing, he became awfully belligerent, I must say."

"Sit down, Jack," Hovey said, easing me toward a chair.

"I won't have him intercede for me with the French!" I waggled a finger at Roosevelt.

"He's already done it," Hovey said, watching nervously for my response.

"You didn't say a word," I said to Roosevelt.

"You didn't give me a chance."

"I'm not a ready believer in conspiracies, but you two have clearly been working behind my back, and I don't like it."

Hovey sighed heavily.

"You want to return to the front, don't you, Jack?"

"The more people who read about what those boys are suffering over there, the more support we'll have when our own boys go in!" Roosevelt bit into the air as he spoke, as though chewing off the end of a cigar.

"If that's the effect I thought my reports had," I said, "I'd hang up my lance tomorrow."

"'It's-Not-Our-War Reed.' Is that how you want to be known in the history books?" Roosevelt chomped the air again. "If anyone pays any attention to you."

"I'd rather die unknown," I said, "than to be remembered as the man who murdered Cubans!"

"They were *Spanish* soldiers!" Roosevelt slammed his fist on Hovey's desk. "And who are you to complain of murder after what you've written about Villa?"

Having overcome my initial annoyance at Roosevelt's involvement in this affair, I was beginning to enjoy the moment.

"I never did have the chance to write about it, but the truth is, Colonel, that Villa rather admired you. In fact, he told me that he modeled himself on your own behavior in Cuba..."

"Hovey!" Roosevelt exploded. "You told me I didn't have to become a socialist to write for this magazine, but you didn't warn me about having to listen to *him*! Forget about asking me for any further assistance in this matter."

Roosevelt started for the door, but before he could leave I stood up and grabbed him by the coat sleeve.

"Exactly what did you do, Mister President?"

He flung my hand away as though I were a leper and stood there a moment, fuming.

"He spoke to the French ambassador about the possibility of another visa for you," Hovey said from behind his desk.

"And what did you say, Colonel Roosevelt? That you highly recommended that your dear pal Jack Reed be forgiven for firing on the *good* murderers?"

"Jack—"

Hovey breathed heavily at my side.

"I assured them, Reed, that if *I* were Marshall Joffre and you fell into my hands, that I should have you court-martialed and shot!"

Mike Robinson, the illustrator who was to do the pictures

for my projected series on the war, stuck his head into Hovey's office just then. Hovey fairly near leaped between me and the former president to usher Robinson inside. Roosevelt took the opportunity to return to his own office. I slumped back into a chair and stared out at the wintry New York sky.

Robinson and I had been out celebrating our imminent departure for Eastern Europe and the war's other front, a trip that Hovey, thwarted in his efforts to get me back into France, had arranged in desperation. I had not been happy about heading that far east but finally agreed to it. My goal was to make the world sit up with the news about the traders battling against each other for markets, using the workers of Europe as cannon fodder, and if I had to go to a backward place like Russia to report it, I would. I had spent the night trying out the potato liquors they drank on that side of the world, and Robinson had kept up with me. On the way home, rambling along the edge of Washington Square like squirrels in search of food, we picked and kicked and bumped into each other, me filling my lungs freely with songs that let all the anger and loneliness and frustration and pain come bursting out into the air.

> *There's a fight in Col-or-ado*
> *For to set the min-ers free!*
> *From the tyrants and the mon-ey kings*
> *And all the pow'rs that be!*
> *They have tram-pled on the free-dom*
> *That was meant for you and me!*
> *But right is mar-ching on!*

Pounding out the simple rhythms on Robinson's shoulders and back, I urged him to sing the chorus along with me.

> *Cheer, boys, cheer the cause of Un-i-on!*
> *The Col-or-ado Min-ers Un-i-on!*
> *Glo-ry, glo-ry to our Uni-on!*
> *Our cause is mar-ching on!*

"Yip-hip-hooray!"

I danced out into the street, back on the curb again, shouting to the treetops. Didn't we wobble!

"Gonna find us a couple of Russky girls, aren't we, Jack?"

Robinson was magnificently drunk, almost as clogged with booze as I had been the night I fell into a basket at the Fulton Fish Market and awoke to find myself embraced by a slithery fresh squid.

"Two apiece, Mike, two apiece!"

And I staggered out into the road again, almost as if I knew what would happen next.

A clang of metal, the roar of an engine, and around the corner a taxi came speeding with its headlights blazing into my eyes.

"Look out!"

Robinson leaped toward me, as if to pull me out of the auto's path, and the cab screeched to a halt just in front of us and a voice called from within.

"There you are! Get in, hurry up!"

I blinked dumbly into the headlamps.

"Inside, quickly!" Mabel swung open the door.

"Tell the cops," I called to Robinson, "political kidnapping."

"Shut up," said Mabel as I climbed inside.

"What kind of a greeting is that?"

She gave the driver her address and we sped away through the Village.

"We have to talk."

"I had that in mind when I came back from Europe. And now I'm leaving again—"

"You are! Oh, I knew it!"

"What's wrong, Mabel? You sound frightened."

"I'll tell you all about it when we get home."

"Home? Is it home to me still?"

She lay a hand gently over my mouth, and I sat quietly for the remainder of the brief ride.

When we entered the apartment, she marched me through

the familiar halls without a word about her purpose. A light thrill of anticipation tickled my rib cage. Since she had fired those shots at me not too many weeks before, there still seemed some chance that she had not finished with me. The slanting geometric gaze of the women on the new paintings that lined the walls of the rear bedroom enhanced my thirsting mood. Like the figures on the door knocker, these were women of the future, pointing toward some kind of life that all of us now might find quite strange.

But Mabel herself, for all her inscrutable kinship with these females, appeared to me as a woman of the past.

"Will you let me in on the secret?" I asked, feeling rather secure now that she had plopped herself down in the middle of her large white bed and kicked off her shoes. I discovered none of the old emotions rising up in me. How strange, I thought to myself, it is as if she actually killed something between us when she fired at me. I shivered, recalling my race through the snow.

"Come closer." She patted a place next to her on the bed.

"All right." Warily, I eased myself alongside her and kicked off my own shoes.

"You're well?" Patting my face, my shoulders, she spoke as if she had some magical vision into my guts.

"Shouldn't I be? You missed me with your gun."

"Jack, don't mock our love. Remember it for what it was."

She trembled, as though a great chill had passed through the room.

"Are you well?"

"I had a vision."

She started to explain. I watched her eyes as she spoke, tiny pupils floating in a sea of green. She had been smoking opium before she hailed the taxi and went spinning about the Village in search of me because she thought I was in danger.

"...it was as though the tissues of my brain and the corpuscles of my blood had been jarred apart, loosening their habitual hold on each other. I felt a new physical contiguity. I felt it possible to see other, different perceptions of reality...."

Her fingers worked on her buttons as if divorced from the rest of her body, and she spoke as if she were reading from a speech held by an invisible hand in the air.

"...last week, and last night it happened again. I went to bed early and fell asleep almost at once. Sometime later I awoke and sat up in bed. The apartment was silent. And yet there seemed to be a presence in the rooms, a presence that called me awake.

"'John!' I called out, forgetting that he was in the country.

"'Galvin?'

"Burglars, I decided and slid from the bed in search of the pistol that you know so well. When I had it in hand, I quietly switched on the lights and went out into the hallway. No one was there. I felt somewhat silly, put the gun away, and climbed back into bed. I lay there awhile until I realized that I was trying to sleep with the light on! So I left the bed and went to the light switch. No sooner had I turned it off than I felt the presence again. And as I looked into the darkness of the hall, I saw a blue-black column of smoldering flame flickering up through space, and when it reached a height of five or six feet, it formed a huge, jeering grin. Faceless, mouthless! In the center of that roaring sulphuric fire this mirthless, devastating grin!"

She flung herself against me, a large-boned woman trembling like a small child.

"Silly Mabel, what do you think you saw?"

"The Devil, Jack, that's who it was! The Devil and the fires of Hell! They're out there waiting for us! All our talk about changing the world, that's what it all means! I had to tell you, Jack, before it was too late. Max tells me that you're going to Russia. Please, Jack, listen to me when I say this, I beg you to reconsider your trip. You mustn't go!"

It took hours to calm her down, and as she grew more sensible, I became more disturbed. Soothing Mabel into nudity and under bedcovers, I fell into the deep emotion which, after she had sent me running into the snow, I tried long and hard to bury. I had returned to where I had started, and knew I didn't want to leave her now.

"I'll be back this evening, dearest," I whispered to slumbering Mabel when at midmorning we awoke, and I remembered that I had a meeting with Hovey before noon. I slipped a gold ring from my finger into Mabel's palm, and closed her fist around it.

That afternoon Hovey handed me our tickets for the crossing.

"I've heard some wild reports about your nighttime activities over these last few weeks, Jack," he said.

"From—?"

"From just about everyone we know mutually. Now please don't get yourself arrested or injured when you have three days before you sail."

How misunderstood I felt! He had no idea that I had found my love again and that the next three days would be a paradise from which I would dare not stir.

"You think I'm a clown who writes well simply by some strange accident, don't you?"

Hovey shook his head in amazement.

"You took the words right out of my mouth!"

"Well you can't have my words without having me, Carl!"

"Don't get all stirred up, Jack. I was only joking. I'd rather have one of you writing for me than twelve past presidents."

"That reminds me. How is the old rough-writer these days?"

"Jack, you know what I think of that arrangement. John Whitney wants him to write for us, and so he writes for us. You can't fight with your publisher and keep your magazine on an even keel."

"And when Whitney says no more of this dangerous anti-war, pro-socialist talk, what happens then?"

"We'll fight that battle when we have to. Meanwhile, you keep out of trouble."

"Aye-aye, Cap'n."

I returned to the Village, trembling with anticipation. How I needed Mabel then to calm my anxious self! The ring I had given her she had nailed to the apartment door. A note was folded up beneath it. I yanked the articles from the wood and read the message. Mabel had left me and gone west to visit family in St. Louis.

> *Hot moist hands on the glittering flanks, and eager*
> *Hands following the chill hips, the icy breasts—*
> *Lithe, radiant belly to the swelling stone—*
> *'Galatea!'—blast of whispering flame in his throat—*
> *'Galatea!' Galatea!'—his entrails molten fire—*

Thump!thump!thump!
Mike Robinson pounded on the cabin door.
"You've only got a few minutes left before the harbor pilot turns back. If you're intent on sending that poem back with him, you'd better finish it!"

> *Far-bright as a plunging full-sailed ship that seems*
> *Hull-down to be set immutable in sea. . .*

When the harbor tug veered from our side, I kissed the old life goodbye. The greatest city in the world receded into the distance, a child's playpen. Ocean opening out before us, long falling miles of air and air, storm winds.

Ship engines shifted to a sweeter treble. An old tune bobbed up out of memory to haunt me as I faced the salt-spray splash of lolling sea.

> *Pull for the shore, Chlistin!*
> *Pull for the shore, Chlistin!*

Here I was again, idiot Columbus, sailing east to reach the west!

Part Five

OF LOVE AND BLOOD

This all began with a head cold, the most common thing in Portland of a wet winter afternoon. Having once again traveled westward by train with all good intentions of cheering Mother, I found myself in bed for several days, and she hovered about my couch, as though I were back in my old Stout Street room suffering from my ailing kidney.

Mother, however, could not cheer me much. Her pained letters, the notations about her finances that Harry had posted, lay as heavily on my mind now that I was here as they had since my return from abroad. The cash I had sent on ahead, nearly the entire proceeds of the payments from the *Metropolitan* for the Eastern European series, had been already paid to creditors who had waited out of a sense of loyalty to what the family used to be, some of them for as long as a year. More bills had piled up in the meantime. Her health was not marvelous. By means of some intricate figuring that had, he claimed, something to do with the war, the landlord had seen fit to raise her rent. And she paid out more for little services, deliveries, and taxi fares now that she wasn't well enough to do for herself all the things she used to do.

Harry helped a lot, of course. But because he was as yet not sure what he cared most about, he was in and out of jobs, never staying long enough at one to build up savings enough to carry both him and mother through his next stretch of unemployment. Since he was a Reed, he did this with grace and, if there was an audience, good humor. But during my first full day in bed—after waiting of course for Mother to leave the room to attend to some business she had at the stove—he lamented the *plans* he had had, and while he wasn't complaining, he was wondering if I truly saw how much he was giving of his time and his life to the care of our Mom.

"Look, Hare," I said, "don't you think I'm aware of what you do for Mother? I cover the battlefront, you cover the home front."

Acheu!

I sneezed: punctuation from the gods. I hadn't lied. I admired Harry for the devotion he had showed to Mother through all the rainy days he'd spent here since his own commencement from Harvard. I could not imagine myself living in Portland, but I suspected that if Harry's willingness to return home hadn't freed me from the day-to-day responsibilities for Mother's care, I might possibly have turned my path back toward the West Coast, might have embarked on a career in San Francisco and paid more frequent visits. But Jack, came a truthful voice that had lived with me often since my trip through the Balkans, you'd stay on the scene for a month or two and then ship out down the coast like Uncle Ray and watch the natives revolute themselves in Bolivia. Or returning one day from covering a tea party where someone lectured about Original Sin, you'd see a sign in a shop window, a sail in the harbor, catch a cup of coffee, buff up an editor with visions of a story, and find yourself on a freighter under a sun dipping into the sea all the way to China.

Acheu!

"If the war keeps up," Harry said, drawing me out of my feverish reveries of alternative presents, "I'll be called up to fight and there'll be no one here to care for her." He paced from one side of the bed to the other, glancing down at last and saying: "It's important for us to try and set up some kind of constant for her. I have a line on some stocks that might do her well. Of course we all know how you feel about capitalistic ventures such as that."

"Cabalistic is more like it, Hare. You never know from one day to the next what kind of magician is manipulating the market. I'm not against capitalism in principle, only in practice. If all the Moms in the world stopped paying out their hard-earned cash for pieces of paper that are traded around until no one knows how much they'll be worth from one day to the next, maybe all the certificate barons would have to practice their chicanery on one another. Then they'd see how they like to get stung. The thing to do is for all of us to pick up and leave all those money magicians high and dry. Why, they'd look around and see that America had gone out from under them, like the tide pulling back at the call of the moon. They'd either have to change their ways or stay out of the wet with the rest of us." My head jerked back as though it were a puppet's in a showman's handglove. "*Ach*—"

"Watch where you sneeze now!" Hare backed away from my bedside.

"—*cheu!* Christ! You've got lovely weather here. I haven't felt so bad since I don't know when. I twice passed through the Valley of the Shadow of Death when I was in the Balkans and drank and ate with the sickliest folks you could imagine until the Czar's boys threw me and Mike Robinson back over the border into Poland. They wanted to bury me several times, sometimes out of concern about my future health, sometimes out of wishful thinking. But I didn't get sick once over there."

"Aw, Jack," Hare said, "You're a lucky man. But we're talking seriously here about a serious subject. How much cash can you spare if I come up with an investment that could give Mom something to grow on during the next five years?"

I patted my dear brother on the arm. "You're talking like one of the Rockefellers. You ought to come to Manhattan and talk like that and you'll make enough for Mom to live a hundred years on! 'Something to grow on!' You're the best investment she ever made! While—I'm her—ahem—her dividend that never really paid off. The cash I sent you from New York was my last penny. I've got enough with me now to keep me for a week and feed me on the train trip back. I know what you're thinking. I've traveled up and down the country, been to Mexico, ridden with the revolutionaries, sailed to Europe more times than you've been to New York City, and put out dozens of articles not to mention two books, and you're wondering why I don't have any more ready cash than a working stiff after he's hit the bars on payday? Because that's all I am, Hare, just another working stiff. I go from assignment to assignment, keep my apartment in New York on the good graces of roommates whose welcome I have long outlived, and don't know how I'm going to be eating come tomorrow. I won't know until I return to New York and pick up some new assignments. And then, chances are, it will be about a beauty contest for turtles instead of an interview with the secretary of state! That's what I have to do just to keep my head above water!"

Harry looked as though he was brother to the boy who assassinated the archduke at Sarajevo.

"So you don't think you can contribute anything toward this? It's an apartment building, five flats, a place for all of us to live as well, me, Mother. You'd have a room when you came to visit, I don't know how I'm going to raise my part of it. I've got a friend who thinks he might go in on it with me. An old friend of Papa's downtown will help us out with the loan . . ."

If Harry was looking at the assassin of his lifetime, I was looking up at the little boy who always got left behind. He had grown thinner since my last visit. The broad healthy face, the husky cheeks that were Papa's legacy to his boys had turned wan and waxy. The time he had passed here in attendance on Mother had taken more than a few years' worth of fire from his eyes, and I blinked out of fear that this was how I would look if sickly or dying.

"I might try wiring the editor of the *Metropolitan* for an advance against an article I could make up real quick. But I'm ashamed to say that would be a pitiful amount."

"It wouldn't be pitiful if you went out of your way to do that. It would be a mighty nice thing, Jack, because every little bit will help. You've always been a good brother, and I've always admired you, Jack—"

I pushed him as hard as I could in the direction of the door.

"Get your mournful puss out of here and buy some apartment buildings!"

I lay abed in solitude, musing upon mother's sad condition, Harry's loyalty, the state of my life. Books I'd never written took shape in my mind and then diffused into the foggy drizzle outside the bedroom window. I had walked over acres of corpses, bodies thick as grass, survived the threat of plague, crossed the border into Russia, been arrested, walked out again. Little could touch me now except mother's plight.

I slept awhile. Upon awakening, I accepted an invitation Carl Walters extended over the telephone. Walters, an old friend, told me that there was going to be a fine group of people over the next evening and that I could turn down the invitation at the risk of finding myself replaced by a sea otter. Colonel Wood and some others I'd like to see would be there. I told him that my head was stuffed but my shirt wasn't and that I'd be happy to attend. If my cold was going to keep me here another day I might as well give the disease to some fellow writers and artists.

Mother took great pleasure in nursing me through the day. By the morning, I felt well enough to get some exercise. I dressed and went out into the fog. The walk downhill went briskly, and with my stuffed head protected by my hat, the venture did not seem so bad at all. Noisome fumes drifted along the roadway as I reached the thick of the traffic. Since I had last seen it, Portland had become not just one of your thriving Western cities but a place like Hartford or Newark, a location with the mark of true progress stamped on it and its inhabitants.

I glanced at father's watch as I strode along. My fingers closed on the ring that had been burning a hole in my pocket ever since I had retrieved it from the nail on Mabel's apartment door. That trinket had traveled with me across the Atlantic and overland into the Valley of the Shadow of Death—the bloody Balkans and the Russian front where flies died with more dignity than soldiers—and out again. It gave shape to my private sorrows even while my eyes, ears, nose were subjected to the greatest public horrors our age had yet known. Mabel's vision of Evil seemed laughable alongside stacks of corpses piled higher than men are tall, and my own fate appeared as ephemeral as smoke rising from the battlefield. Yet the pain remained, and each time I had contemplated flinging the golden trinket into the ocean or the bloody mud I had paused and considered how much worse my grief might be without it.

"Hello," was all she said when I emerged from the pawn shop.

"Do I know you?" I asked, licking the lightest tinge of salt from my lips.

"Possibly."

Her scarlet hair glistened, uncovered as it was to the falling rain. The daring glint I spied in her grey-green glance showed me at once that she was the kind of woman who purposely went out without her hat. Did she like the feel of the rain? Or did she merely want others to notice the way the freshly fallen water illuminated her long, bright mane of frilly, lush hair? But couldn't it be both? Trim in a smooth cloth coat she stood, daring me with her stance as well as her eyes.

"It wasn't in Bucharest, was it? I've just come back from Bucharest."

"I know," she said. "But it wasn't Bucharest."

"You know I've been there? Was it Paris then?"

"Nope."

"You say 'Nope' like a cowboy. Are you a cowboy? Or a cowboy's best girl?"

"A cowboy's best daughter. Will you guess again?"

"What? Oh, the place, the place, sorry. Well...was it Paris?"

"You've asked me that already and I said no."

"Was it Cleveland?"

She laughed, a curling wave of sound that made me shiver.

"You're getting closer."

"Sandusky?"

She laughed again.

"Nope."

"MacDougal Street?"

"Where's that?"

"Aha, you are a cowboy's daughter if you don't know Mac-Dougal Street. I'll try cities farther west." And then I sneezed.

"Perhaps we ought to get out of the rain while we play."

"Not back in there," I said as she stepped back into the entranceway to the pawnshop. "I just had a very bad experience in there."

"Sell your typewriter, Mister Reed?"

"Worse than that. Call me 'Jack.' And will you please tell me who you are and where we've met?" I motioned for her to follow me along the street. The rain had not let up, but I paid little attention to it now, except where it glistened on her hair.

"We've never actually met," she said, "but we came close to meeting one night at the I.W.W. hall when Emma Goldman came to speak."

"Aha! Go on."

We walked in a southerly direction at a leisurely pace, past the court buildings, a little park, and up toward the hills where small frame houses had spread since my childhood. After a block or two, the pavement stopped. Horses and a few wagons, an auto here and there, traveled the muddy roadway.

"I'm suddenly quite embarrassed by this."

"What? By what?"

"Meeting you this way."

"Don't be silly. I'm having fun." I sneezed a monstrous sneeze and she grabbed my arm, as if I might slip into the muck of the roadway. "I have a cold. I guess you'd want to call it a bad cold."

She touched her fingertips to my forehead.

"What's your diagnosis, nurse?"

"Hot and wet."

"I've been worse. Right here in Portland I've been sicker than I've ever been anywhere else in the world. Except maybe for one time in Mexico."

"When you were riding with 'La Tropa.'"

"You read that, huh? and you know I've been to the Eastern front. I guess I'm the one who should be embarrassed now. You're my *audience*."

"You couldn't ask for a better one." She shook her glossy mane. "You'll catch pneumonia if we keep you standing here."

"Well, I wasn't going to give up on you until I found out where we'd met. I am an intrepid reporter."

"Shall we walk back toward the center of town? You really need to get out of the rain."

"If you'll tell me the awful circumstances of our encounter. Was I so drunk that I've obliterated it from my memory? That's the only time your intrepid reporter seems to miss the important details."

"I was the intrepid reporter then," she recounted, calling me back to an evening on a previous visit when Hare and I listened to Emma's speech in the labor hall while a group of students, boys and girls giggling and applauding together, huddled up front near the podium. "I covered her talk for a little socialist newspaper we publish on the campus at Eugene."

"I thought you might be a little socialist."

She tore her arm away from mine and gazed sullenly at the gray and dripping sky.

"Well, wait a minute. I didn't mean to hurt your feelings. It just surprised me."

"Can't a woman be a socialist? What about Emma? Or don't you count her as a woman?" A few passersby looked at us now, thinking, I supposed, how only lovers could find it within them to rush about in the wet on such a misery-making afternoon as this.

"Please, listen, I didn't mean to insult your sex. I was marveling at it, in fact! Emma is middle-aged and weighs more than my brother. I had never met a girl as *pretty* as you who was a radical besides." I tried to take her arm but she brushed my hand aside. "You believe me, don't you? This is so crazy! Dear pretty stranger, we're arguing like good friends, and I don't even know your *name*."

She laughed and looked for all the world like a child at play.

"Louise Trullinger."

"Hello, Louise Trullinger," I offered my hand.

She placed her hand on my arm, and we started walking briskly back toward town.

"So Emma was your hero? Your heroine, I mean."

"Yes."

"But you knew who I was, too?"

"A few of us read everything you wrote in the magazines. I bought your books, too."

"That's lovely. Are you studying politics at the university?"

"You think—?" She burst into laughter again, glancing around at me, laughing in my face.

"What do you do here in Portland?"

She laughed again, that thrilling, rippling, chilling sound. She laughed more than any other woman I had met. She laughed as often as other females cried.

"I write. For my own pleasure. I paint a little, too. And I help out with the socialist meetings now and then. I keep a studio in town."

"That sounds swell. But how do you support yourself? Writing takes so much time. And you have to pay for a studio."

"The oldest profession," she said, her eyes fairly sparkling in accompaniment.

My heart sank like a stone in the muddy roadway.

"I don't believe it." So young, so beautiful, so intelligent. The other prostitutes I'd met had possessed one or two of these qualities but not all of them together. And they had been always somewhat bedraggled, depressed, downtrodden. "You couldn't be a street-walker and a socialist. The two things are antithetical!"

I sneezed violently, feeling her catch at my arm.

"But couldn't I be a *married woman* and a prostitute? Aren't *those* professions one and the same?"

"Trullinger...Trullinger. What was your name before it was Trullinger?"

"Eve. And then I changed it to Mary. A virginal touch, don't you think? Most people called me by me father's name which was Bryant. You may call me Eve Temptress Mary Mother-of-God Louise Bryant Trullinger. Or just plain Lou."

I picked my heart out of the roadway, rinsed it in rain-water, and handed it over to Lou.

I basked awhile in the heat that flowed in waves from the big pot-bellied stove in the center of the room. Two floors above a busy side street near the center of town, the large one-room studio, with its kitchen area and toilet behind a screen in the southwest corner, might have overlooked a warehouse loading ramp in Little Italy in New York City. Covers from back issues of *Blast* decorated the walls, along with a few *Metropolitans* that announced my articles, drawings from socialist newspapers around the country, strands of beads, homemade drawings, old embroidered pillow cases, fresh typescript on which verses lay in irregular stanzas that I skimmed while behind the scarlet screen the scarlet-haired woman fixed me something to drink.

> *Yellow sail on the horizon*
> *A wave curls*
> *Tide draws you close*

Several covers of *Burdick's Pattern Monthly* framed under glass.

Someone's attempt to do Multnomah Falls in the mode of the French light painters.

A pencil sketch of a long-limbed dark-haired woman whose face and breasts pointed toward a sun not visible.

> *Do you know, stranger, whose soldiers*
>   *guard this wall?*
> *His love for the treasure within is*
>   *legend in this province.*
> *Twelve rows of Saracens stand between*
>   *his jewel-box and the avaricious few*
>   *who dare to envy it.*
> *A hundred vicisius Hareem guards block*
>   *entrance to the chamber of his love . . .*

"Sounds like something I once wrote."

Dishes clattered behind the screen.

"What? I can't hear you."

"Nothing. I'm just studying your decor."

> *North-west current,*
> *Flowing toward my beach,*
> *Heat of Nippon.*

"Here you are," she said, coming around from behind the screen. She had changed her long cloth coat for a long blue silk robe. In her hands, she bore a tray with steaming white mugs. "You may sit down, sir."

I settled myself on the broad, soft sofa behind which stood another screen. She sat cross-legged on cushions on the other side of a low stone table. Light from three large windows behind her glazed the air on either side of her pale, compelling face: the sheen of hair and silk, the freckled thighs she showed at the hem of her robe nourished my glance. I wiped my raw, moist nose, smiled, and reached for a mug.

"Looks delicious."

She raised her own cup.

"To your health."

"To my rotten health."

Light fell gracefully on her rounded ankle. When her robe rose slightly at the tug of her upraised arm, I caught a glimpse of freckled thigh. "What is this luscious potion, Madame Witch?"

"Tea, milk, honey, and the gum of a sacred tree of the old Northwest. How did you find me out in my witchery? I usually like to let my victims suffer awhile."

"And am I but a cipher in a long parade of bewitched males whom you've taken out of the rain?"

"You're the second one who has ever entered these secret halls."

My heart leapt! My mouth went dry. Muscles in my calves rippled with a life of their own.

"Is that true?"

She laughed a shocking laugh.

"Oh, yes! But look what happened to the last one before you!"

"What's that?"

She twisted slightly on her cushiony throne and yanked a dull-white oblong object from behind the table leg.

"Yoicks!"

"Yorick, you mean." She held up a grinning skull. "Alas, he didn't measure up to my usual standard and I had to...well, look rather gravely on his love for me."

"Where the hell did you get that?"

"I have another confession to make, mister Reed."

"I told you to call me 'Jack.' Now 'fess up."

"My husband gave it to me."

"Is he a gravedigger?" I sipped at my potion.

"No, he's a dentist."

Now I laughed, nearly spilling tea across my trousers.

"So it's *dentistry* that finances this den of iniquity."

"*Den*tistry of iniquity, yes. But don't you think he's lovely?" She ran her palm across the skull's forehead. "I call him 'Taft,' after our beloved former president. But sometimes I call him 'Daft' and other times I call him 'Drafty.' The wind whistles through his open spaces!"

"And what do we call what we're doing? '*Den*tryst-ing'?"

"Very punny, mister Reed. Your editor must delete those puns from your articles. I don't recall such low play with words anywhere among them."

"Very *den*teresting, your point of view. But why did he give you that? *memento mori?*"

"Is that Japanese? I have a love for the Japanese—"

"It's Latin. Which I have hated ever since college, though I once cared enough to translate Horace. Did your husband give it to you to remind you of death?"

"Not death. Teeth. Dentists don't think of death! Only of uppers and lowers, molars and bicuspids. And roots, there's more talk of roots than you'd imagine. And nerves. *Les nerfs*, *monsieurs, sont terribles.* Actually, I took it from his office thinking that I might stick a candle in it and serve a Halloween dinner. But I've never had the strength or the nerve, *les nerfs, monsieurs,* to cut it open. Talk about nerve. You can really lose it when you're married to a dentist, unless you put your mind to saving it."

"It seems as though you've done a good job of that." I sipped more of the brew. The skull stared inertly at the rain. My new friend sighed and skimmed her tongue lightly across the rim of her mug. "Trullinger is a good person," she said. "I like him a lot. I even love him sometimes. Most of his friends think he's mad to put up with me. He tries so hard. He's changed a good deal for the better since we married." She let the skull fall into her lap where it rested, jaws down, in an enviable location. "He's seen the value in giving me freedom. It's better for his own nerves that way. He's even written poetry in the last few months."

"Aha! Then you didn't write that awful poem on the wall. He spelled 'vicious' v-i-c-i-s-i-u-s." My mug was nearly empty, and I lay my head back against the pillows. I hadn't sneezed since we'd come indoors. I was feeling first-rate.

"You're the one who's vicious. Spell it however you like!" She frowned, creating a picture I did not care to gaze on for too long. It showed the lines at the corners of her eyes and made her long face appear older than it was. (On the walk to the studio we had exchanged our birth dates and it turned out that she and I were almost exactly the same age.)

"Sorry. I'm sure he must be a good sport to let you have your fun. Does he get his fun as well?"

Her smile returned, a puzzled smile but at least it replaced the gloomy pucker around her eyes.

"I can't really say. He could see other women if he liked. But I don't think he wants to. That poem reveals a great deal about how he feels about me."

"But it talks about a 'Hareem.' Perhaps he keeps a lot of other women."

"We'd be even then."

"Do you keep a lot of men?"

She showed me a new face, not a frowning visage but a sly, squint-eyed mask.

"I have my secrets."

"Never admit, never accuse. That's my motto."

"Wonderful. Who taught you that?"

"I learned it myself the hard way."

Now her guarded look faded.

"Please tell me how."

I sneezed furiously, spraying spittle across my trousers.

Lou leaped nimbly to her feet, snatching my mug from my grasp; the skull rolled into a corner and lay at rest once again.

"You'll need another of these."

"I didn't spill it all."

Our eyes met as if in the exotic setting of her liberal husband's awful poem.

"But enough."

"Enough."

Lou swirled behind the curtain to replenish my drink. I lay back on the sofa, running amuck in my mind. Lou reappeared from behind the curtain, holding aloft another mug of the steaming tea.

"Drink."

I sipped, let the hot brew lave my tongue and slip warmly down my throat. My head cleared suddenly, the way a winter sun peeps out from behind dense clouds and warms you well before it slips back into the gloom.

"Did you add rum to this? It's really helping."

She nodded teasingly, retrieving the skull and holding it up before her face.

"We aim to please," she said through the gaping jaw. "Now tell us your sad story and we shall judge it. If it seems appropriate, we shall even offer a prophecy. Why, when we found you standing in the foyer of a pawn shop, were you weeping into your hands?"

"You saw me?"

"You're a bit embarrassed? I thought you were the kind of person who never gets embarrassed."

"That's true. Damn it, you know me better than you know yourself!"

"You wouldn't know that." She placed the skull on the table and stared defiantly across the space between us. "You know next to nothing at all about me."

"I think I know quite a bit by your name, Louise Mary Mother-of-Eve Bryant Trullinger. You're not any relation of William Cullen Bryant, are you?"

"You think you're being cute. But as a matter of fact, I might be. I used to say 'To a Waterfowl' over and over to myself while walking about the desert. *Whither, 'midst falling dew,/While glow the heavens with the last steps of day,/Far, through their rosy depths dost thou pursue/Thy solitary way?* Would you like to hear the rest? *Vainly the fowler's eye/might mark thy distant flight—*"

"Not my favorite poet. Was he on your father's side or your mother's?"

"He never took sides. A fair man, lousy poet."

"Stupid of me to ask. What did your father do for a living?"

"My real father did only one thing that mattered. He abandoned us when I was quite small. We were living in San Francisco. Mother took us to Nevada and married Bryant there. He was a railroad man, built rights-of-way across the desert. My real father died in the San Francisco quake. I always remember that day because I was playing down by the telegraph station when the news came clacking in. The earth had swallowed up my Papa whole. At first I was glad. But I had horrible dreams for years afterward. Mother never blinked an eye. I hated her from then on."

"The aftershock."

"What?"

"The aftershock. You still feel the aftershock of the San Francisco earthquake."

A strange look came into her eyes.

"*Thou'rt gone,*" she chanted, using the skull as a megaphone, "*the abyss of heaven/Hath swallowed up thy form—*"

"Appropriate! Your father and the waterfowl!"

"*—yet, on my heart/Deeply hath sunk the lesson thou hast given./And shall not soon depart.*" She paused, as though out of breath from running.

"Might as well finish it," I marveled at her pluck as she plunged back into the poem, like a swimmer into a broad, swiftly moving stream.

"*He, who, from zone to zone,/Guides through the boundless sky thy certain flight,/In the long way that I must trace alone,/Will lead my steps aright.*" She took a breath and, once more, lay the skull aside. "Not my favorite poet, but we must honor our ancestor, mustn't we?"

"You learned about ancestor worship from the Japanese fellow who wrote those cute short poems, I'll bet. They're nice, for free lines. Is he?"

The lady actually blushed, yanking nervously at the drawstring of her robe. "No wonder the French wanted to shoot you as a spy!"

"Doesn't the dentist want to shoot the Japanese for pinning his poetry on your walls?"

"Trullinger is a nice, understanding soul. I told you, he wants to be a free soul. And so do I. We help each other in our struggles. As you can see, he even writes poetry, and you know how the average bourgeois detests the stuff. They'd make a law against it if they could."

"Now if you want a dangerous poetry that speaks to life, I'll quote you Byron."

"Quote away!"

Her eyes blazed as she deposited herself lithely alongside me.

"Eighth canto of *Don Juan*, stanzas fifty and fifty-one. The battle sequence. Waterloo."

"You must have a good memory."

The delicious fog of her scent enveloped me.

"*God save the king!—*"

"Did Byron say that?"

"Wait! *—and kings/For if he don't, I doubt men will longer—*"

The sofa shook as she laughed.

"*I think I hear a little bird who sings/The people by and by will be the stronger....!*" She recited along with me.

"You know the lines!"

"Of course, I do," Lou said. "I live that poem!"

"You love it, you mean."

"I *live* it."

She forthrightly rearranged herself so that nothing more than the length of a butterfly's wing kept us apart. Then the width. She trembled, as a bird about to sing sometimes trembles. Our lips touched, held: we spoke in tongues.

"You have now been awarded the Jack Reed Memorial Head Cold," I teased her when I broke free. "It has been a pleasure to bestow it upon you."

She touched a finger to my lips.

She slipped off her robe. The pale-white bodice that sheathed her showed pearly in the glow of the stove.

Beyond the window the rain had stopped. Twilight yielded to evening.

"'*That day they read no further,*'" she said, propped up on an elbow and looking quite puckish.

"You know your Dante and your Byron. But if your logic were correct, after reading the Byron we'd rise up from our couch and make revolution, instead of lying down and making —"

"We *will* make a revolution, Jack. One thing at a time. To-day you've got a cold, and you barely have time to embrace me before you have to get dressed for dinner."

"How'd you guess that? I have a dinner invitation. Or did. But I'm going to take you out instead. If you tell me where *the* place to eat is these days, we're on our way."

"You can't turn down your invitation at this hour, can you? Not for an old pickup on the street like me."

"Of course, I can. I will. If you're just a pickup, it's pickups for me from now on."

"Well spoken, parfit knight. But let's get dressed for dinner or our hosts will wonder where we are—"

Lou planted a kiss on my forehead and leaped nimbly from the bed.

"How did you . . . ?"

"You goose. I'm invited there myself. They think we'd make a match!"

On our way to dinner, Lou admitted the truth. She had been walking along, turned at the sound of a loud sneeze. She recognized me and followed me for several blocks and decided to speak to me only when she saw me weeping in the alcove of the pawn shop.

"Are you ever going to tell me what that's all about?"

I told her about Mabel and the ring, and how I dared myself to get rid of it.

"If you gave me a ring I'd never return it."

"If I gave you a ring, and you gave it back, I wouldn't pawn it. I'd give you one you couldn't give back."

"Through my nose?"

My head suddenly felt clearer than it had in days.

"You've cured me!"

"The rum does it every time."

"It wasn't the rum."

Her voice dropped suddenly, like a sail when the wind fades.

"I know, my darling Jack."

"My lovey."

"Sweetest sweetness."

"Daring lover."

"Hairy lover."

"Honey lover."

Dinner was a marvelous charade. Lou and I staggered our arrivals and played the night out as though we had just been introduced. Trullinger was not present at the meal. Our hosts clearly wanted to see how we would react to each other.

It was difficult explaining my absence to Mother the next morning. But she was pleased that my cold had subsided. The intensity of my affections for Lou escaped her until the next day when I introduced one lady to the other. She sighed, smiled, kissed Lou, and blessed me. Harry was pleased to receive my token contribution (the proceeds from the ring) toward his project. He lent us his car for an excursion to Astoria. While waves roared in on us, we talked about the past.

"These spaces"—Lou swept her arm toward the ocean—"they remind me of the desert."

"Is it high desert?" I took her about the waist and pretended to lift her as a dancer might.

"High, yes." She twisted about to kiss me on the lips.

"Hi."

"Hi."

We walked about, kicked at the sandy slope of beach.

"Did you love your old desert a lot, sweet dearie?"

"I loved the air, the light, and the sounds of the desert, Jack, sounds you'd never think to hear there or anywhere. The call of—"

"Mating rattlesnakes! Looopa-looopal-loooo!" I patted my hand over my mouth like an Indian and danced around her on the sand.

"You don't want to listen?"

"I do want to, very much. Go on."

"I loved the light at sun—"

"Looopa-looopal-loooooo!"

She started running, flailing her arms about like windmill blades and pumping her legs like faulty pistons. I gave her a minute and then went after her.

"Got you!"

"How dare you tackle a woman!"

"I learned it at school."

"I'll bet you did! Let me go! This sand is sticky!"

"It's winter sand." I released her, helped her to her feet.

"Now I'm full of sand."

"So am I. Let's swim if off."

"You don't dare! The water's freezing!"

"The Japan current's in. It won't be too bad. And what if it is! We've got each other."

"Are you warmer than the current?"

"Try me."

"Swim first."

"Let me help you—"

She swatted my hands away.

"I can do just fine by myself."

"Not always."

"In most situations. Go on, you're not just going to stand there and gawk, are you?"

"Nope."

"Off!"

"Sorry. Jes' can't help musself."

"How silly men look in their undershorts!"

"You've never noticed that before?"

A rumor of nipples stirred beneath her shift. She caught me staring and shoved me over onto the sand.

"Last one in's a ninny!"

She showed me her half-moonlike buttocks as she headed for the surf. I tossed the remainder of my clothing aside and hurried after. We reached the water at the same time, dodging icy waves hand in hand until we fought our way past the first row of breakers.

"God, it's COLD!"

"Let's swim to Japan and complain about the temperature."

"I'd rather swim to China if I had the choice."

"You would? You're a girl after my own heart!"

"How'd you guess? Oh!"

A wave washed over us, frightening me for a moment when I came up but saw no Lou.

"Lou!?"

"Over here!"

"Don't swim out too far!"

"Daring lover, try and stop me!"

Another roller came smashing down.

"Help! Jack! Is that you?"

"Wasn't a shark!"

"Oh, you scared me, Jack!"

"Jes' nibblin', honey, jes' nibblin'!"

Kicking my legs strongly, I never felt so free.

"But there!"

"What's that?"

"A shark!"

I shivered as a dark shape floated up out of the fourth wave ahead of us, then dipped under.

"Don't panic!"

"I love you, Jack!"

"Lou!"

"If I go under, remember! I—"

"Lou! It's all right."

The dark body of the sea visitor swept past us through the waves. Its round white eyes sparkled, its mouth agrin.

"A seal!"

"I told you, darling!"

Returning to shore, we built a fire out of driftwood, sheltering the flames behind a high dune.

"Did you ever do this in the desert?"

"Swim nude with a lover? Awfully difficult to do out there, dearest."

"Not enough water, of course."

"Not enough lovers."

"Did you have any there?"

"Jack Reed, do you know how old I was then?"

"Old enough I'll bet for everyone to look around when you

came into the room."

"We had no rooms."

"When you came into the desert."

"You don't come 'in' to the desert, silly. You're just there."

"There." I reached for her hand. "Darling, before, in the water, you called out to me."

"I called out to you because I thought I was going to be attacked by a shark."

"But nonetheless you called. Tell me again what you called."

"Did I call?"

"Tell me!"

"Don't twist my arm! I'll tell! I called 'Get your red hots!' That's what I called."

"You didn't, sweetest. You called something else."

"I cried 'Shark!'"

"You cried 'Love.'"

"Did I? I must have been delirious from the waves."

"From the waves?"

"From the salt."

"From the salt?"

"From the spray."

"From the spray?"

"From my love."

"From your love for me?"

"From my love for you."

"You've cured my cold and given me a fever."

"Let me feel your— My God, Jack, you are burning hot!"

"Get your red hots!"

"Put your coat on before you catch pneumonia! Please!"

"You care, you care so much!"

"Of course, I do, dearest. Now...There...."

"She cares! Do you hear, winds! She cares!"

"But Jack, you haven't said a word about what you feel about me."

"Not in the last ten seconds."

"Not in the ocean you didn't."
"'Get your red hots!' I love you!"
"I'm your 'red hots.' Come love me!"
And the ocean kissed us with a seal.

I wrote to Max, I wrote to Dell, I wrote to Steffens; I wrote to Hovey, I wrote to Bobby, I wrote to Mike; I wrote to Copey, I wrote to Jig and Susan, I wrote to everyone with whom I was friendly at the time announcing my new-found love. I even dared the Fates and wrote to Mabel. Even after sending my letter about Freddie Lee, I dared to compose this new note because I wanted her to know the truth about my life. Never had a woman made me feel anything at all like this! Not Mabel, not Freddie, and certainly not any of the little women I had played gallant with prior to my arrival in New York. This was the real thing; sea, land, air, this was fire! Lou was the first person I had ever loved without reservation, none of mind or body, none for the past, none for the future. The present was all, a series of gloriously happy moments: romps on the beach, hikes in the hills, a boating trip up river that took us past scenes where once I had played as a boy.

Then came the day of my departure for the East. Mother wept, but Lou was ecstatic. We vowed to meet soon in New York and then we would never part again. She had only to make some arrangement with Trullinger and then entrain herself for the City.

"Take care, my loves, my dears!" I embraced them both and shook firm hands with Hare.

Two women hugged each other on the platform while the steam hissed, the engine choughed and puffed. They looked more like mother and daughter than strangers. The bond was formed all 'round! Lou and Hare embraced. The train rolled forward. I waved madly. Family! Love! The bond that Lou and I had formed between us in a few short weeks made me privy to a condition I had only read about before in poems! The train trip East was all a blur. During the weeks of separation, I wandered about the city in a daze, stirred by no live woman and no memory but that of Lou. Lou, Lou, Lou! Aroused by the letters she wrote daily, I pictured the great stream of love dammed up in me, enough to irrigate all the parched valleys of the West!

Friends took me out to dinner just to marvel at my conduct, as though I were a new breed of beast escaped from the zoo. Had I forgotten Mabel that easily? All queries were answered, all qualms dispersed, all doubts subdued by Lou's arrival in New York.

Mother's letters had left no doubt in my mind that Lou was truthful when she told me she was coming. The breakup of the Trullinger marriage was the gossip of the season, and Mother felt ashamed to hear my name linked with that story and, at the same time, pleased that she could supply the details firsthand for her friends. With Lou still in Portland, I learned later, she made some effort to defend our affair, but once my lovey boarded the eastbound train Mother gave in to the tea-party morality of her daily companions and let me know how much she disapproved of our "modern" ways.

We did not seem at all "modern" to us. We felt downright primitive! From the night Lou leaped from the train into my arms, we never stopped showing ourselves the turns and nuances of our great new passion. We made love until our bodies turned raw. Lou sometimes had to excuse herself four or five times during a dinner, and one afternoon while playing softball on the street in front of the *Masses* office, I was taken with such a pain in my walnuts that, after I reached second base, I had to have someone run for me. We clung to each other constantly as we walked about the city. I was so attentive to Lou's kisses that once a rude passenger on a Fifth Avenue bus ordered us to sit farther apart (and I got into a shouting match with him until he threatened to call a policeman and I threatened him with an article in the *Tribune* and the rest of the passengers looked the other way). No amount of late-night carousing in the Village kept us from making love on our return. Yowl for yowl, we matched the cats in the alley, biting and kissing, licking and sucking, fondling and foraging, in different light, different tempers, different paces, positions, but never straying, in those early days, from the mood that had enveloped us at our first meeting.

Gradually, the world outside our love bubble returned to haunt me. The week that Pancho Villa invaded New Mexico and headed south again with the American army on his trail, it was difficult to keep the world away. Wilson's intervention was not easy to ignore. But my feelings sustained me, and on those lonely nights when I had to travel to Washington or Detroit or wherever to work on a story for some magazine, I felt as though work and the world were a dream conjured up by us two lovers, and that the real life waited for me in our Village bed. I resisted all efforts on the part of Hovey, Max, the editor of the *Tribune*, and other news boys to send me back to Mexico and report the progress of Pershing's quest for Villa. I swore that I was never going off on a foreign assignment without Lou.

Out of respect for our love, the spring of 1916 offered pleasant, warming days. The Botanical Gardens, Harlem cafes, midtown shops, Brooklyn's Bridge, the docks, our Village with its welcome Washington Square, dance halls, jazz bins, hop joints, Italian, Jew, Southern, German, French, and low-down Irish restaurants: we toured around the town. By showing Lou such sights I reignited a passion for the city that had first flared in me when I came down from Cambridge six or seven springs before. Now and then I'd take time out to work, or to speak at a rally against American intervention in the European war. (With the publication of *The War in Eastern*

Europe, I received more invitations to speak than I could answer, not to mention accept.) A great deal of hoopla about "preparedness" echoed throughout the country. A big stir came up at the *Masses* when some of the staff claimed that Max was too tyrannical and should be overthrown, but I tried to keep myself apart from all that. Though Max pronounced to me over many beers that love and revolution would one day have to mate, I found that at that time they didn't mix well for me at all.

One night we took a ride on the Staten Island ferry with flaming-haired Vincent, the prodigy poetess. Lou and I were so much in love, Vinnie told us, that we inspired her right then and there to make a poem about how we made her feel. It was bitter-sweet to see Vincent so inflamed by our love. She had had an affair with Seeger, who had seen the war as a chance to practice knighthood and gone to France as a volunteer. That night she seemed so lonely, clinging to Lou. I kissed her now and then to cheer her up. Lou kissed her as well. No one on the ferry seemed to care.

Spring gushed along toward summer, and we were caught unawares by the first truly triumphantly warm day of the year.

"I can't wear any of the clothes I brought with me from Portland," Lou complained. And we went uptown to the best Fifth Avenue shop and spent everything in our pockets on a new blouse and skirt. Money mattered little to me (us). Lou received an occasional check from Trullinger (the remarkable liberal dentist!) and was writing verse and taking notes for a series of stories about the lives of lonely women of Nevada and the Coast. I was working on a number of bread-and-butter pieces for various magazines and sending back to Portland as much money as I could. If we had enough cash for dinner, we figured that breakfast would somehow turn up. It usually did.

Only a few things intruded on us in those days, and one of them was a particularly immediate problem intimately connected with our love. We felt destined to love each other and live with each other for the rest of our days: should we consummate our love by having children? The question first came up somewhat playfully while we were out for a stroll on Fifth Avenue and passed by a dowdy woman herding several small, push-faced youngsters ahead of her.

"Nasty," Lou said. "Just think of the poor woman chained up with them all day. I can't see myself getting trapped into a situation like that."

But later at home she gazed at me hypnotically while in the midst of love.

"I wonder what ours would look like."

"Darling dear, I think they'd look just beautiful, with your eyes and your face and my bones and dash. But it just doesn't seem like the right time to bring kids into the world. We've got to clean the place up a bit first."

"I feel the same way, Jack. Don't you think I'm too wild and sensual to be a mother—just yet?"

Peace reigned in my life. I never wanted to stray far from home again. The only one of my friends who hadn't yet come to that conclusion was Mabel. She hadn't yet had the chance to see us together until one weekend in Croton when Lou and I were tramping about the woods.

I can't speak for how Lou felt about the meeting, but I was nervous. Mabel, however, was polite and confident in her own powers. She was living with Maurice Sterne the painter, and this had apparently smoothed the edges from her manner. She did not jangle herself and others with her usual nervous energy—to live! to see! and, above all else, to do!—that had kept me clinging to her for as long as I had.

"I'm so pleased to meet you," she said to Louise (who was unable to match the face and the manner with the stories I had told her, it all happened so quickly), "you seem to be such a fine complement for Jack."

"Should I change my name to Jill?" This sent us into a tumble of nervous laughter.

"You're a Westerner," Mabel said. "Do you see a real difference between the light out there and here?"

It went along like this for a while. "Why didn't you tell me she was so fat!" Lou scolded me as we continued along our own way through the flowering wood. "Not to mention her age. Well, you told me about her age, that's true. But her weight! Jack, for a writer you certainly missed out on giving a true description of that one." For Mabel's part, I had a note from her several days later, in which she praised my choice of Lou in the most complimentary phrases, knowing full well that I would show it to my lovey and that Lou could only feel bested by this tactic. "She may be fat, but she has good taste in women," Lou said.

My encounter with Trullinger did not compare well. Lou and I had been staying in Provincetown for a few days. Trullinger, meanwhile, had come into town looking for Louise. A note from the dentist greeted us when we returned to the city. Sure enough, that night, the door buzzer intruded on the usual mood of solitude-in-tandem that Lou and I found in our evenings at home.

"It's him!" Lou started up out of her chair. Pages from her notebook fluttered to the floor. I bumped my side against a desk chair and hovered at the railing while Lou, throwing a light shawl about her shoulders, went down to answer the door. I heard her muffled greeting at the bottom of the stairwell, listened for a moment, and then returned to my work. After several minutes, I decided that she had taken him away somewhere to make private speeches about the end of their marriage, and focused my attention once again on a novel I had begun about the life of the young anarchist who had assassinated the archduke at Sarajevo. But facts, I had discovered, were one thing and fiction another. News fairly well spills in bright, attractive sentences from my pen. Verses flow in rivers. But stories show my failings. And since what I do badly never interests me for very long, I put aside the novel and scribbled out verses in honor of Eastman and the life of action he led on behalf of all the good things we believed in.

> *There was a man, who, loving quiet beauty best*
> *Yet could not rest. . . .*

The words came easily for a while, but then my hand began to tremble so much that I had to stop writing. The night was growing longer, and I missed Lou madly. I loved her so! I loved her more than any egoist could ever love himself! One great heap of home-boy American loving! I loved her body! I loved her soul! I could not tell the difference between them.

It was nearly midnight when she returned out of breath from her hurried climb up the stairs. River scent clung to her clothing. They had taken a walk, she told me, to the Gansvoort Pier and then to several low dives along the waterfront.

"He was pitiable," was all she said in answer to the question in my eyes, pulling off her clothes with the speed of someone about to rescue a drowning man or who needs to be rescued herself.

Out went the lights and off went my own clothes. The scent of rut lay thickly on the air. Had Lou gone to bed with Trullinger one last time in some little hotel along the docks? Did she use that way to say farewell to the lanky, long-jawed dentist, with close-cropped blond hair—I had seen him once at a distance in downtown Portland two nights before I entrained for the East. It didn't occur to me then that her direct and almost brutal command—"Come in me now!"—may have resulted from her desire to dissuade me from exploring where traces of her husband's presence still lingered. It became clear to me that I didn't dare predict anything she might do or say. Never accuse, never admit.

The world meanwhile continued its chicanery in the form of political conventions. And I had to raise some cash to buy breakfasts. I entrained for Chicago and St. Louis. The pols strutting about the platforms, the hypocritical endorsement Roosevelt made of Cabot Lodge's nomination on the Progressive ticket, the rebuff given to me by Henry Ford when, during an interview, I asked him if he would finance a campaign to help alert the American people to the dangers of getting dragged into the European war, all of this took a great toll on the insular feelings engendered that spring by my love for Lou. I returned to our house on the Cape with a stink in my nostrils that took large amounts of ocean air to cleanse.

"Here we are cracking lobster and loving each other," I remember saying one night over dinner with the Cooks. "But just across the ocean the shells are still flying. And down in Washington all the folks who said they'd keep us out of war are preparing to send American workers in to kill German workers. Why? Because their bosses want to pick up the pieces of the Kaiser's empire once he gets smashed."

"You're turning as red as this lobster, sweetie," Lou told me.

"And she doesn't just mean in the face," said Jig Cook, his brow crinkling in amusement beneath his great thick shock of white white hair.

Susan Glaspell spoke up just then.

"If America gets into the war, that means you'll be going back to Europe, Jack. Will you take Lou with you? It would mean a lot to all women if one of us went to the front lines along with you."

"That's a swell idea. But I'm not going to write about war anymore. Revolution, maybe, but no more war. Hovey and I have talked about my going to China."

"Jack's always wanted to go to China," Lou put in. "Once he even tried to get me to swim there along with him."

"Where I go, Lou goes," I declared with a snap of a claw.

"Bravo!"

Both Cooks cheered. More shells cracked. Wine flowed. The moon showed us its smiling kisser over salt waters flecked with incandescent froth. We continued into the night a dialogue about the founding of a new theater.

While I was out in St. Louis, Lou had given up prose and thrown herself full tilt into a play for the group Jig was calling "The Provincetown Players." This was the dream-group he had made real after leaving a Washington Square theater earlier that spring. America wasn't getting the kind of drama it deserved! Besides Susan Glaspell, four other writers had promised him one-act plays, some of which Jig hoped to get on the boards before summer's end. The boards themselves were literally boards, the plank flooring of an old house built out on the end of a local pier that we had been renovating. Jig's idea was to renovate American drama itself. When I first heard the plan, I began a satirical play that I hoped would show my disgust at American politics, national and international, in a sharp and delightful way.

"A political play!"

"A political play?"

Cook was not so sure when he heard about the project. Drama to him meant booted figures in masks raging about a stone amphitheater in Athens.

"And Aristophanes?" I reminded him.

"Jack, are you comparing yourself to Aristophanes?"

"I'd compare him to Dionysus." Lou piped up a little praise of me, knowing how much I loved to know how much she loved me. She had in fact called me that beautiful name early that very morning while out on our daily swim.

Time: Sunrise.

Setting: The dunes.

Character: A tall beefy fellow with bright eyes characteristic of enthusiasm and peeling skin characteristic of a sunburn. A willowly, shoeless dune-nymph dressed in flowing gauze.

She: Is it you, Dionysus, come on the rays of the early morning sun?

He: Yes, 'tis I, your deity come to claim the bride my followers have put up for me.

She: Welcome, O Glorious!

He: Good morning, darling.

They splash about in the surf, then swim vigorously back and forth for nearly half an hour. Then as the sun comes up full and eye-piercing from behind the bank of easterly clouds, the nymph makes a dash for the dunes. The beefy fellow follows in swift pursuit.

The wind sprayed sand on her tan belly, golden grains nesting amid the sea-tangle of her thatch. Dark stones on light hillocks, her nipples hardened in the breeze. I knelt alongside her, kneading sand with my knees, licking her breasts with my tongue. Soon she softened, though the sand remained hard, and gently held me erect and trembling in the soft palm of one hand while lightly playing the other across my thigh. Just then, as if to prove that all was radical comedy, I lost control and farted.

"Clown!" Lou shrieked in mock-disgust. She released me from her grip and rolled away from me. "Such a vulgar god!" She stuck out her tongue and then leaped away over the sand.

She ran lithely, like a boy, and I pursued her, my kidney keeping time with sudden pain. I tracked her over the sand back toward a row of ramshackle buildings that fronted on the beach, but she was nowhere in sight.

"Lou?" I shouted into the wind.

"Dionysus..." Her cry blew back to me over a dune that stood between me and the makeshift houses. I stepped around the reed-covered mound and saw her stretched out on a ragged clump of blankets, the remnants of some beachcomber's encampment. She smiled blissfully at my approach. My foot came down on something sharp and I yowled in pain.

"It's bleeding, poor Dionysus's foot is bleeding!" Lou helped me hobble to the blankets.

"Some bastard's broken whiskey bottles," I cursed. The cut hurt so much that my self-pitying thoughts of possible kidney relapse soon faded.

Lou squeezed a splinter of glass from my left sole. The wound stung awfully. Lou distracted me by painting in blood two small, red crosshatches on each of our chests.

"Confess now!" she suddenly commanded. "Did you ever love Mabel here on the beach?"

"Has that been on your mind all this time?"

Lou nodded, looking out over the waves.

I forgot about my pain and cuddled her on the blanket.

"But that's all old news, isn't it, darling? You won't want to worry about that again, will you?"

The sea flashed silvery and gold in the fresh light of a full round sun. Each wave of wind that played across the beach soothed us both, and soon we had nestled down amid heaps of books and newspapers scattered about the campsite.

"Couldn't we pick up fleas from this?"

"That's the kind of question you-know-who might have asked."

"That's all old news. Don't talk about her."

"You're the one who asked first. I'm not the kind of person who cares about old loves, mine or anyone else's."

"You didn't care that I'd been drilled by a dentist—"

"Hussy!"

"Dionysian brute, unhand me!"

"Never!"

"I'll scream!"

"Don't! You'll upset the seagulls!"

"You love to work me into corners like this, don't you?

Mean old tomcat!"

"I won't hurt you!"

"I'll squeal!"

Lou rolled away from me and, before I could stop her, raced into the dunes in the direction of the water. I hauled myself to my feet and lurched after her but not before catching a glimpse of a lanky, dark-haired fellow in worn shirt and trousers ambling across the sand in my direction. Figuring that he might be the resident of the campsite (and the owner of the bottle I had speared my foot on), I hobbled off in a hurry after my little dune-nymph.

Lou was putting on her clothes when I caught up with her.

"We'd better hurry back, darling," she said, "or our friends will make the American theater without us."

I thought no more about the dark man on the dunes until the next day, when on the way home from the theater to work on my play I caught a glimpse of him in an alley near the house.

"Did you see him?" Lou stuck her head out the door.

"Who?"

"The beachcomber. I caught him staring at me from the street."

"And I saw him staring at me. I think we invaded his little campsite yesterday."

"Wonder what he's doing here. Don't you wonder how people like that stay alive?"

"I've seen a lot of them, darling. In the mining camps, down in Mexico. The social system cuts them out to brand them, and then lets them drift away from the herd. He was probably once a stockbroker or a store manager; now he's the mysterious dark man of the dunes."

"He reads Shakespeare."

"Does he?"

"I saw one of the old books lying around his camp. If it was his camp."

"That deepens the mystery, doesn't it?"

"He reminds me of the Ancient Mariner."

"If you find him that interesting, I'll invite him in for a drink."

"The Ancient Mariner was an opium eater, I've always thought. You think this man eats drugs to get that haggard look?"

"It was whiskey, remember?" I pointed to my wounded sole.

How much whiskey it actually required to create an Ancient American Mariner we found out soon enough. At around eleven that night with Lou tucked into bed and me seated at my desk at work on my play, there came a knock at the door.

"Jig?" I figured Cook had come to repent for his misgivings about my political play and take a walk around the dunes as sometimes was his wont.

I went to the door and opened it to discover the beachcomber leaning against the porch rail. The fellow looked me over with his deep-set, searchlight eyes and then handed me a package.

"Carlin said you'd read this."

A tide of whiskey rolled in on his breath.

"Terry Carlin?" This was an acquaintance of mine at The Liberal Club.

The dune man nodded, waiting for some sign from me.

"Did you follow us home?"

"It's a small place, here."

I didn't know at first whether he meant the village or the house. Then I noticed that he was looking over my shoulder, and I turned to see Lou peeking through the slightly-opened bedroom door.

"Ancient Mariner!"

The lanky man lurched sideways in the doorway.

"What'd she say?"

"What do you have here?" I tapped the package.

"You read it?"

"Sure. Uh...you want to come in?"

I heard the bedroom door close shut behind me.

"Read it first." He stumbled around toward the railing and, without further announcement, shuffled down the steps and into the dark. I went back inside, and while Lou in her nightgown looked over my shoulder, I opened the mysterious package.

"A bomb?"

"A manuscript."

In my hands I held a tattered copy of something called *Bound East for Cardiff* by Eugene O'Neill.

"He's not the son of Coleridge," Lou said.

"But still a mariner of sorts if the title means anything."

"And by the smell of it."

It was true. The odor of whiskey tempered with sea water hovered over the battered script.

"Let's see if the rest of it smells as bad."

I turned the title page over and began to read.

By the end of the hour Lou and I were dancing around the house.

"Wait'll they hear about this one! Talk about Dionysus, we've found American drama washed up on the beach!"

I put aside all my work the next morning and hurried over to the theater as fast as my sore foot could carry me to show the script to Jig and Susan. We had gotten little sleep. But when O'Neill shuffled in through the doorway of the building, he looked as though he had been awake the entire night. His breath reeked and his old shirt bore new tatters and stains.

"You read it?" He spoke in a low, whiskey-dulled guttural.

"I have," I said, "and I think it's the best play I've ever read by an American!" I offered my hand. "I'm happy to meet you, O'Neill."

He looked at my hand as though it were too clean to touch and gave it a rough squeeze.

"You think they'll do it?"

He rubbed his hand across the back of his dirty neck, toying with his shirt collar as though to shake loose sand fleas or mites.

"The company is reading it right this minute," I nodded toward the interior of the theater. But when I turned back to him, he was already striding off toward the beach.

"Lemme know," he called to me, his voice doubly slurred by whiskey and wind.

I limped after him, the gash on my sole still plaguing me. But he disappeared over the dunes.

Later that day, charged by our fellow Players with the task of telling our marvelous new playwright that we were in fact going to produce his one-acter, Lou and I set out in search of him. Almost as though they could tell something about his personality from the work itself, the women had been less enthusiastic about it than the men. But this could have been the result, I thought, of the all-male cast the piece required. However, Lou was deeply thrilled about staging it. Even though there was a good chance that her own one-act play might not make our summer program because of it, she argued fervently for adding the O'Neill to the repertoire.

"You don't mind its smell?" I joked with her afterwards as we made our way slowly across the dunes.

"Actually I'm beginning to find it rather appealing. Very sensual in its own way."

"Raw life. The scent of things in the raw."

"Don't joke."

"Who's joking?" I kicked up sand with my good foot, blinked out over the sun-silvered waters. There was something in me responding to the black-haired playwright that was at once good and bad. His play about shipboard life cried out to me in thrilling ways. We needed to see life as it was, as it really was. Good! But the texture of his own life, beginning with the smell of him and ending who-knew-where—somewhere deep inside the blackness of his dead-eyed gaze—made me wonder. I had never read anything by an American that set off such wild and deep emotions about the world, and I had certainly never *met* any one with the talent to stir up such feelings. For a traditional kind of writer, O'Neill was in his own way an anarchist who'd just as soon destroy the world as mirror it.

"And that's what scares you?" Lou asked after I'd explained some of my feelings to her.

"I wouldn't call it scared. But he makes me think we're all standing on the verge of something we don't know exactly what."

I looked down at the small, ratty encampment where I had cut my foot. A pile of old clothing and the same worn blankets lay heaped up against the side of the dune. Old newspapers and empty whiskey bottles littered the sand around the charred space where someone had cooked the night before. Here and there books sprawled broken-backed among the reeds; a piece of cutlery, a shard of pottery, a scrap of metal, remains of food. I looked closely at all of the furnishings now that I knew to whom they belonged.

A shadow appeared on the sand alongside us. Here stood O'Neill wearing nothing but a brief swim suit. His pale, thin frame looked less pathetic bared to the sun than it did when draped with his worn, filthy clothes. Bearing scars of toil at sea and barroom brawls, he looked somewhat more heroic than he did the night before.

"Welcome to the Players." Lou offered her hand.

O'Neill looked at it for a moment and then gave it a feeble shake.

"I've got to swim. I can't do anything before I swim."

He turned and trotted off toward the water.

"Wait!" I stripped and followed after.

"Don't leave me behind!" I turned and saw Lou pulling off her clothes as she ran in our direction. O'Neill was already wading into the gently rolling surf. I waited for Lou, slipping my arm about her slender smooth waist and together we trudged our way forward into the waves.

"The anointing of the playwrights!"

We found our new companion floating on his back, like a sea animal at rest, just beyond the edge of the breakers. When he saw us approaching, he spun about and started swimming strongly toward the horizon.

"O'Neill!"

I found it difficult to gain on him.

"Watch the undertow!" Lou called from behind.

I turned to assure her that I could handle it, and when I looked back toward the horizon, I couldn't see O'Neill anywhere. A slight edge of panic stabbed my side. I knew enough to fight it back and kept swimming smoothly in the direction of the deep. I sometimes felt more at home in the water than on land, and my instincts told me to keep stroking. O'Neill gave me the feeling that he was, also, the kind of person who'd buoy up in heavy tow. Still I couldn't catch sight of him even when I strained my head up, gazing seal-like toward the blue-white horizon. Nothing but the heavy roll of waves lay between me and Europe. Where was he? Drowned? Were there sharks? Or German submarines? The wildest pictures flashed through my mind as I found myself straining forward into the rollers. I looked back at the land, a thin strip of sparkling sand against an equally brilliant sky. Resting, I let the rolling swell lift me up and then roll me down, lift me and then roll. Who now was Dionysus, the god pulled back into the sea? I swam out farther, breathing well.

Ree!ree!

Shore birds skimmed the water, crying out encouragement as I cut sidewise through waves.

"Reed!"

I scouted about for O'Neill.

"Here!"

My heart slowed, rested, floating. I frog-kicked my way toward his head floating on the waters. I could scarcely catch my breath, swallowed water, spat, bobbed up on the swells.

"You're crazier than I am! Think you're a seal, do you? I thought...you'd swim right out to sea!"

He looked at me as though for the first time, with an animal stare that faded into a human look as a wave's rim passed over us.

"I...just...wanted to be...alone...."

"He just wanted to be alone." I repeated his remark to Lou when we staggered up onto the beach.

"I should dress." Lou's voice sounded awfully wistful for a woman who had watched us nearly drown. Walking delicately across the sand, her hands clasped demurely over her trim backside, she led us away from the water.

We never saw O'Neill so athletically inclined again. Once he began his daily drinking, he turned into another variety of being. Later that same day, my story about cutting my foot on one of the bottles in his beach cache sent him into a ten-minute tirade on the subject of American manufacturing, American distilling, filthy beaches, the problems of human balance ("—down in fucking Argentina, and that's with a soft g as in gents, *ladies*, they brew the goddamned stuff in their maiden aunt's assholes and it comes out tasting peppier than the 'Merican piss-swill-pig-blood-plantwater-gutter-slough they sell over the counter or under the table in, what we're calling these days, our native land, our native goddamned American native country 'tis of pee, piss, stinking lousy country of pig-swill liquor—") and various and sundry other subjects that had nothing whatsoever to do with my original remarks. His voice was thickened slightly by the liquor. To see him standing tall, his hands wildly waving about his head, and his long legs pumping up and down, up and down, both when he wandered about the stage or remained in place, you would have thought of a prophet, if you believed in prophets, and madmen, if you had ever had the chance to see one, and bad Shakespearean actors, most of all.

Day after day, once we had put his play into rehearsal, he delivered long, bitter, brutal monologues on a string of subjects: the theater—"...haven for every frightened human chicken-hawk too talentless to live as a normal human being, thick-headed dogs, smelling each other's assholes and calling it praise!"—art—"...fart! Dribblings and droolings from famous pens that couldn't draw ten holy cents from a bank account in a small town in Utah! These scribblings you read, Henry James, Howells, who else you got there in your god-damned shelf? Ten people out of ten million understand that pocked-marked pebbly-shit style and they ought to hang themselves in the morning for having that on their minds! One person out of ten million talks the way they write, and he ought to have his tongue cut out and dried in the sun for bird-feed!"—America—"Land of the fee and home of the knave! I've been happier spending days in a freak's lavvy in a Buenos-Aires-whore's kitchen than one hour I've ever passed in this wretched foul-ball filthy mouth-and-rust-eaten stretch of Indian-fucked pasture land where you couldn't graze a cow that didn't ask you for a dollar to smell its droppings! The day my poor belly-swelled granddad sold out his birthright for a mess of Yew Ess Hay he damned the rest of the line to the daily buggery they call living. Those that can't tell their own dead selves in the mirror from the ghosts of their children-to-come deserve to live here! Sell it back to the dinosaurs! Give it away to the Kaiser! Ask the niggers to plant it over with cotton and the rest of us catch the next boat for Timbuktu where at least they call a desert a desert and the weather's nice for dying quickly all of us food for the buzzards when you've done it all amd said...!"—politics—"Show me an anarchist and I'll show you a gentleman at heart, an honest guy who wants to keep things quiet 'round his person, you can sympathize with that, bombs blowing up around the states, just to make things quiet once the bodies settle, the blood congeals, the cries of pain cease forever and the dead join the dead in the ether; but Demigods, and Republic-kins, those itchy-fingered swole-wallet pea-eyed ass-wipe honey-browed bank-robbing bastard children of a democracy created in the name of all those who hate the king because he's the only one can steal. Chop 'em up for fish-bait and throw 'em in the sea and the only thing you'd do is kill the sharks, poison the dirty fishes with a stench of flesh no self-respecting carrion bird, animal, even the coyote, the native American dog, would stand for! And shouldn't we put him on our emblem instead of the eagle? Not even the jackal in darkest Africa who lives on the stool of ape-men suffering from the last stages of leprosy-deluxe would touch a tasty bit of the hide of Ammurican politician! Give me the anarchists any day! All they want to do is bomb us into the grave, and isn't that better than living in it without dying!"—women—"Cunts! *Culs!* Cave-quiff! Cess-pond! Quicksnitch! Bifbams! Snatchwitches! Cleft! Puling, pustulant slack-tit—"

"Enough, Gene!" Lou called out toward the end of one of these evenings. We had been going all afternoon and night at the final scene of *Bound East for Cardiff,* and those who weren't acting, such as Lou and Susan, were even more anxious than the rest of us to close up for the night. It was only a few days before the opening, and we still had part of the set to complete, and more signs had to be posted on walls in Boston and its environs. Whether anyone was going to buy tickets to see a new play by an unknown playwright performed by a new theater company full of mostly amateur actors didn't bother us. We had quite enough worries. I had lost more than a few pounds in the flurry of it all, and the number of cigarettes nervously smoked by men and women alike made a pretty pile each night.

"It beats war but it's not peace," I joked as we went through the fifteenth run-through of the final scene. Waves crashed against the rear wall, which faced on the ocean, the pressure of the tide seeming to dramatize the surge of onrushing hours that all of us within the theater had felt for days on end. The play was draining away all of our energy. For a week now Lou and I had fallen asleep without anything more than a gentle flurry of kisses. My kidney woke me each morning with the painful notice that time might not be on my side in my race to keep my health until the opening of the play. Jig, fortunately for all of us, possessed enough faith in his vision of a new American theater to keep us working, but he showed the strain of our final week of preparations, wondering out loud to me about the worth of the drunken lout's play, after one particularly clumsy run-through, in which my lines went up in smoke and Gene raged about the hall waving a bottle and cursing us all for mucking up his drama. Gene had left the beach for the last week of rehearsals and had moved his filthy bedroll into a corner of the theater that, as a result, now smelled like a sheep ranch.

"Better there than with me," said Susan, cleaving to her husky director husband with a grip more than playful. Gene had sneaked up behind her one afternoon and grabbed her, swearing later that he was so drunk he did not remember doing it. Nor did he feel embarrassed when she dared to raise her blouse and show him the dark bruise just below her left breast. She was truly a modern woman, proud of her sex, and had lectured O'Neill on the necessity of understanding the relations between men and women. But it was like trying to explain the glories of the telegraph to a monkey. Gene, beginning to drink again in response, it seemed, to her increasingly more strident lectures, removed himself from us all during the aftermath of rehearsals, preferring to curse and rant at the stars glittering over Cape Cod Bay than put up with the criticism of females.

Thus it was not much of a shock when Lou had shouted at him to stop his rant against women, but it was unusual that he did not spit in her direction and storm out of the hall. Instead, he hung his head like a boy who had just been caught with his dingle in the honey-pot in the middle of a church supper. He sniffled through his perpetually runny nose and sat down to watch the latest shading of the scene currently being hatched on stage.

"Lovey," I told Lou in bed that night, "you have a sobering effect on such genius. It's a case of beauty and the beast."

Lou laughed, gave me a squeeze. "Let's sleep now, I'm so exhausted."

"I'm seasick from our rehearsals, I don't know if I can sleep just yet."

"Please, Jack, let's do."

"You're not tiring of this sailor, are you?"

"Not in the least. The truth is, Jack, I feel my capacity to love expanding."

"And I mine."

I dreamed that night of swimming while storm clouds bustled overhead. The voice of Lee Sing, the chiming of gongs. *Pool for the shore, Chlistin. . . .* Seals, mobs of lumberjacks, the gathering of the strikers. I speak for you, I heard myself shouting in a speech delivered from a fir tree. But who speaks for me? Booming of big guns in the distance. Boom doom boom doom!

Pounding on the door.

"Jack, what's that?"

I shook myself awake.

Boom boom!

"I was dreaming."

"There's someone at the door."

I climbed out of bed and went to the door. I opened it to find O'Neill, breathing hot and heavy, smelling of liquor and burning wood.

"What's the trouble, Gene?"

"Fire!"

"Gene?"

Lou called lazily from the bed.

"Hurry!" He ignored her, urging me to dress.

"Back soon, honey!"

I raced out the door close on the heels of O'Neill, who ran, as it turned out, as well as he could swim. The guns in my dream and O'Neill's fist on the door continued to pound in my back. I pushed myself harder when I saw the black smoke rising from behind the theater.

"Christ! Call the others!"

"Too late!" O'Neill raced up the wharf and around the side of the theater. A small paper fire smouldered in the wind and spray. Fortunately, the planks, though blackened, hadn't yet caught.

"We'll get it!" I danced on the flames, and he joined me in stamping and stomping until nothing but smoke rose around us.

"What a crazy place for a fire! How the hell did it start?"

O'Neill kept on stamping as he gazed out to sea.

"I burned my manuscripts."

"With a little luck, you could have taken the theater with you."

"No loss. My play is rotten. I couldn't get it right yet. I never will."

"You'd better take a swim, pal. Clear your head."

O'Neill glowered at me, spitting into the smoking mess on the dock.

"What do you know? You're a journalist. You don't care if you get things right or wrong."

"Whatever we do, Gene, the idea is to make the world better, not burn it down."

"Better—shit! You eat, you drink, you screw, you write! The Greeks knew all about it. One kind of action, that's all! Better—the whole goddamned mess wouldn't fill up half the ocean! Swim? Remember how you felt all alone out there in the currents, ocean dragging you down, the bliss of sinking, end it then, wish for all of us...?"

Waving me away, he stumbled across the dock and leaned against the wall of the theater.

"Essence...essence..." he muttered the words into the wind.

"I'm going back to bed now, Gene. You can have your

solitude. Just don't burn the building down this time."

"Wallow in the trough...pigs' party...." Suddenly he whirled around and challenged me.

"What are you waiting for, journalist!"

He lumbered toward me, his arm pulled back as if he were about to throw a punch.

"Tyrant! Bully! Dare to strike a blow against the artist! I've read your cant, your frilly pig-swill poesy. Bring it over and make a fire 'long with mine. You dare me, dangerous Dan from the western can?" He dropped his fist to his side, spun around, and walked off the edge of the pier.

Good riddance, I said to myself, and then looked down over the edge. O'Neill lay on his side half in, half out of a pool formed by the incoming tide.

"Hold on!" I called, but he gave no notice that he heard me. I took the length of the pier at a trot, leaped onto the sand, and within a minute knelt at his side.

"Gone?"

The body stirred in the wash of the surf, rolled over, and blinked its eyes open, then shut them against the rising sun.

"Sea scurf...flotsam and scummy bowels of ocean....catch the nigger octopus by the tide and send him out to suffer...Oh, my islands! where, WHERE did you wander? Father, forgive them..." I grabbed him by the ankles and dragged him up the beach to avoid the tentacles of the incoming tide. I stopped to urinate before heading back to bed. Something sprang loose again inside of me then. Jabbing pain. Water poured out of me onto the sand. Except that it was blood.

Blood became a sign of the times: no amount of frivolity with my lovey or pleasure with the Players could stand against it. A doctor on the Cape gave me some powder for the pain but told me I ought to get on down to the city and see a specialist. After the opening of *Bound East for Cardiff*, a great success for us all, I returned by myself to New York and had a checkup. It was then that I discovered how far outside the magical circle of romance I had strayed.

First, I had a horrible afternoon in the doctor's office, feeling like an infant, wearing nothing but a smock, and wondering what the darling nurses felt when they heard the verdict.

"This kidney's infected and it's going to get worse."

My heart sank.

"Will it affect me...in any way?"

"Affect you? Oh! That way? I didn't see the connection. Must be on your mind, Mister Reed, because it wasn't on mine. No, it shouldn't in the least. There's a surgeon down at Johns Hopkins I hear does the job just fine."

I wandered downtown, passing through the arch at Washington Square, then flopped onto a bench in the park. I felt like a dashing young college fellow I had once written about who made a failure with the capitalist system and ended up sleeping on benches under the trees. Except it wasn't any system but my own body that was giving me pause. And I'd have a hard time struggling against it if I wanted to.

The lazy life of the park suddenly became an insult to me. Leaping from the bench, I hurried out through the criss-cross patch of streets that led to Vincent's apartment. I rang the bell over and over without any success. I shoved a note into her mail drop and wandered back toward the park. I could have gone to the *Masses* office where I might have done some work. But I didn't want to see anyone from the magazine. A quiet place, warm arms to enfold me, a bosom to weep on—that's what I needed. Mabel? Fortunately, she was out of town, and so I saved myself another awful scene.

As I was crossing MacDougal Street a familiar voice hailed me.

"Jack! Jack Reed!"

It was Lippmann, hurrying his slender self across the roadway.

"We've got to talk."

I glanced in at the empty stables where peddlers' horses had only recently been quartered. It occurred to me that it would make a perfect home for the Players, if Jig wanted to bring the group back to New York in September. The Players! I shuddered at the physical memory of my lovable Lou. If only she were with me I would be able to bear the day.

"Hello, Lippmann. How's life?"

"Seeger's dead."

"What?"

"A shell blew up in his face. I just heard the news."

The news exploded on me. I needed a place to sit. The last person I wanted to share the time with was Lippmann. But since he had brought me the news and seemed intent upon acccompanying me, I led the way to the Liberal Club, which, fortunately, we found empty. Seeger dead. The first of us to go! The only thing Lippmann and I ever agreed on was the nobility of our classmate's manner. Lippmann ordered coffee; I ordered tea (no alcohol the doctor had warned me). It tasted bitter.

"That was something you probably expected of me, wasn't it?" I said. "To ride like a knight in shining armor onto the mechanical battlefield and take a piece of metal in the face?"

"At least he was consistent. He never pretended to be anything else but a chivalrous dreamer."

"Yes, of course, you think that I'm a pretender."

"Not a pretender. Just a bit muddled, Jack."

"Life is muddled, Lippmann. What you want is everything neatly laid out in rows, all logical. So now you've got Seeger all neatly laid out in a row. You'll never have to ponder over his behavior again."

Lippmann picked up his cup, as though to read my fortune in the leaves, hesitated, then set it down again. His looked past me toward the street.

"I did think a lot about him, you know. And about you. I still do. I think a lot about all the men from our class and where they've been going, what they've been doing. We're not just an ordinary mob. We're men who can affect the times we live in, men who'll move history. I always used to enjoy watching you lead the yells during football games, Jack. There's a real enthusiast, I'd say to myself. How I envy his ability to get that unruly mess of drunks and old boys shouting with one voice.

"You've told me all this before, Leap. Tell me something new."

"Have I told you? I've thought about it a lot. Perhaps you just pick up my thought waves or—"

"I read the piece in *The New Republic*—"

"—and I read your lines about me in your poem about Bohemia. So...we're even. But let's talk about life." He squinted up at me through his small, clear-rimmed spectacles, not yet thirty but looking like the pundit he wanted to become. "I've read your book on Mexico, and I've read your reports from eastern Europe. Both of them are vividly written, and yet both of them are pathetic in a way."

I chewed my lip, feeling the table edge under my fingers. I might have snapped it in two.

"All men are pathetic and vivid at the same time, Leapman. Voltaire Leapman."

He did not even blink.

"That hurt you, didn't it? But I wanted to tell you the truth. Jack, you want so much to be part of a great movement, to make your readers tremble when they read your pages. But instead you whittle away your time with Mexicans and Slavs...."

"I don't count out the greasy little people as quickly as you do. You're supposed to be a socialist of sorts yourself, yet you do."

He tapped his cup with a spoon.

"I've got the system and you've got the passion for it. Isn't it a shame that we couldn't put the two strains together, Jack?

Nothing against all those other peoples, but our country can master the flow of history. We're going to be riding the wave for a long time to come, and it disturbs me to see you divorcing yourself from your own greatest possibilities."

"Leapman, get to the point! Are you suggesting that I run for Congress? Perhaps you're just too subtle for a western boy like me."

"It's Seeger's death. And the death of a lot of other fellows as well. Deaths that will haunt us all if we don't face up to our responsibilities...."

"I see."

"Do you, Jack? Do you see that it's becoming more and more our war? Your slogan stood us in good stead for a while. But the times are shifting...."

"Wilson is campaigning as a man of peace. He doesn't seem to be ready to lead us into Europe. Not on white chargers, not in armored wagons."

"I don't care that you believed Pancho Villa, but must you believe Wilson?"

"What precisely is the message you're trying to convey to me? That I shouldn't believe Wilson when he says he wants to keep us out of war? I've always been a damned fool about taking people at face value, Leap, and it's too late for me to change now. You sound as though you're about to offer me something if I'm prepared to say the right things. What exactly is it that you're going to offer, Leap?"

"You are a fool, Jack, a holy fool. This is what I have in mind—"

I slammed my cup on the table.

"*I'm* the only one allowed to call me a fool, you ass!"

The air sizzled with our anger. Hyp Havel came in off the street, did a turnabout when he saw me and Lippmann sitting together, and then hurried through the door connecting the place with Polly's restaurant.

"We're about to write a major editorial on the war...."

"'We' being *The New Republic* gang?"

"That's correct."

"And the pitch of this 'major' piece?"

"We think we ought to go in."

"In?"

"To the war. Send our troops."

"The President doesn't, but you do. And, naturally, since you went to Harvard and he was only President of Princeton it makes sense to follow your advice."

"It sounds to me as though you won't be interested in the rest of what I have to say."

"I'm interested. Confused, but interested."

"Then give me a chance to explain. The *Masses* is continuing to take a stand against American entry into the war, correct?"

I nodded, feeling my back, where a thick pocket of pain had come to establish what seemed like a permanent residence.

"If you were to change your own views on the fighting, you'd have to find another place to publish."

"I see."

"Do you? Do you see a place in *The New Republic* for your articles about the American boys in France?"

"The French will never let me return to their lines."

"They'll be Allied lines in the future."

"A hell of a future."

"A hell of a future if we don't take it into our hands."

"We?"

"The Americans."

"Rah! rah!"

"We're drifting as a nation, Jack. Drifting slowly now, but if we don't soon become masters of our own destiny we'll have no reins to grasp."

"You're mixing your metaphors. You should have studied with Copey."

"It's not writing you ought to worry about, Jack, it's thinking. Copey helped you to see but not to think."

"I'd *rather* see than think!"

"That's the kind of impulsiveness that gets you into hot water. I'll bet you fired at the French lines for the same reason. Because someone told you not to."

"That's right, Leap. I'm just a plain old American rascal. But what are you? Pure cranial matter! A dull gray mass. Go ahead and play prophet. Come out in favor of our going into the war. Argue in good logical socialist fashion that we ought to have our workers fighting the German workers because the French workers and the British workers are fighting them already. That's your kind of logic, isn't it? And we'll toss the Russian peasants in for a little extra cannon fodder? Fight the bloody thing, and when we're finished, the socialists, like the rest of the good Americans, will have a piece of the Kaiser's pie to munch on? Meanwhile, I'm going to try to go to China and report on a real revolution instead of just your usual capitalist's war."

"You've got fine sentiments, as usual, Jack. But no arguments. China would be a good place for you, with all its bandits and gongs...."

"And the *Masses* will be a good place for my stories from China. They might consider them too inflammatory over at your rag. You ought to ask Colonel Roosevelt to report the war for you if we go in. He likes to bang drums and shovel manure." I stood up to leave.

"Let's face it, Jack. You haven't changed a bit since we first met. You'll always be a cheerleader for one cause or another. At least this time you ought to consider leading the yells for the right side."

"Did you follow me across the park to insult me like that?" My kidney throbbed like a bass drum on the Fourth of July. It was all I could do to stand and speak.

Lippmann's eyes lighted up as though he were watching the flight of roman candles. But he wasn't looking at me. Rather he was looking past me, and I turned to see the wraith-like red-bobbed woman standing in the doorway swathed in batik.

"Gentlemen..."

She paused lightly on the word, like a forest creature about to bound lithely from a glade to the cover of trees.

"Vincent!"

Lippmann stood. He didn't mind poets if they were women.

"Come help us! We were just summing up history and we need a voice like yours to help us do it properly."

"My squeaky old voice? You don't need that."

"Did you get my note?"

"Why, yes, and I was coming over here to look for you. What was it that you wanted to see me about?"

"We're going to be expanding the Players."

"You don't want to talk about history?" Lippmann still looked hopeful.

"Walter, I love history. But I love theater more, and if the choice is between that and the other, I'll choose theater."

"If the choice is between talking to me or Jack, you'll choose Jack."

"You said that, she didn't."

Lippmann blushed.

"'Prick him does he not bleed.' You're human. What a surprise. Seeger would have been pleased to see you this red." I bowed my head.

"Seeger? Have you heard from Seeger?"

Vincent still fluttered in the doorway, a butterfly in batik.

"He's dead," said Lippmann.

"You've done it now!"

I rushed forward to catch Vincent as she slumped over in a faint onto the pavement. Her eyes twitched open, shut, open, like a swimmer's just up from underwater.

"I want air, space!" She trembled when I lifted her in my arms.

"Can you walk, Vincent?"

She nodded feebly. "Take me away."

"We'll walk a bit in the park. Goodbye, Leap, and have a happy war."

We left Lippmann standing in the doorway of the Liberal Club and walked slowly up to the park.

"I want you to take me away," Vincent said in a whisper when I tried to get her to rest a moment on a bench.

"But where shall we go?"

Her eyes opened wide as though she might be emerging from deep waters, or sleep.

"We'll find a place," she said, tugging at my coat-sleeve like a small child intent upon an errand.

"Had he written to you recently?" I asked as we started walking again.

Vincent delicately kicked at leaves, head bowed, her shoulders momentarily slumped forward.

"In fire," she said.

"He was a powerful writer," I said.

"Did I love him?" Vincent asked. "Or just the idea of him? Now I'll never know."

She paused—we stood in front of a small hotel on University Place. She led me up the steps.

"What's here?" I asked.

"My sister's at home. We can't go there."

"Is this what you want?"

She nodded vigorously, throwing her flaming hair forward across her slender shoulders.

I registered us as "Mr. & Mrs. W. Lippmann." When I told Vincent she laughed and squeezed me as hard as her frail little arms could.

"Seeger would have wanted it this way," Vincent said.

I agreed. I hadn't seen Seeger much since Harvard, and I didn't know that the special feeling I felt meant that I mourned him or the idea of him. But short of a birth, there was no better way to celebrate a death than the way we spent the next hour.

Part Six

ALMOST THIRTY

On a brilliant September afternoon in 1916, while troops on both European fronts killed each other in the mud (and Americans prepared to join in the killing), we picnicked upstate, gamboling away our last Bohemian days while green grass still showed beneath heaps of crackly, bold gold leaves. I dove into a chilly pond, swam too long into the waning day, contracted a cold and then a fever. Back home in Manhattan, I suffered a series of nightmares unlike any I had known before in my adult life.

The first took me suddenly, with Lou still awake and reading by the light of our tiny bed lamp. I dozed off. Fog swirled up out of murky depths of ocean. I wandered alone along a narrow embankment, waves splashing at my shoes.

Ass-Storia

A sign appeared in the mist.

Home! How cheered I felt at the idea that Oregon embraced me.

But watch the crack in the wall!

Lou's voice crept upon me out of the sea foam.

Darling, it doesn't matter, I replied. I'll be leaving you soon for a voyage of long duration.

But you're ill, you can't go.

Lou fluttered her hands in distress.

I've got a fever, no matter, I said.

Everything matters, Lou told me, stepping back along the wall.

Watch your step! I cried. She fell forward into the waves, I lunged for her and found myself on board a fishing ketch. Up from the storming darkness, a familiar tune arose.

> *. . .for the shore, Chlistin*
> *Pool for the shore, Chlistin*

Lee Sing! You've come back!

Po' Mis' Leed, you can' tell goo' fro' bed, the smooth-yellow-skinned man laughed at me as I reached for him, and much to my horror, my hand passed right through him and touched the mast.

Lee Sing! Lee Sing!

Be big boy! I see no other you big bill! No touch a lack, little Leed child. I see, O you go now fly bye!

A wave came up and washed me overboard and I screamed *NooooOOO!*

and woke in a pool of sweat, Lou shaking me by the shoulders.

"Big Bear, are you all right?"

I shook off the dream fear and asked for a drink.

Lou slid out of bed and poured me a whiskey. Next she picked up a book from the bedtable.

"Go to sleep, Jack. I'll stand watch."

"You're a good trooper."

"I'm a soldier of love."

"May I salute you?"

"You're sick and you've got nightmares galore. I don't think you ought to confuse yourself anymore than you need to."

"Then you refuse me?"

Lou smiled maliciously.

"Sir, you haven't asked."

Lovemaking seemed to soothe me, especially the gentle loving that Lou gave back that night. But after I dozed off again, I was awakened by an ache in my back so terrible that I twisted sharply about and fell onto the floor.

Lou gave me a helping hand, hauling me back into bed.

"It's all right, darling," I said, "When this nasty cold leaves me, I'll feel much better, I'm sure."

"You'll see the doctor again is what you'll do."

But the cold stuck with me for a few days more, forcing me to remain in bed. Lou's attentiveness pleased me. I was sure that if love could heal me, she was my cure.

A few mornings later, I awakened feeling quite odd. Something inside of me had changed, whether for better or worse I could not say. I got out of bed, showered and shaved, dressed, and called the doctor. Made an appointment for later that day. Stopped at the *Masses* office, on the way uptown, to check a few matters with the rest of the staff...had my latest examination.

Lou was out at the Players until quite late. Fortunately. I was a bad fellow for rehearsing any kind of decision, and it took me quite a while to go over the matter in my mind.

"Marriage!!"

Her eyes lit up when I said it.

"We'd be the only ones in our crowd besides Jig and Susan."

"We'd be shunned, ostracized."

"AND stoned! But we'll be suffering all that for love, and that's the important thing."

I put my arms around her.

"Isn't that why we're here in bed in the first place?"

"I do feel at home with you, Big, more at home than when I'm all by my lonesome."

"And so we'll marry?"

"But what will that do to our freedom? It's not what the crowd thinks of us but what we think of ourselves. Can you picture yourself as a married man? I know what it did to the dentist. When we first met, he considered himself quite a dashing creature, a sort of hussar of the drill-and-fill brigade. You can bet he changed mighty quick." Lou squirmed from my grasp and lit up a cigarette. I studied the pattern traced by the smoke on the ceiling of our little room.

"Darling, when I was at the front I saw hundreds of fellows like myself, all of them ready to throw themselves over the edge of life for a cause greater than themselves. A damned stupid cause, but one that meant a great deal to them nonetheless."

"Darling—" she wrinkled up her long face in a question.

"Let me finish, dearest. When I was in jail with the strikers and out in Ludlow after the Rockefeller massacre and down in Chihuahua, I always noticed the special look about men who have grown in a single day in ways it takes most others years or even decades—"

"Big Bear—"

"Darling, wait, please listen. This must come out right now. You see, I saw myself in the mirror in the doctor's office today and noticed that I have that look about me. Perhaps you haven't seen it. You've been busy with the Players, busy working on your own play, but it's there."

Lou took another puff and regarded me in the fading light of late afternoon.

"So? I know who you are."

"Lou, I'm going to have an operation. I'm not afraid, but I'm aware of how it's already changed my view of things. I just might not come out of it intact."

"Intact? Or alive?"

"Alive."

"I've never known you to look worried."

"So you can see it now. But it's not worry. It's recognition. I see the difference between the way I've lived until now and the way I'm going to live after the operation. If there is going to be an 'after.'"

Lou stabbed her cigarette in the air.

"There had better be. I have too much to give you, Bear. It would be shameful to waste it all."

"You'd find someone else."

"No one like you. I've looked."

"But you'll change your taste. You'll need someone."

"Suggestions?"

She sat back on the bed now, holding her cigarette with one hand, stroking my palm with the other.

"Max?"

"Too flighty for me, darling. Even flightier than myself."

"Dell."

"Too much of a plain Joe, for all his learning about adultery, and besides, he leers."

"Does he? I hadn't noticed. But I want you to answer my question. Will you marry me?"

"When I left Trullinger, I thought that I was saying good-bye forever to marriage and all that."

"I'm not asking if you want 'all that.' I'm asking you only one slim thing."

"Some slim thing. This means, doesn't it, that I become heir to all of your vast royalties in case of your, as we used to say around the campus, Untimely?"

"Heir to my vast royalties and all of my minions."

"Millions?"

"Minions. You inherit my quarrels with all the magazine editors in town."

A harvest moon shone down on us on our return from Poughkeepsie. We were married there in a quiet ceremony without any friends for witnesses. The local clerk had to scurry about through the offices to find two employees who could attest to the coupling between Louise Bryant Trullinger, who fortunately had packed her divorce papers for the trip, and the marriage-virgin John Reed. For a while, I thought they were going to have to fetch me a doctor. My knees trembled, my heart shuddered. Though the foliage attested to the presence of autumn, I sweated enough for a mid-summer day. I was glad that we had done it this way. How foolish I would have felt standing up, trembling as I was, in front of a pack of our friends. How that crowd would have howled!

And yet they might have swooned at the sight of us kissing before the justice.

"This same J.P. who might be leading a lynching if we preached a non-preparedness sermon in the square."

"It didn't look like such a bad town, dearest," Lou said as the train clacked us back toward the city. "We could retire in a place like that one day. People'll come from all over to talk with us. Newspapers will send their top reporters for inter-views. We'd put Poughkeepsie on the map."

"Perhaps I'll buy you a house there."

"You? Buy a house!"

"I was just thinking, dearie, that I married you to be able to sign my property over to you, and now I've realized that I don't own any property. I'm going to have to see about that first thing tomorrow morning."

There was some other business I had to attend to im-mediately as well, and that was Vincent. Our one desperate afternoon in memory of Seeger had turned into something neither of us had bargained for. Once a week for the past month, we had been meeting at the same hotel.

Lou was a gemstone of a woman, diamond-hard, rubylike in her fury, emerald-witty, sapphire-ethereal.

Vincent was all motion, the noise of her own voice saying poetry with an unceasing passion, the rush of her long pea-sant skirt across paving stones, the spectral flight of her rosy behind. At twilight or just after breakfast on mornings when Lou went to work at the Players and I was on my way to or returning from work at the *Masses* or some magazine farther uptown, we cavorted in our hotel room. Because she practic-ed at seeming so ephemeral most of the time, Vincent surpris-

ed me with her substantial passions. Loving Lou was like being embraced by angels or falling with ferocious velocity into
a forest of welcoming fire; loving Vincent made me feel like a
fat lake bass who'd just been gill-hooked by a master.

"If I could only make poems about this!" she cried out one
October morning, pounding her fist against the pillow.
"About this! About this!"

Her frustration was artistic rather than physical. Vincent
had become, in a short time, my affectionate little sister of
the bedplace, one of the few stays against the pains and aches
of both my body and the body politic that existed outside the
walls of my household with Lou. It upset me that we were going to have to break it off. But I resolved, after Lou and I had
vowed our vows, that nothing should ever come between us.

"And so you believe that it has ended?"

Vincent's small, insistent voice caught me off guard. Gazing out the window over the rooftops, she might have been a
schoolgirl trying out for the part of a woman far beyond her years.

"It has to," I said.

We had both just gotten dressed. It seemed to me the proper time to speak my piece. But this made Vincent stand her
ground and recite several of her own poems which she considered appropriate to the occasion.

"Now I'm ready," she said when she had done, as though
she needed to rinse her soul as others sometimes need to
wash their hands.

"It's been a great lot of fun," I said as we left the hotel.

"Like an ocean cruise or a night at the theater?" She took
my arm as we headed west on Eighth Street. "Jack, you certainly have a way of saying things. Have you thought ever of
writing poetry?"

I was pleased with what I took to be Vincent's mellow air
and bantered a bit with her as we approached the corner at
Sixth.

"What a pity!" She suddenly exhaled. "Poor Seeger. If he

had only lived a bit longer he might have known so much more of life. He understood a great deal about what it is to fall in love, but he never felt the pain of having it end."

"We were in love, Vincent, weren't we?"

"Oh, Jack, you're such a cad! Some of us still are!"

"In love with love!"

"In love with you, you bastard!"

And with that she pushed me so hard that I nearly stumbled off the curb.

"Vincent, sweet, you'll be fine, you'll be swell. As for me, I've got my own pains to ponder...."

"Well spoken, *hypocrite*"—she gave the word the French pronunciation. "You're doing fine yourself. I wonder how Lou is going to take it."

"She's taking it just perfectly," I said. "She doesn't know a thing. And you won't tell her?"

We started off across the avenue, on the lookout for motorcars.

"I'm sorry, Vincent. I didn't know that it was going to end this way."

"You have no good reason for not wanting to see me anymore, Jack Reed."

We reached the corner of Tenth Street and Sixth, only a few yards away from the entrance to the alley where Lou and I had made our nest.

"Vincent, Lou may be home from the Players by now. I don't think that you really want to come upstairs, but if you do, I'd like to ask you to have some sympathy."

"Mercy, you mean, Jack? Why must we part?"

"Vincent, please."

"Why, Jack? Why?"

She beat her palms against her chest, as though to press more air into her lungs.

"This was something we wanted to keep to ourselves, Lou and I, but the fact is, we're married."

"How could you! It goes against everything we believe in!"

A police van pulled up before the steps of the courthouse and gave her an excuse to turn away.

"Come upstairs, Vincent," I begged her. "I'll fix you a drink and explain."

Lou wasn't going to be home for several hours. I decided that I could avoid a scene on the sidewalk and calm Vincent with whiskey. But by the time we climbed the steps to the apartment and shut the door behind us, I realized that I had made a mistake. Within a few minutes she had polished off several stiff drinks.

"This'll be the last one, Vincent," I said, joining her in a third.

"The last one for me and thee, is that what thou say'st?"

Her slender neck throbbed as she swallowed. Lying back on the sofa, she began to recite.

"Vincent?" I stood up.

She went on reciting.

I fixed myself another drink.

She went on reciting.

"This doesn't seem to be doing either of us much good."

She stopped reciting, sat up and grabbed the whiskey bottle, took a long swallow, and sagged back against the sofa.

"Where's your potty?"

I helped her to her feet. She rolled her eyes at me as though I had commited some disgusting act, yanking her hand from mine as soon as she gained her balance.

"Very well," she said with a decisive nod as she followed me toward the bath. "Very well," she repeated as she slammed the door shut in my face.

I poured myself another drink, sipping it slowly while looking out at the courtyard beyond our window. Since my last visit to the doctor, the neighboring maple had turned from green to gold to brown, most of its leaves already littering the pavement of the little alley below. My condition had worsened considerably. It could all make my head spin if I let it. But on the verge of my twenty-ninth birthday, with the prospect of serious surgery less than a month away, I pledged that if I survived—hadn't I decided all this before?—I would give up on the lyric and fight the epic way.

Meanwhile, in the bathroom, comedy: a woman was running the tap.

"Vincent?"

I knocked softly on the door.

The gurgling tap answered my call.

"Are you all right?"

Pressing my ear against the wood, I could hear her reciting over the sound of the water!

"Vincent! For Christ's sake, the joke has gone on long enough!"

The apartment door opened and in walked Lou.

"What joke, dearest? I could hear you from the stairs."

"An impractical joke. A very impractical joke."

I gave her an impatient kiss on the cheek, drawing back when I saw O'Neill standing behind her in the doorway.

"We didn't expect to find you home so early. Gene was going to go over some lines with me. He wants them just right."

"I didn't expect to be home so early myself."

I stuck out my hand.

"Gene."

"Huh." That was O'Neill saying hello, his head cocked toward the rear of the apartment, listening intently.

Lou looked at him then at me.

"Are you getting ready to take a bath?"

"No," I said, staring dumbly at the dour O'Neill. "Gene, can I fix you a drink?"

Lou shook her head.

"That's the last thing he needs," she said, moving past me toward the bathroom. I caught her around the waist.

"Wouldn't you like a drink, darling?"

"One or two."

She shook her head. "What is that, Jack? the plumbing?"

I was sweating like a ditch digger.

"*Gene* must have a drink."

"Gene doesn't need a drink, sweetest. Gene needs famously not to have any drink ever again. You know that."

"Huh!"

O'Neill grunted again and sat down on the sofa, sinking into some reverie that resembled sleep. Lou wrestled herself free of my grasp.

"What's going on here, Jack? There's someone in the bathroom!" In a few quick strides she was at the door, trying the knob.

"I think at this point in the drama I'm supposed to tell you that I can explain all of this," I said, joining Lou at the bathroom door.

"Who's IN there?"

Lou pounded on the door with both fists.

"No use," I said, "she's locked herself in."

Lou was about to speak when she turned to see O'Neill lurch past us, heading for the kitchen.

"Gene, that's enough!"

"You said he didn't drink anymore."

"We had just one together after rehearsal."

"Are you sure you want to play this comedy in front of such an unappreciative audience?"

"*Eyes!*"

O'Neill's voice echoed through the apartment.

"What's he saying, darling? You understand him better than I do."

"*Eyes!*"

O'Neill moaned again.

"He wants ice," Lou said.

"I'll get him some."

"You will not.

"I will."

"*Who* is in the bathroom?"

"Yes! Yes! *Eyes!!*"

"He's having a fit," I said, pleased with the distraction of the drink-starved (or crazed?) playwright talking to our icebox.

"He's perfectly numb. Now who?"

"*Eyes!*"

"We'd better help him."

"You'd better help yourself, Jack! I want to know who's in there."

"Vincent. She's locked herself in. I *tried* to throw her out."

"A likely story!"

"*Eyes! Eyes! Eyes!*"

"I didn't bring her here for what you're thinking."

"You can't even speak coherently, can you? Guilt is twisting your tongue!"

"I don't feel any guilt! I haven't got anything to feel guilty about!"

"Soon you will!"

"What does that mean? What does 'soon I will' mean? Lou?"

"*Sí, sí, sí, sí, sí!*"

"Shall I get that wretch a drink?"

"He musn't have one!"

"How about you? Don't you need one now?"

"I want to settle this bathroom business."

"*Ice! Ice, sí, sí, hello, hello!*"

O'Neill staggered out of the kitchen and collapsed on the floor in front of me, his hand clutching my cuff. Lou fell to her knees alongside him.

I yanked my leg away.

"Don't hurt him!"

Lou jumped up and smacked my face.

"Christ!"

"*Sí, sí, sis, sí, sí!*"

"I'm sorry, Jack."

She sobbed her apology as our drunken friend crawled toward the bathroom door.

"Goddamnit, everybody wants to get in there!"

Someone came storming up the stairs. The door flew open and in rushed a chubby fellow in an apron.

"You drip!"

The man waggled a beefy fist in the air.

"Get out!"

"You stop da drip?"

"What drip?"

"Gene!" Lou screamed. "He's bleeding!"

The fallen playwright sat up, his face smeared red where he had wiped his hand across it. From under the door seeped a reddish pool of—

"Dat's no blood!" declared the beefy man. "You dripa da wat' on my market! Turn it off righta now!"

"It's true," I said, "it's not blood. I've seen it in the trenches and *that's* not real."

"*Ice!*" moaned O'Neill.

"Shut up!" the beefy man said.

"Who are you?!" Lou shrieked, "Get out of our house!"

"Stop da drip, lady, I get out."

"*Ice, yes!*"

I tried to haul O'Neill away from the front of the bathroom door.

"Upsa-daisy, Gene!"

"*Sí, sí, señor, el hielo es de mio!*"

"I guess there's nothing left to do but break it down."

"I suppose we might as well get it over with," Lou said.

I immediately lay my shoulder to the door which bulged inward, buckled, splintered!

"Help!"

The naked poetess in the overflowing bathtub screamed at the sight of us.

"What the hell are you doing, Vincent?"

My voice rose in indignation.

"Composing!"

"You've bled all over my house, you filthy bitch!" Lou shouted.

"I have bled, Louise," said Vincent in mock-regal tones, "but I have not bled for thee." Stepping out of the tub, she looked about for a towel, and finding one, she patted herself with regal disdain. "I have changed myself in order to rid myself of bitter memories accrued by the person that I was."

It was then I realized how different she appeared.

"Vincent, you washed out your red hair!"

"I dye. I fall upon the thorns of life...."

"You folks no drip no more? You clean up and get dressed?" The market owner patted me on the shoulder. "*La commedia est finita, sí?*"

"*Sí*, and thanks," I said.

"*Sí, sis, sí, sí, dama con hielo! Eyes!*" O'Neill raved from his place on the floor.

"Some neighbors you have, eh?" The market owner glanced around the apartment, taking in Vincent, who was now dressing under Lou's vigilant eye, and O'Neill, who still burbled on through the haze of his boozy perception. He winked at me and went out the door.

"What are you waiting for?" Lou asked. "You can just follow him right down the stairs."

"I live here, dear, and we're marrried now, don't forget!"

"Marry yourself and this bitch out the door. Or else *I'm* going!"

"Vincent!" I grabbed her arm. "Tell Lou! Tell her that nothing happened here between us."

Vincent, languidly brushing her long (now straw-brown) hair, smiled at Lou as though in a dream.

"Nothing happened here."

"Or anywhere!" I put in.

"I want you both to leave," Lou said.

"*Si, si, con hielo!*"

"I thought we loved each other like sisters," Vincent said, handing me the hairbrush. "I'm going to tear up the poem I wrote about you!"

"You can eat your poem, for all I care," Louise said with a terrifying grin. "Now both of you, git!"

"Now that's a fine fix we're in," I said to Vincent when we reached the bottom of the stairs.

"A fix you're in," she said, slipping out through the gate that separated Patchin Place from Tenth Street.

"Wait, I'll walk you home!"

Vincent turned the corner and was gone.

I walked swiftly westward toward the docks, walked to the end of a pier. My life. Such a joke. And yet so serious. The war. The bathtub. Silliness. Suffering. Tough-minded. Tenderness. If old James hadn't died, I might have entrained for Cambridge and plagued him with such questions as harried me now. Such a mixture, neither comedy nor pathetic tragedy, could only have occurred during our modern times. Lyrics, bloody urine. How could anyone put a tag on this before it ended, comedy or tragedy? Life came first, style later, and that was that was that.

The sun settled behind the Hoboken tenements, factories—New Jersey's finest hour. The Hudson gushed with the news of the incoming tide, giving off the aroma of deep ocean seamusk. A tug commented in the distance on travels yet to be. I pictured the sun still high above Pennsylvania, over Iowa—over the Rockies, Nevada, the sparkling Willamette. Ocean to ocean, my mind raced with the light. And as if I could somehow overtake my idea of my own best self, I stripped and dove into the Hudson and swam twenty-nine strokes out, in honor of my impending birthday. Stroke, kick, stroke and kick, what now wouldn't I do to bring my honey home to me again? Oh, phenom, oh, epiphenom! I trod water at twenty-nine, thinking how Byron would have plowed on all the way to the New Jersey shore. Byron at least had a myth to inspire him. All I had was my lonely, hurting self.

Part Seven

PROGRESS OF AN ILLNESS

Death comes on like this, I know.
Snow-soft and gently cold;
Impalpable battalions of thin mist,
Light-quenching and sound-smothering and slow.
Light as a wind-spilled sail
The spent world flaps in space—
Day's but a grayer night, and the old sun
Up the blind sky goes heavily and pale.

Out of all circumstance
I drift or seem to drift
In a vague vapor-world that clings and veils
Great trees arow like kneeling elephants. . . .

Lee Sing tinkled tiny bells in my ear. I pushed on through the mist. The first person I encountered was President Wilson dressed in an old bathrobe that I recognized as having come out of Steffens's closet.

"You're taking notes?"

"Of course, I am, Mister President. A good reporter never wants to forget."

He led me through a tangle of berry bushes to the base of the Washington Monument.

"This is where we'll place his memorial."

"Whose?"

I seem to have dropped my pencil and note pad.

A voice drifted over the foggy grasslands, its booming bass-notes coinciding with the beating of a drum. I shivered, anticipating some uproar I could not yet explain.

> Tippecanoe and Tyler Too
> Parlez-Vous
> Tippecanoe and Tyler Too
> Parlez-Vous

I struggled to run across the flat space in front of the hill. The singing grew louder, acting as a prod to my sluggish frame. Rose petals floated down through the mist, now here, now there. In the distance a tug called its sad, hoarse mate.

"Ladies and gentlemen!"

President Wilson was perched on a platform several feet above the ground. He had exchanged his pince-nez for a telescope and was peering anxiously through the instrument.

"It's all a sham, isn't it, Jack?"

"Seeger!"

"The sensation of life, the pulse of perception...."

I followed his shade to the other side of the monument.

"Lou!"

She struck a wicked pose, elbow against the stone.

"He brought you to me."

Grinning lasciviously, she began to undress.

"Darling, won't you be cold?"

"Not as cold as he is!"

She stopped her peep show long enough to point an enameled fingernail at the shape wearing Seeger's mask.

"He knows nothing."

"But the dead have special feelings!"

"Jack, you're such a sport!"

After revealing her breasts to the crowd, she proceeded to shimmy out of her slip. I hurried to her side, though ownerless hands reached out for me.

"Hush now! Our leader makes his speech!"

On the platform, Wilson poked the telescope into his trouser pocket and proceeded to urinate onto the crowd. Screams! Panic!

And then, in the distance, the faintest music of a bugle—*d'ta-d'ta, d'ta, d'ta-taaaaaaa!*

A three-masted schooner, sails filled by invisible winds, cut swiftly across the plain.

"Old salt! Old sailor! He's come, he's come!"

I left Lou behind as I raced with the crowd toward the oncoming ship. My heart beat wildly. From the decks, crewmen fired at us with pistols, and I ran for cover at the sound of their reports.

"In here, young rabbit!"

Cooney Washington appeared at my side, grabbed my hand, and yanked me in the direction of some berry bushes.

"I've got to find Lou," I said.

"Aw, she's just stark raving naked. She'll be jest fine. I wanted to tell you a story. Are you ready?"

"Can't now, Cooney. Got to get out of here."

"Now listen."

He took me by the shoulder.

"I was up Alaska way one dark summer, and summer in Alaska is a sight you—"

I yanked myself free and started running back toward the monument. The schooner had foundered on the hillside. Nothing but wreckage remained of its once gallant, though menacing, facade. Tall thick-stalked sunflowers marked the place where its fo'c's'le had stood. Smoke floated thickly across the already cloudy horizon. Looking about for Lou, I found her dressed in nothing but a spangled skein of snake skin.

"Help me!"

Some sailor lay moaning amidst the debris.

"Help me, comrade!"

I thought his voice sounded familiar, but it was hard to see him in the growing dark.

The bugle in the distance—*d'ta, d'ta, d'ta, d'ta, d'taaa!*
Shapes shifting—
"Help me, son!"

> *Out, out*
> *Swish-swish—flash by the spokes of the Wheel of pain;*
> *Dizzily runs the whining rim.*
> *Way down in the cool dark is the slow-evolving sleep,*
> *but I hang heavily writhing in hot chains*
> *High in the crimson stillness of my body,*
> *and the swish-swish of the spokes of the Wheel of pain.*

Such was the course of my dreams during the winter of 1916. Biting cold and several heavy snowstorms ravaged the east. Europe heaved and twitched under the burden of new militarized murder. But after emerging from surgery with one kidney fewer than when I went in, I discovered that I had my own little battle to fight at home.

A visit from Carl Binger, a Jew whom I'd known years before at Harvard, should have cheered me. Binger was now a surgeon at Johns Hopkins. He had seen my name on the patient list and looked in on me during my postoperative troubles. I apologized for my past sins and offered to write an article about his experiences as a surgeon. Binger laughed and gave me advice about how to convince the night nurse that I needed more medicine for my pain. However, the physical torments were not as unsettling as the mental. I had roughed it before in Chihuahua and the Balkans. The doctors here seemed like angels compared to the ogres in white who attended the weeping, screaming wounded on the Eastern front. (One bearded gent wearing a bloodstained smock and a monocle refused to treat me for a bad case of dysentery. When he had asked me about my previous medical history, he became insulted when I did not mention syphillis. "Come, come," he had chided me, "I'm a busy man and I don't have time to treat liars. Everyone has had syphillis! I won't be lied to by an American! Good day!")

My doctors chuckled when I told them that story. The nurses blushed.

Heady still from the ether, I floated again on the verge of a dream, feeling Lou's presence alongside me even in those moments when I was clinically unconscious. Marvelous that without any rehearsal Lou played the role of comforter so well. While cradling my head in her arms, brushing her breasts against my lips, taking the sponge away from the nurse—dismissing her, in fact—and bathing me as though I were her newborn infant, Lou convinced me that, her own protestations to the contrary, she would make a wonderful mother. She enveloped me in such a healing embrace that I could think of nothing else more important to tell her when I emerged from my postoperative stupor.

"It's true, sweetheart," I said. "You've got the touch! I can feel it."

She looked around the room as though she thought the nurses might be spying. Then she grasped my hand and squeezed.

"You're embarrassing me, Jack."

"Honey! We'll have a child, we'll do it, we'll give up waiting until the war is over, we'll make our own little peace and tranquility, we'll do it, just as soon as I'm well . . . . "

Lou frightened me when she burst into tears.

"You're not telling me something! What is it that you're not telling me, darling? Was their operation a failure after all? Am I going to die after all?"

She released my hand and promptly rubbed her knuckles into her eyes, murmuring, "No, you're well. That's why I'm weeping. Because you're well, and I'm so cruel to you . . . I was so mean to you about Vincent, and I know I shouldn't have been . . . . "

"What are you talking about? You're the sweetest, kindest...that's why I want us to have a child!"

"We'll have plenty of time to talk about that, Jack," Lou said, her tears drying up as rapidly as they had come. "Now you need your rest. Don't worry about me. We have to take care of sweet you."

She fondled my chest beneath the bedcovers.

"Your heart's beating so fast."

"And one part of me is feeling like its old self. Of course we can't do anything about that until I get out of here."

"I'll come back tonight. We could shut the door."

I lay my hand atop hers on my heaving chest.

"We could invite the nurses, too. And have a real Village party. We'll call Dell and get him to write about it. Say, where is that lunk and all my other friends? Couldn't they find the train fare to come down and take a look at me?"

"One of them's waiting downstairs. Do you want to see him?"

"Who? who?" My excitement cost me a sharp stab of pain.

"I didn't realize you'd be so lonely or I'd have brought more people with me."

"Who came with you? Is it Dell? No. Max! Oh, Max?"

"Walter."

"Voltaire! That cretin! I hate him, I love him. Oh, darling, please tell him to come up. I need to talk to him. I had a historical dream. I have to talk to him about it."

But on this occsion all Lippmann wanted to do was talk about my operation, my pain, my recovery. At first I thought Lou must have warned him—or could he have warned himself?—about how to treat a patient coming out of surgery. After a few minutes of inconsequential chat, I realized, when our Harvard friend in white stuck his head in the door of the room, that it had been Binger who had advised him.

"How does he look to you?" Binger called to Lippmann.

"He looks just fine to me," replied the tough-hearted ideologue, adjusting his spectacles on his nose.

"I feel rotten!" I said in a kind of croak.

"You do? You don't sound it."

"Shall I go?" Lippmann asked after another few minutes of chat.

"Leap, I want you to stay forever."

"I'm on my way to Washington. I don't think I can stay that long."

"Practical man, Carl, yes?"

Binger shook his head.

"I've always admired both of your styles."

"Can you arrange to remove Leapman's liver? That way he can stay awhile and show you more of his style."

"My liver is fine," said Lippmann.

"I'm sure it is."

"And I really do have to catch a train."

"You just arrived."

"Good night, fellows," said Binger, "I have to go back to work."

"You always were a real cut-up, Carl."

"Thanks, Jack!"

"Goodbye, Carl," Lippmann said.

Outside the hospital window, thick, frothy gobbets of snow floated steadily down.

"It's going to be a frightful day in Washington," I said.

"It's been that way for a while," said Lippmann.

"Is Wilson really going to give us that war he promised he'd keep us out of?"

Lippmann snapped his fingers at the window. "You know what promises mean in politics, Jack. They come down like the snow on the roof."

"And they pile up?"

"And they drift."

"And they melt and run down the gutters?"

A few days later, O'Neill shuffled into the room and enclouded me in the gloom of unknowing that followed him about like a mascot.

"I hate this place," was the first thing he said.

I patted the edge of the bed.

"Sit down and tell me why. I learned some techniques from Mabel's Doctor Brill. They might help you."

"Fuck Brill." He pulled up a chair. "I have a potion I bought from an old sea-dog down around Cape of Good Luck and the recipe's never failed me." He dug into his coat pocket as though in search of subway fare and withdrew a small flask. "Can you drink?"

"Are you kidding? I'm wired up and full of tubes. One slug of that stuff and I'd explode!"

"You don't mind if I do?"

"Be my guest. They'll get you back here one day and put your liver in a glass jar."

Gene took a stiff slug from the flask, shuddering as he swallowed. He gazed at me with blood-rimmed intensity.

"That what they took out of you?"

"Liver? No, a kidney."

He made a noise in his throat.

"One organ or another has to go. It's just chance which one goes first."

"Not with me, pal. I had that bad kidney ever since I was a boy. But I don't have the damned thing anymore! Oh, I'd love to have a drink of that rotgut to celebrate!"

O'Neill shoved the flask toward me.

"Worried?" he asked. "If the operation doesn't work, you can't have too much longer anyway. If it works, you can drink. So drink."

"I don't want too much longer. I want only just enough."

"Haven't you got it? You're famous. Nobody knows me from driftwood."

"Feeling sorry for yourself? That's one thing I never learned to do. They cut me open to the bone and core, old boy, and I still didn't feel sorry for myself. That's something I inherited from my father, I suppose. He was a great good man and people kicked him for being his best, but he never felt sorry for himself, not for one Indian minute."

"Fathers! Fathers! Let's not doodle on about fathers! Let's drink to sons! They're the best, don't you know!"

"To sons!" I took the flask and raised it to my lips.

"Drink!"

O'Neill's eyes met mine, and if a stare could have an odor, his look matched the smell in my nostrils. I'd sipped home-brewed whiskey in the Balkans with the worst of men, bandits and officers, sickly and incorrigible boozers. I'd chanced picking up the spores of the worst diseases and laughed at the prospect—flung the empty bottles into the air and called for more! So it was neither fear nor timidity that kept me from closing my lips over the rim of the container. I had the sneaking suspicion that once I drank I'd have entered into a pact with the boozy Irishman whose terms I knew not of.

"Drink already goddamn it, Reed! I want another belt."

I took a sip at last and pushed the flask back into his hand, while a burning tide in my chest flowed down to my bowels.

"Darling!" Lou entered the room just at that moment in the company of a new doctor. O'Neill took one look at the man and hurled his flask to the floor, with a clang and a crash as the metal object, trailing its fluid, came to a halt at the door.

"If thine flask offend thee," he announced, staggering into the center of the room, "cast it out!"

He bowed slightly toward the astonished doctor.

"Doctor," Lou began, "this is a friend of ours, Gene O'Neill, Doctor—"

But O'Neill cut her off with a wave of his hand.

"And if thine brain, thine BRAIN, offend thee! What, doctor, doest thou then?"

"Now, Gene!"

Lou spoke to him in the same tone she had used to control him during the summer at Provincetown, a sharp, commanding voice that suggested a lion tamer speaking to his beasts. "You go on over to that chair and sit down."

O'Neill's usually rough and ragged baritone turned whiny.

"I hate hospitals! I spent six months in a prison like this!" He punctuated his words with a thrust of his foot in the direction of the abandoned silver flask. "Six months! You ain't been here, pal, no more than a few weeks!" His eyes narrowed, like an inquisitive ape's, and he leaned his lanky figure toward me. His voice now seemed less childlike and more the put-on expressions of the rough drinking crowd of the Bowery and the washed-out souls of the cheap rooming houses along the way where he sometimes spent the night. "It's me that's really been sick, mate! Six months in a monkey house! I taught my lungs wid burst!"

"If you've been sick, Mr. O'Neill," said the doctor, "perhaps you'd like to lie down and take a rest. I have a perfectly comfortable office where—"

"Nix!"

O'Neill spluttered at the amused physician, swaying over the empty flask and, finally, bending over double and picking it up and turning it over as though it were an object he'd never seen before.

"I've been sick but I'm not sick now. He's the sick one!" He pointed, of course, at me. I glanced over at Lou for some reassurance that she retained control of our friend but she merely blinked and looked away. "I still got both my lungs! You took out his offending organ! I'm one up on him. Ain't it so, Jack? Ain't it so?"

"If you say so, old boy," I replied, fatigued by his overlong performance. I wanted to rest, I wanted to hold my honey's hand and dream of a trip to China. I wanted to imagine the end of the war. I wanted to soothe myself with empty, dreamless sleep, and make sharply contoured poems that dealt in comedy rather than sorrow.

As though he'd been reading my thoughts, O'Neill let out a derisive howl.

"He's been lying in bed like a sultan while the rest of us have been slogging through the blizzards! Right, Lou?"

"Keep your mean old thoughts to yourself, Gene. Jack's just had a serious operation."

"Was I being mean?" He lurched toward my bed. "Awfully

sorry, old sport. Old bean. Old piss pot, wot? It's just my dumb flair for the melodramatic. Now how do you like that? Oh, I wish I could get rid of it just as much as you do. It's cost me! Do you know how many pages I burned last week? Fire and toil, boil and trouble, if thine page offend thee, cast it off! Isn't that right, Lou? Don't answer. I know. Too frail. Too weak. Doctor, get thee to a surgery. This poor boy, his offending organ...."

The doctor tried to assert himself then.

"Perhaps we ought to—"

O'Neill spun around to face Lou and the physician.

"Never cogitate neither! That damned cogitation, costing us millions in tribute every year! Our boys will never go to the front, and never will they cogitate!" He spun dervish-like around and addressed himself to me again. "Millions for a fence and dog turds for the tribunes! How's that for a motto, Jack? We'll never go to war and we'll put a fence 'round them that wants to."

"I'm glad we agree, Gene. But now the doctor wants to do his duty with me here. You think that you and Lou could—"

"Cast me off? Fend the boat off when they've come to rescue ye? Oh, the ironies of it all, Jack, the offending ironies." He planted one long, bony hand on the bed to keep himself upright. "You didn't know that I was sick myself. Hospitalized for half a year! The doctors hovering over me; TB or not TB, that was the question."

I couldn't help but smile, but Lou and the doctor remained unnaturally solemn.

"Visited by the angel of death at least twice, the ugly bird sitting on the edge of my bed, peering over the covers at me, waiting for me to expire."

"I didn't know that you'd been that ill, Gene. So you know what this is like?"

"Yes, I know, I know, mate. And no, you din' know, I told your woman but I din' tell you. More bravery, eh? The female of the species more sympathetic, while the male, the male, aha!"

He suddenly reared his head back and sneezed. We remained

silent as he wiped his nose with the sleeve of his ragged jacket.

"This is a pathetic performance, isn't it, Lou?" he said.

My wife nodded firmly, her eyes showing not a whit of sympathy. But, instead of stopping him, her coldness only seemed to drive him further into speech. Words tumbled from his mouth like apples down a chute. The doctor pressed Lou's arm, then moved toward the door.

"I know it was down in Buenos Aires," he was shouting when the doctor left the room. "I know that when I touched my lips to that rotten mate's bottle was when I picked up the bug! We were sitting in the park, I didn't even have a pair of socks to call my own, no *socks*, and he passed the rotgut along to me—I know, Jack, just the way I passed my flask along to you, but don't think I've infected you, because I'm cured, oh, yes, I'm cured—six months in the monkey cage, nothing but white women in white gowns and snow all around in snow-white buildings and white floors and black was I inside but oh my gums were white! This nigger passed me the bottle, and the air was perfumed with flowers we never see up these parts, smooth music in the breeze, my socks were missing, I felt a terrible itching in my balls, and I was miserable. What a wretch I was! Swallowed up in the whale of the world! Nobody to mourn me, nobody to mourn for! Mate, I was lost, lost in Patagonia, Antarctica called out to me, the Southern Cross winked at me at night. Come hither, come hither, come hither! That's how I picked up those tubercles down there! Come hither! Come hither! Come hither!"

He shuddered, as though passed over by a violent windstorm, and I swallowed hard at the sight of Lou taking him in her arms like a mother embracing a child in the throes of a nightmare. Two orderlies entered the room followed by the new doctor. But they had no trouble with O'Neill, since Lou led him quietly into the hall.

She caught me with my pants down when she returned.

"I'm sorry, doctor," she said to the man examining me. "Our friend seems to be calmer now. I'll take him back on the train."

"You're not afraid?" I asked.

"No, sweetie, he's fine, he's just been drinking. You know how he gets."

"He needs treatment," the doctor said.

"He won't see anyone," Lou explained. "I've been trying to convince him of that since the summer."

"Lou's playing Beauty to his Beast." I rolled to one side at the urging of the doctor's strong fingers.

"I like the way the scar is healing," he said. "Perhaps we won't have to do anything more with him."

Lou leaned over and kissed me.

"Ugh," she moaned. "You smell awful."

"That's Gene's doing. He gave me a drink."

The doctor looked at me incredulously.

"You Bohemians!"

"Can it hurt him?" Lou frowned.

"Probably not," said the doctor. "But how could he take a chance like that?" He tossed my covers back and motioned that I could pull my gown down over my dressing.

"You Bohemians!" he said again.

"I know," I said. "The next thing you know we'll be sailing to China."

Lou returned to New York that evening. Soon after that a letter arrived from her that caused me distress. She wrote that she had been feeling a lot of physical pain and her doctor told her that her ovaries and such were inflamed and infected, possibly because of some kind of chemical response to my own condition. I called for the nurse because I wasn't going to lie in bed in Baltimore while my honey had to undergo surgery in New York City. They tried to get me to take some pills to calm me down but nothing helped until Carl Binger agreed to telephone Lou at home and find out more information about the diagnosis.

"Minor woman's troubles," was what he reported to me. "You wouldn't want to know all the boring details, Jack. She's got a good doctor and she ought to know a little more in a couple of days."

I raised myself up from the pillow, still a painful act.

"Did she sound well? Is she still hurting?"

Binger gave me his profession's dismissive wave of the hand. I'd never felt so helpless in my life. I suffered through another letter in which Lou described the trouble in greater detail, and then learned from the next telephone call that they had decided against surgery. One more visit to the doctor's office and some medication already had helped the condition a great deal. After the news, I fell back into my bed relieved and hardly noticed the exploring fingers of a group of student doctors whose teacher had decided to let them feel inside me before and after the operation to help them notice the difference between a sick Reed and a mending one.

When Lou arrived at Hopkins again two weeks later, she was the one who looked as though she had been through the major ordeal.

"We're both so tired," I said, cradling her head in my arms on the train trip back to New York. "We'll go to Croton for a while. The old hustly-bustly Village, that's all too much for us right now."

The train lurched forward. I looked outside the window at the hundreds of white marble stoops crouching before the lonely, square wooden houses.

"And you're feeling better, lovey-honey?"

Lou looked up at me with her inscrutable green eyes.

"It was so sweet of you to ask that doctor to call, darling. It cheered me up so much in such a bad week!"

Her voice was soft, appreciative, but even as she spoke her eyes showed me the inner motion of her mind in some flight I could not follow.

"You did tell me everything I should know, didn't you?"

"Everything."

She burrowed deeper in my arms as the train rushed northward. Her drowsiness was contagious.

"You've been asked to speak here at a rally next week," Lou said when she discovered us sitting in the Philadelphia station. "But I don't think you should go."

"I may be rested by then. There's a fight and I want to be in it."

"The fight not to fight?"

"You can put it that way."

I had been reading newspapers again during my last week in the hospital. The struggle to keep us out of war was becoming quite a battle itself, a battle of words, however, rather than bullets and bombs, though often just as fierce. The distant towers of Princeton recalled me to my mission. How many hundreds of men who walked and studied and swam and prayed just beyond those trees would soon lie mangled on a battlefield in France? While we changed trains in the city, I explained to Lou how I felt about the struggle to keep us out of the war.

"But how can we keep that up and go to China at the same time?"

"I don't know, but we'll do it! I feel so much better now. I'm ready for anything!"

"If you are," said Lou, "then so am I."

Life in Croton consisted of simple hours of reading, writing, and indoor gardening. By day, I talked poems to our plants. By night, I discovered that the ghosts from my past remained unquiet in the afterworld—

"*You come watch me home! You come watch me home!*"

Lee Sing gave his pigtail a gleeful shake, and I sat upright in bed.

Lou teased me while I shook off the dream.

"If your friends could only see you this way!"

"It was just as if we were back in Portland talking to each other and nothing had happened since. Maybe I've developed some kind of brain fever from my operation. I swear to you I saw him so clearly I could have reached out and touched him!"

"You were dreaming, sweetness. And you'd better go to sleep again if you want to feel rested in the morning."

"Can we—?"

"You needn't ask, darling. You know it's still not safe yet."

We embraced. Now and then I glanced over at the wall near the window where I had first seen the figure of the Chinaman appear.

In the morning, I decided that I understood the meaning of the apparition.

"Something's up with the China assignment," I explained to Lou over breakfast.

She looked as though she were about to laugh in my face.

"You don't really believe in these things, do you, darling?"

"I don't know whether I believe in it or not. But I saw the thing."

"You had a dream, darling."

"Don't you believe in what I'm saying?"

"Must I believe everything you say just because I love you?"

"But I saw it! Something is going on about China, I know it. Lou, if O'Neill came through the door screaming that he'd just kissed Jesus, you'd—"

"I would make him a strong cup of coffee! Jack, you're not jealous of him, are you? That poor dilapidated man!"

Lou's long mouth pursed up and she might have been about to weep. As I reached around the table to caress her, she slid her chair away and hurried into the bathroom. I turned around in my chair when I heard her come out, but before I could catch her, she had thrown on her coat and left the cottage.

It turned colder that afternoon, making a chilly though snowless twilight, but because of the uncommon intensity of the sun as it sank beyond the Hudson, it seemed that winter might somehow be on the wane. I was watching the dark come on, wondering if I would ever follow the sun around the world to China, when Lou returned.

"Where have you been?"

"You sound like a dime novel," she said, hanging up her coat and hat. "I thought that someone like you could make better dialogue than that."

"I never claimed to be a fiction writer. I just report what people say. Where have you been?"

"Out."

"Ta-da! My lady love hath told me something that is news to my ears. I know you've been out, Lou. Where out?" I studied her face. "You just wanted me to mope around all day and miss you, didn't you?"

"What if?"

"That means you wanted to hurt me. Why do you want to hurt me? We've both been hurt, honey. We've both just been cut up and poked by all those ugly doctors. Why do we need to hurt each other?"

"So you admit that you might have hurt me, too?"

A dour look flickered across her face, and then her visage turned into a mask of shadows.

"We'll just have to keep on loving each other extra hard until we can come together physically again."

"I'm ready," I said, squeezing her hands.

"But I'm not," she said. "I have to see my doctor again next week. And then we'll know."

"There might be other things to do. We'll just play," I said, taking her by the hand.

"We won't!" she shouted in my face, and twisted away.

I squinted at her in the deepening darkness, while she poured herself a glass of whiskey.

"Pour me one?"

She peered back at me across the shadowy room.

"Did the doctor say it's all right?"

"I drank with Gene in the hospital, remember? It didn't do any permanent damage. The pain is lousy today. I need a drink."

She shrugged, poured me one. Her hand trembled as she handed me the glass.

"Can we talk some sense now?"

"Not when you speak to me like that we can't."

"If I only knew what 'that' was...."

"'That' is the tone you take when you've decided that it's

my privilege to tell you about everything in my life, like it or not."

"Darling, I'm really all at sea now. I don't know how we started talking to each other like this. I'd love to end it. Can't we sit—?"

"I'll remind you how we got started, Jack. It got started when you made that remark at the breakfast table."

"Remark?"

"You're so stupid you don't understand even now. Don't ask me anything more about it."

Lou spilled whiskey over the lip of her glass. Looking down at the deepening stain on the rug, she behaved as though she had no recollection that she had made it. She raised her glass and drank off the rest of the liquid.

"Salud," I said, drinking mine in turn.

She kept her lips tightly closed.

"Getting hungry?"

She laughed then, and for a few seconds I felt better.

"Hungry? You think you can change the subject just like that? You're such a simpleton, Jack Reed, I swear to Christ!"

"Is the subject my insulting you at breakfast? If it is, then I'm sorry."

"Are you really? Well, then I'm glad. And will you cook us some chops now? And shall I bake a cake? And shall we stroll down the hill in the gathering dark remembering how it was when we first met?"

"What the hell is going on with you? Is Vincent still on your mind? She's not on mine, I can swear to that."

Light suddenly flooded the room as Lou switched on a floor lamp.

"I don't want to talk about it anymore," she said.

"Then you do really want me to cook the chops?"

"I'm not hungry." She poured herself another drink. "I think I'll just get into bed and read."

She left the room. After a while, I heard the water running in the bathroom. I pressed my forehead against the window, wondering why I could not think of what to say or do that would mend this, whatever repair was needed. I heard Lou shut the bathroom door. Then came the creaking of our closet door. Something flitted across the snow, a rabbit or a squirrel, then raced away across the blue-white silence of the field. There was a half-moon, its light almost strong enough, it seemed, to stir what few dead leaves dangled from the branches of our maples and elms. Some lively shadow flitted between trees and moon.

"It's a lovely night outside," I heard myself saying as I walked into the bedroom.

"Good, darling, I'm glad," Lou said.

She sat propped up on several pillows, a glass on the bedside table, a book in front of her face.

"I had a kind of vision, darling."

"You're having a lot of those lately, aren't you? First your old Chinese man. Now something else. What was it?"

"Do you really want to hear?"

Lou put down the book and stared at me without expression.

"Let me guess. That old woodsman you told me about?"

"It was a child."

She reached for the glass from the night table.

"I had my face to the glass. I couldn't see much through the window because of the light behind me. But I did catch sight of something moving on the snow, some animal, a rabbit, I think. And then—in my mind—I saw a child running after the rabbit, running it to ground. It was a boy, a big, blustery, sandy-haired lout, but with a narrow face that kind of centered on his upturned nose and sparkling eyes. A beautiful child, Lou, let me tell you! I could tell that he was pretty beefy already, even at his early age. He ran like a miniature bear. Still, he had a certain delicacy about him, a strength in his smallness that he must have gotten from—"

"No! We said we weren't going to talk about this. Jack, I warn you, we're not doing anybody any good by this."

"It was just a vision, Lou, that's all. I wanted to tell you about it."

I lumbered over to the bed, feeling young and clumsy, raw, tender, and with more pain than before the operation.

"We've talked and talked about this, Jack," Lou said. "We decided that we won't have children now. Do you bring it up just to torture me?"

I sat down on the edge of the bed.

"It doesn't have to be torture, sweetie. It shouldn't have to hurt us to talk about it."

"It hurts me here"—she touched the rim of the glasss to her breast—"because it hurts me there." she glanced down between her legs.

"Did the doctor really say that I infected you with something?"

"He said it was a good possibility."

She sipped her whiskey, a habit that was beginning to upset me.

"But now you're almost well."

"I'm not so well."

"Is there something the doctor said that I don't know?"

"Nothing the doctor said."

"You're talking in riddles, sweetie."

"To myself as well as you, Jack."

That was a strange winter. We lived in patterns that reminded me too much of my life with Mabel: there was public time, work devoted to the problems of war and peace, specifically in those months to the writing of articles and speeches through which I hoped to rally working people to the cause of keeping us out of war; and there was the private time, hour after hour given over to the curious and rapidly growing struggle that had developed between Lou and me and Lou and herself. The worst and most torturous aspect of this period was that there seemed to be absolutely no connection between the two realms. Some other shrewish girl might have called me down for all of the hours I gave to the campaign against the campaign to bring us into war. Not Lou. As I regained my strength, I put it into this fight at the expense of a great deal of frivolity—dramas, musicales, and the usual high jinks that took place—and Lou worked right along with me. On the front lines of this struggle, at rallies, meetings, debates, and marches, she stood at my side. When the catcalls and hooting from our opponents grew louder, she laughed above the din. When the police swung their clubs, she was happier than I had ever seen her since my return from the hospital.

But at night in the privacy of our love, we seemed at times to behave as antagonists rather than comrades. Still prevented by our respective ailments and recuperations from coming together physically, we found ourselves standing on either side of a chasm of doubts and misunderstandings. The smallest problem—breaking a dish or mislaying a book—became the cause of a great outburst and that outburst the preface to an outbreak of verbal violence.

One night in late February, after Mr. Whitney, the publisher of the *Metropolitan*, had personally informed me that he had decided against sending me to China, we left for Croton on the late train in the midst of a heavy snowstorm.

"There'll be other adventures, sweetie," I said, watching the large flakes of snow flutter past the train window. "Hypocrites! They want to jump on the war wagon! I've written all we need to know about the killing in Europe! They say that they might want me to go over there again. But we have to wait and see if we come into the war. What a runaround! Hypocrites, bastards!"

"I. . .I had counted on it, Jack, I had." Lou's hand draped lazily at the wrist, brushing my knee. "And so had you! Admit it! You dreamed of your old Chinese man. Admit it!"

Like a sick, tired horse, I nuzzled her neck.

"I would have loved to have gone, sweetie, you know I would have. If we're lucky and we work hard enough we can keep Wilson from sending troops over. That would end the war sooner than most people think. The French and the Germans will have to make a peace agreement if we don't come in to keep things stirred up. And then we'll go to China."

I slid my arms around her, but she shook herself loose.

"Not in public!" She glanced about the half-filled car.

"Since when are we ashamed of loving each other in public?"

"Since my sickness. I'm just more sensitive about it now, Jack. I don't know why."

I sulked all the rest of the trip.

"You'll undress me," Lou said as we trudged slowly up the hill toward home.

"I guess I will," I said, confused but nonetheless ignited by her request.

"I'll build a fire," I said when we got inside.

"I can't wait," Lou said. "I just want a quick drink."

I poured us each a shot and led her into the cold bedroom and undressed her.

"Come under," she ordered, burrowing beneath the bed covers.

I stripped and, shivering, rooted after her.

"Your hand's cold," she complained.

"Shhh."

"Don't you hush me! Now do this for a while!" She moved my hand in a special motion, stalling me, then hurrying me, when I lost the pace she enjoyed.

"Harder! harder!"

"I don't want to hurt you."

"I love it! You left me behind in Portland all black and blue. Remember?"

"No!"

"Harder!"

"This?"

"Yes! Yes! No, turn! Hurry!"

"Watch out, I'm a bear, a monstrous bear!"

"Bite me, bear!"

I pummeled her, lost control, things turned rougher! We rocked and whirled, yanked and slapped.

The next morning, Lou sat up in bed and shrieked, "You've killed me!"

Throwing back the covers, she revealed blood, caked brown and ugly, on the inside of her thighs.

It was not the blood—I had seen enough of that—but the bruises on her battered face and chest that upset me.

"Lie back," I said, going to the bureau. "I'm going to fetch a doctor."

"No!"

"But there's something wrong."

"I know what it is. Stay here."

"If you know what it is, then tell me."

"It's just some bleeding."

"I can see that, sweetie. But why?"

"Why do you think?"

Her puffy cheeks made her look terrifying.

"I was too rough with you last night all around. I want to get a doctor."

"I'm not in pain. I just need rest. I'll stay in bed today." Gritting her teeth, she lay back on her pillow and closed her eyes. "Jack, I want you to leave. I'm not blaming you for last night. I just want to be alone for a few days. I need the time alone."

"As long as we agree that it's only for a few days," I said. "I'll stay in the city until after the *Masses* meeting on Friday. But what about a doctor?"

"I've seen the doctor about this before. I know how to take care of it."

"Why didn't you tell me about it?"

"Would it have mattered?"

"That's a rotten thing to say! Do you think I wanted to hurt you for real?"

Her eyes turned glassy. "I don't know. No, I don't think you wanted that. Go on. You'll miss the early train."

I walked away from the house with melancholy strides. There was still snow on the ground, but the air was mild with scarcely any wind to chill the somewhat sunless day. Looking down over the bare stand of trees that guarded the far hillside behind our cottage, I watched crows scavenge for some invisible bit of carrion. Few other living things stirred. Whatever animals lurked in our woods had made their accommodations for the season. A light breeze rolled in from the west, and I shivered. Crows mocked my thoughts with their insistent speech. *Caw, caw, caw, caw!* I glanced at my watch. I felt empty, superfluous, undone. The doctors had saved me from death by faulty organ. For what, what? A gust of wind rippled my hair. Writing was empty, the government was winning, the *Masses* was our hope and our joke all in one. My wife had thrown me out again! *Caw, caw, caw!* I shook my fist at the mocking crowd of birds and walked, less than triumphantly, down the hill.

There came one of those meals that friends take together from time to time when they realize how much they have been missing the warmth they give each other. Somebody at the *Masses* office had said "Italian." After haggling for a while, we all embarked for Mama Cartelli's on Prince Street, a little place with the largest platters in the neighborhood. All, that is, but me. I was to have met Lou at the apartment, and so I hurried back to Patchin Place, hoping to head her off and lead her down to the restaurant before our friends' spaghetti cooled. But the apartment was empty. I waited a few minutes in the dark. Then I turned on the lights, thinking that I would leave a note for her on the door.

Since her desk was closer than mine, I poked through the drawer in search of a sharpened pencil and it was there that I saw the manuscript. Glancing over my shoulder, like some burglar who has sneaked into the house in the middle of the night, I listened nervously for footsteps on the stairs. Then, breaking all the promises that two working writers make to each other when they live together, I began to read.

It was fiction, but fiction with only a thin layer of make-up covering the real face of the first-person female narrator. The opening section described her girlhood in the Nevada desert where her father worked for the railroad. Her mother did not fare well in this section. An Eastern-born woman with great hopes of finding a new life in the West who marries a man whose only love is railroading in the dustiest, driest and loneliest part of the new territory, she came off as silly and pathetic. The tone was wrong. Lou seemed to be trying to build up and attack her mother at the same time. There was a sharp page where she wrote about dressing herself in her best clothes in imitation of her mother and then sneaking out of the house to parade down the burg's one main street in the style of Mama herself. And meeting her father who is just stumbling out of the local saloon after a hard day's labor at the railroad office. I shuddered at the description of the beating he gave her.

I flipped a few pages, stopping at a scene with her family. The young Lou has a terrible fight with her mother about a trip she wants to take with her father up the rail line to Reno. The parents argue. Her father gives in. Lou, in tears, rushes out of the house. I could nearly taste the dust that rose at her heels, and smell the sweat on her teary face. Her father calls after her. But she runs and runs. Familiar landmarks fade away. A wind stirs, as though the sun were pulling all the heat of the day westward as it descended. Her throat aches and tastes of alkali and the bitter truth that her father will not fight for her. The sky darkens. Her strength dissolves. She sinks to her knees. A strange feeling envelops her. It has something to do with the great spaces surrounding her and with the fact that she is female. She senses chaos! Furious boiling bubbling outrageous chaos! If she weren't kneeling on the desert floor she might have guessed that the very bottom of the earth had fallen away, spilling cactus, rocks, and desert rats into the blackness of the other side of the moon! Yet she remains there, while the world spins around her, and she saves herself by her act of patience. It will yet come, it will yet come! She'll travel to Reno and farther west and east and south and north despite their objections! This is not a prayer (she hasn't been raised to say prayers) but neither is it a threat. She vows that she will become the mistress of her own life. Yes, that was it, she understood then. Outwardly, men triumph, but inwardly, the pernicious system damns them to eternal capitulation. It was a rotten way to exist, and she would not live that way herself! She pledged her life to making something more of herself than a captive captor like her mother. She rises, stretching out her arms toward the departing streaks of day. Spitting wrath, something sizzles past her shoulder. The rattler slams against the ground and regroups itself with the agility of a cat. But by this time, Lou, miraculously saved because she stepped out of the reptile's path just as it sprang, Lou is running, Lou is running back toward town.

I kissed that page. It was sweet writing. But how little I knew about my wife's past! I wanted to savor her story, but, instead, found myself turning pages swiftly. I didn't have much time. She might return at any moment and catch me in the act. I rushed through scenes from her school days, her time at college in Oregon, and caught glimpses of references to our romance in what she called the "city of many hills" and the "Spit." Some of the writing seemed more like code than finished fiction, but then this was an early draft. It surprised me that the earlier scenes were sculpted as convincingly as they were, when the pages about her life, as it came upon her day by day in the present, were merely notations of events without any shape or form.

The narrator was living with a world-famous reporter named Joe. He went into the hospital to have a lung removed. The narrator was disconsolate. Her entire world seemed overturned by the possibility of his dying.... I skipped more pages, anxious to reach the end.

"Something strange happened," she wrote. "I came to town one day and going to the Village I decided to look up John O'Flaherty. Harry, his older brother, had told me that they were worried about him and couldn't get him home. His parents were living at the St. George Hotel. So I went to Hell Hole. John was there—I don't know how long he had been there. He hadn't washed or shaved for days, but I managed to get him to go with me. We went outside and tried to find a taxicab, but none came along. So we got onto an uptown bus. When we reached 28th Street, I wanted John to get off the bus with me. He was in an ugly mood and said he wouldn't get out because he knew 28th Street, had been born in New York, and this just wasn't the right street. I finally got him out and to his hotel and to bed. I was going to take the subway to the 42nd Street station, and just as I was stepping into the car, John came running down the stairs of the station, shouting and crying. But the doors closed after me and off I went. A few days later, he telephoned, very sober, and apologized, and said that he would like to see me. So I came into town again and we had a serious talk. He decided that he would go to 'the Spit' to work. He'd be all alone up there and could settle in and write poetry."

There the manuscript ended just as Lou turned her key in the door. It might have been the surgeon's knife in my belly. She burst into the apartment, hair flying behind her and threw her coat on the floor. At first, she didn't see me leaning against the wall behind her desk.

Then she gasped, "I'm late!"

"Very."

"It was a long, difficult rehearsal, darling. There's a hole in the middle of the new play big enough to walk an elephant through."

She picked up her coat and tossed it onto the sofa.

"I just want to wash before we go out. We are going out with Max and Art, aren't we?"

Her voice was high and tinny, the way it sometimes got after an afternoon at the theater. Smiling at me in silly, tipsy fashion she waltzed past me into the bathroom and closed the door behind her.

The sounds of Lou washing echoed through the small apartment: Lou urinating—Lou flushing—Lou splashing water on her body—Lou humming to herself (humming!)—Lou brushing her teeth—Lou gargling—Lou calling out to me.

". . .the meeting?"

Like a young doe bounding into a clearing, Lou blithely emerged from the bathroom, transformed by her ablutions into a fresh-faced, fresh-smelling incarnation of the innocent heroine of her own story of the encounter with the rattler.

"Where're we going?"

"Italian." I explained that our friends were waiting at the little restaurant on Prince Street.

I squeezed alongside her as we descended the steps, madly trying to catch a whiff of something incriminatory. She grabbed my hand and swung it back and forth as we walked to the corner of Tenth Street and Sixth Avenue.

"I feel quite young and gay today now that I've washed my face," she said.

"Good," I said. "Good, good. Good, good. Good."

"If it's that good, why don't you kiss me?"

"Why don't you ask 'John O'Flaherty'?"

"Who?"

Lou walked calmly with me across the street and glanced up at the courthouse, as though someone might have called to her from an upper window.

"Oh, 'O'Flaherty.' My 'O'Flaherty'? You've been sneaking in my drawers—"

"Who else has been sneaking in your drawers!" I slapped her in the face, and she staggered back against the steps of the court house, her eyes wide with surprise.

"You talk to me now," I said, blocking her escape.

"About what?" she said with a cough and a sob.

"You tell *me*."

"It's a novel I'm writing."

I yanked her toward me by the arm.

"You hurt me!"

"Tell me about it."

"It's a *novel*, Jack. You hurt my arm."

"What's behind the novel?"

"Nothing's behind it."

"There's a father and mother behind the early part of it. There's a rattlesnake behind the middle part of it. What's behind the end?"

"There's nothing there, Jack. It's fiction, I swear." She touched her tongue to the roof of her mouth. She was breathing hard, hard, hard. "I'm hurt, Jack; my arm hurts."

"Where were you this afternoon?"

"At the theater." She rubbed herself gingerly through her coat sleeve.

"You broke my arm."

"I broke nothing."

"I want to go to the hospital."

"No more hospitals for a while. Talk."

"Not to you, you beast!"

She jumped past me and started walking down the street, hugging her arms to her body.

I chased her and caught her by the coat.

"Tell me where you've been today."

"At the theater."

"The entire time?"

"Yes."

"You were drinking."

"Who says we can't drink during a break?"

A little man wearing a bowler tried to step between me and Lou.

"Say," he said, "don't you think you'd better leave her alone?"

"Go away," I said, "we're having a discussion."

"Miss, are you all right?"

"Go away," she said without looking at him.

"You heard her," I said.

"You're both crazy," he said. "I'm going to get a policeman."

"Bourgeois pig," I spat at him through my teeth.

Lou laughed, despite her pain.

"We're being silly."

"You are," I said, unamused.

"You really have hurt my arm, Jack."

"And you really have hurt my life."

"Such maudlin dialogue, Jack. Please take me to the hospital now."

"Will you tell me about it?"

"Tell you about what?" Lou scowled, almost convincingly. "About my feeble attempts at novel writing? You've read it already and you haven't liked it much, I can tell."

"I liked the early parts. I liked the part about running off into the desert and seeing the snake."

"Expulsion from Eden."

"You're Eve, of course."

"Without an Adam. Then."

"Now I want to hear about the snake."

"Wouldn't you prefer to hear about the bear?"

She smiled feebly, trying to make me give way.

"I didn't see anything about a bear."

"You must have skipped those parts."

"The snake. I want to hear the truth about the stinking, drunken snake."

A policeman, a stocky young fellow about my age who sported a thick handlebar mustache, came walking rapidly toward us.

"Got trouble, mister?"

He squinted at me suspiciously as I explained that Lou and I were having a family quarrel.

"Lady," he said, "is this man your husband?"

"He certainly is."

"Ask her if he molested her, officer, ask her."

This came from the little man in the bowler who was standing behind the policeman.

"Just a minute," said the cop. A small crowd had gathered around us by now, and he was moving them back with vigorous movements of his arms. He asked me my name. When I told him, some of the passers-by were close enough to hear.

"The pacifist!"

It was a knowledgeable Village crowd, except for the little man in the bowler.

"He's not a pacifist," he said. "I saw him molest his wife!"

"Leave this to me, mister," the cop announced in a loud bullying voice. "Now, do you think that you and your missus can go along quietly?"

"We can go, officer?" I had never before heard myself speaking so passively to a policeman.

"Yeah," he said, "let's all move along now, folks, let's all move along."

"Anarchist!" the little man called after us as we walked briskly across Greenwich and continued south on Sixth.

"Do you really need to see a doctor?" I asked Lou when we had recovered from a fit of laughter.

"My arm hurts a lot," she said. "But maybe you can apply some spumoni to it and make it feel better."

I held her close to me as we walked.

"I'm really sorry, sweetie."

"Then kiss me."

We stopped and kissed in mid-sidewalk. People flowed around us, oblivious now to our family activities.

"And I'm sorry that I wrote what I did," Lou said when we were walking again.

"Never accuse, never admit."

"Just a minute ago I thought you'd forgotten that maxim."

"Only a temporary lapse," I said.

"Will you tell me what you think about my manuscript now that you've seen it?"

"The truth?"

She nodded appealingly.

"I think that you need to work on it a lot more. But the kernel of good writing is there. The passion, the visual insights. If it's got a fault, it's that it gives the impression of being too close to life. I said 'impression,' remember. I'm not trying to accuse you of anything when I say that. You'll want to work it over again, you'll want to work on it every day."

"That's good advice, lovey."

"I wish I could take it myself. I haven't finished a poem in weeks. Articles, articles, it's only articles they get out of me these days."

"Some of your articles are closer to poetry than the work of some poets," Lou said.

"Do you want to be kissed again?"

"Are you sure you want to kiss me?"

"I am."

"Then you can."

And we stopped once again and kissed once again, again without gathering a crowd.

"They all left. I thought I might wait for you."

This was Art Young who had remained behind after the rest of the diners had given us up for lost. He made us laugh a lot that evening with his dry voice, his cultivated face. I felt as though I were back in college again, out on the town with my true humorous friends.

February yielded to the gusty plaints of March. Our magazine was besieged—the Associated Press threatened to sue for slander because one of Art's cartoons showed a puffy, ugly tycoon (labeled "AP") poisoning the waters of a reservoir labeled "truth in reporting." Our President was continuing his new crusade against peace, though I must admit that I had not yet lost all hope that he might still change his mind. But then I remained innocent about a number of important matters. I believed that most socialists with whom I found myself rubbing elbows at anti-war meetings would stick to their principles even though it seemed that the President was moving toward a call for all citizens to put aside their differences and come out on behalf of the slaughter. I believed that since my physical illness was behind me, I could tackle the higher problems head on. I was even so foolish as to believe that the changing of the seasons would bring on a corresponding change in the feelings that passed between me and Lou.

But I was disastrously incorrect. My anger at being shunted aside at the *Metropolitan* was getting the best of me in public as well as private, and I found myself subject to strange impulses that I had associated with my college days. At a meeting of various sympathetic groups on the question of intervention in Europe, I leaped from the stage to battle with a heckler who was sitting down front. Before we threw him out, he kicked me in the stomach, which kept me in bed for a week. My stomach turned inside out every morning for another ten days. Then came the night Lou and I went uptown for the Broadway premiere of O'Neill's *The Moon of the Caribees*. I had not wanted to attend since this was a play that O'Neill had originally promised to Jig and the Players. For the sake of the glory and a few dollars more, he had sold it instead to a big producer. To me this was not a great triumph. I was ashamed to be in the house since Jig had been disconsolate at O'Neill's betrayal. But Lou would not hear of missing the premiere.

When the curtain went up, I must admit that I was charmed by the plaintive Negro music that drifted across the stage. The artificial dusk in which O'Neill's untutored, husky-voiced sailors talked about booze and their other wants and lacks set the stage for recollections of my own early silly little playlets. Lou, by contrast, seemed to be focusing all of her energy on the goings on up on the stage, as though missing one word of the gutteral exchanges that passed among O'Neill's seaboard working stiffs might deny her entrance to the heaven of the saints. But what were we watching? The actors moiled about on the deck of the *Glencairn* in unclassical disarray. Here was a mob scene out of Shakespeare turned into the main event. The audience, mostly from Madison Square, with a scattering of eccentrics looking remarkably like former classmates of mine, had never seen the likes of it. Serious drunks and would-be fornicators at center stage in a Broadway theater. It was a revolution of sorts, though a shabby one.

"He's certainly for the underdog," I whispered to Lou, "though it's a dirty dog he's got under...."

As for myself, I saw little but the carnal fantasies of a fallen Catholic. No Negro or sailor I knew had ever behaved this way. I tried to say this to Lou, but she shushed me down. No doubt that there was something about the unsculpted speech of O'Neill's actors that had great appeal. When I was performing in his first play (on board the same *Glencairn*), the words had come to me as easy as breathing. He had a way of making the roughest talk behave on stage. When the sad, baffling, dark blue music came up at the end, I was moved more than I had wanted to be.

"They're more shocked than excited," I said, after the vigorous applause had died down.

"Let's go back," Lou said, caught up in the mood of the music.

"I don't know that I'm ready for that."

We stood next to each other in the aisle while the opening-night audience streamed past us. Had the play opened in the Village at the Players, I would have been cheering.

"Poor Jig," I said, taking Lou's hand in mine.

"Poor Jig? Why mourn for him? He had his moment of glory

with *Bound East for Cardiff*. You couldn't expect Gene to turn down the chance to have his night on Broadway?"

"It would have come. He might have waited."

She entwined my fingers in her own.

"Oh, Jack, you're not jealous, are you?"

"Let's not go into that," I said. "I'd even rather go backstage and pump the hand of the alcoholic beast himself than talk about that."

"You won't be insulting, will you? It's his night of triumph."

The fact that she felt as though she shared some of his triumph was apparent from the speed with which she led me into the wings.

We found O'Neill slumped in a chair in the little hallway that connected the dressing rooms to the stage. He seemed more exhausted than drunk, though the odor that clung to him announced that he was probably both. Alongside him stood a heavy-shouldered, gray-haired man with the same gaunt face, a slender, stately woman who looked as though she suffered O'Neill's fatigue for him, and a tall dark fellow with slightly more wolfish features than O'Neill's. Lou made the introductions, but they weren't really necessary. A cloud of gloom and debilitation hovered over the family. They posed as if at a wake rather than an opening. The cast and the crew, their friends, acquaintances, and admirers, kept their distance.

"Mr. and Mrs. O'Neill," said Lou, making the introductions, "this is my husband Jack. Jamie O'Neill, Jack Reed." I didn't like her familiarity with them, but I could do nothing but suffer it while we chatted in the theater hallway.

"You're the journalist, of course, lad, aren't you?"

The elder O'Neill's dolorous voice enthralled me with its immense depth and distant horizons. I had never heard him declaim the famous role of the Count of Monte Cristo, but hundreds of thousands had over the years, and it was as if I knew his performance merely from having lived in America. When he spoke, he opened a window on times past. In a way, he was more an institution than a man, and he appeared to suffer from the realization of this. After listening to him talk for several minutes about his encounters with journalists throughout the years and the effect of uninformed reviewers on the state of the theater, he suggested that we all might like to go out for a celebratory glass.

Lou, who had been earnestly trying to revive the nearly unconscious playwright, looked up at the rest of us then and added her agreement on this point.

"That would wake Gene up, I'm sure."

"I don't think I'm for it," I said. "I have a meeting tomorrow early."

"You never mentioned a meeting to me, lovey." Lou glared at me.

"It slipped my mind."

The old man coughed a large stage cough. He might have detected my discomfort or, perhaps, was merely aware of his own momentary loss of audience. For whatever reason, he deftly hoisted his younger son to his feet and announced that whoever was going to the trough had better get along.

Gene sprang suddenly into action, lashing out at his father with his arm. "Let me alone!"

The older man stepped farther back into the shadows of the corridor, which was rapidly emptying of actors and visitors.

"For Christ's sake, Gene!" Jamie showed his teeth in a snarl. He appeared as though he were about to slap his brother's mouth.

"It's shit," O'Neill said. "Give me a match!"

Lou patted him on the arm.

"Gene! Stop talking that way! It doesn't do you any good. It was a wonderful play, the audience—"

"Shit!"

"You won't talk that way in front of your mother!" bellowed out the eldest O'Neill.

"Shit!" repeated his son, a slight smile on his lips suggesting that he was, despite his slumping posture, as wide awake as his impromptu audience.

Mrs. O'Neill slid back along the wall until the darkness masked her face.

Lou, meanwhile, led Gene down the hall in the other direction murmuring into his ear while the besotted playwright raised his hand as a shield against the bright bulbs near the entrance to the stage.

"My son has his moods," said the eldest O'Neill. "And I sometimes think that growing up amidst the Shakespearian repertoire has its drawbacks as well as its rewards. It imbued him with his love of theater but I believe that it may have infected him with a great sense of. . . ." He stopped, flirting in his mind with several possible words and smiling as he did so, revealing by the curl of his lip the kinship of father's face and son's.

"Inferiority?" I posed.

"Humility is the way that I would put it," he said.

"He's a royal pain in the hump, if you ask me," said Jamie O'Neill. "He's got everything he wants for the taking, right now, and he'd rather drink himself to—"

"James!"

The father interposed his booming voice.

"We won't be talking about such things at this moment and place. These are family matters, not a public performance."

"Tell that to Gene," said Jamie, revealing by his twisted features that he himself felt publicly admonished.

But Gene was not to be admonished. He pulled away from Lou and staggered out onto the stage, now lighted only by a solitary bulb on a tall metal stand.

"Yank!" he called into the darkness of the pit. "Driscoll! Smitty! You hairy crew, where the hell'd you go? Deserting me at the last rope! Hairy bastards! Come on out and help me! I don't want to go home!"

"Can't you do something?" Lou demanded of me.

I wanted to shove him off the stage. But instead I crossed the stage and confronted him.

"Gene, shut it off and let's go for a drink."

"Shut up and buy me a drink!"

"Gene!" his father boomed from the wings. "Cease this foolishness and come along!"

"Shut off! Shuffle off this Buffalo coil...."

"Easy," I urged as he lurched toward the pit. I slid my arms around him from behind and hauled him back from the edge.

"Easy for you, you impotent dastard!" he shouted at me as he struggled a moment and then went limp in my arms.

"Don't hurt him!" his mother called out to me from the wings.

"Don't worry, Mrs. O'Neill," I said, leading the unresisting playwright from the stage.

"Thanks a lot, Reed," said Jamie, as he helped me lower my burden into a chair. "I'll call us a cab, father."

"That would be best," said the aging actor, with a flourish of hands. "We thank you kindly, lad, for your assistance," he said to me. "I think we'd better take the triumphant artist home and put him to bed." He took Lou's hand and his performance turned paternal, soothing, calming, totally satisfying, totally false. In a minute, Lou and I stood on the street, plotting our own direction.

"Now you see a little of what he goes through," she said.

"Poor O'Flaherty-O'Neill," I said, "he can't look his Papa in the eye."

"It's not funny," Lou said, as we set off toward the Village. "They have a terrible love for each other, but they can't get along. He won't try psychoanalysis. I've suggested Doctor Brill to him but he won't hear of it."

"The father or the son?"

"Don't be *funny*. Gene doesn't believe in it. It's worse even than that. He doesn't believe in *believing*. I'm afraid he's going to keep on drinking until he kills himself."

"Or someone kills him," I said, remembering the action of the moody little play we had just seen.

"That could easily happen. Don't you see why I've been

spending so much time with him, Jack? He needs someone to take care of him until he can take care of himself."

"His mother seems to love him. Why don't we assign that part to her?"

"He doesn't do well at home, Jack. You saw what happened."

"That was with his father. His mother watched out for him."

"She's a stick, Jack. She sits and sits all day. It's the father, he's run her into the ground."

It was raining when we reached Patchin Place, and cold enough to remind us that winter had not yet ended. I had to admit that I liked the direction O'Neill's work was taking, and that I believed it proper and, in fact, quite thrilling that he was putting such extraordinary ordinary characters on the boards. But as much as I believed it was good for that as-yet-loosely-conceived thing I thought of as our "cause," it didn't warm me much to talk about his work.

"He doesn't treat Negroes very well, does he?"

Lou was shimmying out of her clothes. My comment caught her off guard.

"He doesn't know very many," she said, gazing at the stocking she held in her hand as though it were a foreign object. "But neither do we."

"He's sailed about the world. He ought to know the difference between an animal and a man." Thoughts of the coffee-skinned actresses on the foredeck of the S.S. *Glencairn.* "Or a woman."

Lou frivolously tossed the last of her underclothes onto a chair near the bed.

"He knows."

"How much do you care about him?" I demanded, advancing across the room in the crouch of one of O'Neill's hairy stokers.

"Do you want to measure it? You're a poet! Do you want to measure feelings? Do you want me to measure my feelings for you?" She sat down on the bed, legs crossed beneath her, her breasts and arms stippled from the chill.

"Come love me," she said. "Please, love me now."

"I can't," I said. "I feel too bad."

I shuffled back toward the window.

"Damn!"

I punched the wall and the window-glass jangled in its pane.

"*He's* loved you, hasn't he?"

"You idiot!"

"Hasn't he?"

"Fool!"

She rolled herself up into a protective ball as I charged over to the bed.

"Hasn't he?"

I slid my fingers around her throat.

"Stop that—"

"Tell me!" I applied more pressure.

"I can't talk—"

"Talk!"

"Please!"

She nearly screamed this as she raked my cheeks with her stinging nails.

"You love him?"

She twisted her head from side to side and pounded on my chest with her fists.

Just as suddenly as I had attacked her, I let her fall back onto the bed.

"It's true, isn't it?"

She couldn't speak. Her eyes boiled up in fear, and then she wept, and I embraced her, and a truce prevailed. I nursed her bruises and she washed my cuts. She slept in the bed and I slept on the couch. The next morning, before I got out of the bath, she was already packed and gone.

Max Eastman!

There was a man, who, loving quiet beauty best,
Yet could not rest
For the harsh moaning of unhappy human kind,
Fettered and blind—
Too driven to know beauty and too hungry-tired
To be inspired.
From his high windy-peaceful-hill, he stumbled down
Into the town.
With a child's eyes, clear bitterness and silver scorn
Of the outworn
And cruel mastery of life by senile death;
And with his breath
Fanned up the noble fires that smoulder in the breast
Of the oppressed....

How I loved that man! And how he sustained me through the worst hours of my spear wound of a separation from Lou! When I walked into the *Masses* that morning, my face a map of the terrors that had struck us the night before, he immediately ushered me out for a medicinal drink.

"To look at what you've done, what you do, a body wouldn't guess how much love means to you," he told me. "But I know, I know...."

"It's true, Max, it's true, to look at me you'd think it was all racing about and jokes and reporting and riots...."

This took place in a booth in a Cedar Street tavern. I wept on his shoulder. He soothed me with his mellifluous voice and patted me paternally on the head.

"The whole thing has fallen apart...."

"There, there...."

"I'm so ashamed, Max...."

"That's okay, Jack, that's okay."

I pounded my fist on the table. "Why should I be proud? Tell me, Max, the thing with Lou and O'Neill...."

"Another round," Max called to the bartender. "Wait, I'll fetch it."

"Feeling a little better?" Max asked when he returned with the foamy glasses. His buoyant figure, bright hair, in bright sun—How I envied his gift for floating from girl to girl, like a bee to the many blossoms on which it feeds. Somehow he kept a deep and abiding affection for each and every one, the legacy, perhaps in some odd way, of growing up in a house of ministers. This pastor of promiscuity raised his drink to me. "Sure you are, Jack."

"You never answered my question!"

"We do want the truth all the truth all the time, yes?"

"Yes!"

"Then I'll give it to you."

"Wait!" I shouted. "Another round."

"That's what? The fifth? Do you want to come across like the rummy slob you've been railing against?"

"Have I been railing?"

"Wailing. Like a Banshee."

"Who do I hate more? Him or me?"

"That calls for more ale."

He motioned for me to drink. I slopped my muzzle into the foam.

"How could the boozy animal even know that someone loves him? How could he write a line? That's the bigger question. He must be a fake or monstrously insane. Call the doctors! They've got to examine him before he gets away! Call the keepers! He's loose, the boozy ape, kill the thing with stones!"

"That's what I mean about wailing and raving," Max said.

"I didn't mean to hurt her, Max! I swear I didn't! But she's run down to Hell Hole, Max, lying with the scum of the oceans! We've got to save her! Damn it all, she doesn't know what she's doing! That boozy bastard, he's showing her to freaks and mongols! Oh, Max, Max," and I hung my head and sobbed, ashamed of my shouting and dreaming.

Hours later, I found myself in the tub in my apartment, Max, smiling, at my side, while I felt my life break like a fever.

"Did you carry me up here?"

Max nodded.

"I must have been raving. My head feels like a squashed melon."

"Can we continue our discussion?"

"What were we talking about?"

Max shook his head in amazement.

"You don't remember? I was asking you if you were having any . . . trouble with your health besides your kidneys this fall."

"Why do you want to know? Only my kidney."

"Nothing else?"

"Nothing. Why, Max?"

"Hold onto the tub."

"I'm holding. Well?"

"Now look down between your legs. What do you see?"

"What's the joke, Max? I see the humiliated standard of a love that has been *dashed* against the rocks."

Max coughed a laugh.

"How long has it been humiliated? That's the question."

"What the hell—"

"How long?"

"How long? I don't know what you're getting at. Since I discovered that my lady love was going me wrong, that's since how long."

"And not before?"

"Max, you'd make a wonderful state's attorney for sex. Maybe you'd like to prosecute Margaret Sanger. What's the point?"

Max sat down on the edge of the tub and dipped a hand into the soapy water.

"About the same time that you checked into the hospital for your operation, there was a story going around—I can't even remember who I heard it from, but let's say that it was probably someone at the magazine or its environs—something to do with your—sexual health—about your ability to—now I never listen to talk like that—I guess I just knocked it out of my thoughts—never paid any attention to it—and when you explained your operation to me one time it never occurred to me that the other thing might be the case—"

I lay back in the waters, a chill creeping along my soaking limbs.

"I feel so bad, Max. I want to drown."

"A swimmer like you going under in a bathtub? Wouldn't that be a fine piece of fun. The story was that you and Lou were living more like brother and sister than anything else. It's a wicked story, Jack. But I suppose that I ought to finish it now that I've begun. And that Lou was taking up with O'Neill because, though she deeply loved you, she couldn't get any satisfaction from you. And that you were going into the hospital to try and have it fixed."

"Did that bastard have to give out such filthy stuff in order to run off with my wife?"

Max fixed his eye on the swirl of soapsuds curling about my toes.

"I don't know where the story came from. I suppose that Gene must have talked up such things while he was drinking. But who knows who thought up such a tale!"

"You think it was Lou, don't you?"

I gripped the edge of the tub so hard that my hands might have fused to the metal.

He nodded.

My ears rang, my head spun. In the mirror, a red-faced, red-chested demon of jealousy, spite, and justice squinted back at me, his lips curling up in anticipation of the revenge he would take. I convinced Max that he could safely leave me.

As soon as he departed, I dressed and then I emptied the

closets of Lou's clothing, heaping skirts and coats and boxes of shoes in a pile on the floor. And then I urinated on them and went about breaking up the furniture.

The bed was my initial target. We had no axe, since that instrument was better used in Croton where we needed firewood, so I ripped off the covers, still steaming, I imagined, with the fumes of my unfaithful love, and whacked at the headboard with the desk chair. The chair fell apart but the headboard was undamaged. I tried a heavier chair, managing only to dent the headboard this time. I then yanked the mattress onto the floor and leaped onto the springs, throwing myself against the board until it cracked.

Reports of shattered wood like small arms fire echoed through our little apartment. I destroyed Lou's desk and then my own. The typewriters smashed against the walls; papers, books, and writing gear splashed about the floors. After I had finished two rooms, I could scarcely move my arms above my waist. It was at that moment, glancing back into the room where the rubble lay scattered about the floor, that I noticed the photograph that must have shaken loose from one of the many overturned dresser drawers.

Stretched out against the backdrop of the dunes, leaning back on her hands, Lou lay naked in the sun—hair streaming behind her like a great web of seaweed—her pubic thatch boldly revealed to the eye of old Helios—and the expression on her face showing what her cunt could not reveal: that she had reached a new stage of satisfaction which she had not even known she had been looking for.

Her first letter arrived the next day in Croton.

I looked at the Connecticut postmark and threw the thing unopened into the fireplace.

A second letter came a few days later. The same postmark. I threw it into the fireplace.

Meanwhile, I worked a bit in the house and a lot in the garden. Digging in the newly thawed ground behind the cottage, I felt as though my head were floating off into the thinning blue air above the pines and red maples and elms. My limbs trembled, and I heard, at some distance, what could have been the bellow of a sick and injured animal—the noise of a man weeping hoarsely, me.

Part Eight

AFFAIRS AND
UPHEAVALS

In the doomed and gloomy weeks of my separation from Lou, I found it fortunate, in a curious way, that so many of our countrymen frothed at the mouth at the prospect of joining the mad dog fight in Europe, since their beastliness diverted my attention from my own pains, which otherwise might have served as the news of the day.

The mortgage fell due on the little house on the Cape where all my troubles began, and I couldn't make the payment. Even as I signed papers that turned the house over to another, I wondered if perhaps Lou was hied up there in her seedy little tryst, and a certain pleasurable plain played over me as I screwed my pen up and pocketed the copy of the paper. It was our friend Margaret Sanger who took the mortgage over, she, the prophetess of the free loving that had led me to so much pain.

And then came a letter from Portland with news of mother's increasing financial troubles intermixed with harangues against those she called my foreign Jewish friends (Oh, Max, if she could only see your noble Protestant profile!) those so treasonous as to speak against our entry into the war. Harry had joined the army and would soon be leaving for his training as an officer. Mother needed more money for the house. I sent her more than I could spare. I was losing assignments. (Editors were snubbing me because of my anti-war stand.) One bright, warm afternoon, I found myself on the sidewalks of lower New York in front of a pawnshop with my father's gold watch in my hand, weeping as I recalled an encounter before in a pawnshop in Portland.

"Meester Reed?"

A jewelry-bedecked girl, her head covered with a neckerchief, greeted me with a wide-eyed stare as I approached the pawnbroker's cage.

"Do I know you from somewhere?"

I tried to recall at which rally or meeting we had brushed elbows, exchanged shouts or views.

"You don't remember me, Meester Reed. I once peeked at you from behind the curtain in a very old house."

"*Malka?* What a coincidence! Last time we met, your bomb-making friends tried to steal my watch. And here I am giving it to you."

"Not so much coincidence," she said, lowering her voice. "You want to pawn this timepiece, and that's good, because this terrible old gold time is not going to be good no more." Smiling conspiratorially, she rubbed her fingers across the crystal, toyed with the gold band, turned it over on its face to trace the initials with her fingernail.

"It's just as good as it was when your friend tried to steal it," I insisted.

"No. No," she protested. "The time of old gold is over and the new time of the people has arrived. Dot is why I am here, to make dollars to buy boots for the people's army! For the army that will fight not one stitch for the Czar but will gif everting for the dictatorship of the proletariat!"

"You're turning over your earnings to the revolution? What revolution?"

"News reporter, you don't read the news? There is a new world born in my home country! Don't you talk to Mother Emma? Don't you read what she writes?"

"I've been sick," I said. "I've been cut off from many things."

"So get well! So get going! Find out about it!"

"I suppose I've heard a little about it from the folks at the *Masses,* but most of us have been worrying about America going into the war and other things."

"Tell the troops here to be like the revolutionary army of my country! They must not fire a shot at other workers!"

"I wouldn't be here pawning this watch of mine if I hadn't been saying the same thing a little too often for the capitalist publishers to take."

She peered professionally at the watch.

"It's worth nothing and also much. I'll give you a good price if you want to sell it."

"I just want to pawn it, Malka. It belonged to my father—"

"I see by the writing," she said. "Sentimental value...what's that worth in this world of capitalist merchants who make money from war? I'll gif you twenty dollars."

"It's worth ten times—"

"Twenty-one!"

I slammed my hand on the counter.

"Thirty!"

She banged her hand on the other side of the bars.

"Twenty-five!"

"Done," I said.

"I didn't know big reporters was so poor," she said, as I slid the timepiece under the bars.

"Big reporters who oppose America's entering the war in Europe don't get so much work these days. Big reporters whose brothers go to war and leave their mothers alone and penniless have to find cash to support them."

She was counting out the cash and paused. "Life is dot bad for you?"

"That's why this big reporter is down here selling his father's gold watch. Swell, huh?"

"Take fifty. I'm collecting for the revolution. What you write against the war is a weapon. Take fifty and don't complain. Keep writing."

Later, heading to the Canal Street Station to post the money to Portland, I wondered if perhaps I had dreamed that meeting. But in the station, as I wired fifty dollars to my mother, I knew that the encounter with Malka had been real. As I turned to leave, a familiar figure passed by.

"Vincent!" I called to her. "What are you doing here?"

"I just had my fortune told in Chinatown," she said. "I wasn't sure what it meant until just now. Have you given up, at last, on that bitch?"

"Please don't call Lou a bitch. If that's what she is, then I'm a bastard."

"Well, aren't you?"

She cocked her red head at me at an angle that made her look more like a rooster than a hen.

"I suppose . . . ."

"He who pays the piper calls the tune, and he who calls the tune pays the piper. I've had my fortune. I've come to buy some postage. Now I'm on my way home. My sister's away for a few days. Will you come back with me?"

"You want to know if it's true, do you?"

"Want to know if what's true?"

"The rumor about me."

"Rumor? Oh, yes, well . . . ." She leaned coyly against a row of post boxes.

"Let's go," I said, leading her by the hand onto Canal Sreet.

"About that rumor . . ." she said later in her apartment as I was getting dressed.

"Now you know it's just a lie, don't you?"

"I'm not sure," Vincent said.

"You're *not?* What do I have to do to . . . ."

"I'm not sure what rumor you're talking about."

"If that's true then *you're* the bitch," I said, standing up and putting on my shirt.

"But I don't know *what* you're talking about, Jack."

Wearing nothing but her long red rug of a headdress—which I knew all too well was enhanced by dye—Vincent went to the window and looked out over the rooftops. "Two things make me hungry—making verse and making love. Shall we find some place to eat?"

The expression on her face when she turned around was something less than convincing. "I've made up my mind about you, Jack Reed. I don't want you around forever, but it would be nice to see you every now and again."

"Isn't that what you've been doing?"

Her little mouth twitched, and her look of certainty crumbled like a sand castle as the tide comes in.

"I'm not sure what we've been doing, except making me unhappy enough to write."

We chose an out-of-the-way place in Chelsea, far from my usual haunts, for dinner. Vincent recited some new poems to me, but she couldn't help but notice the distance I kept.

"You don't like my verse, you don't like to be with me. All you want to do is take me!"

She said this in a voice so loud that several other diners turned to look.

"I admire your poetry a great deal," I said, patting her hand.

"Let me help you, Jack," she said. "I'll take you away with me, upstate or to Maine where the surf kisses pine line—"

"Not upstate or anywhere," I said. "I've had to sell the house on the Cape. I don't want to be reminded of it by spending time in other people's summer houses."

"You'll be a better socialist for selling the house," said Vincent.

"My kind of socialism calls for everyone to own houses on the Cape," I said.

"That will take some doing," Vincent said.

"If we weren't about to throw the nation's millions and all its strength into the war, we could do it, easily."

"Jack," she said, "you've so much fire when you dream! I don't care that you're playing with me. Come take me home again! I can do so much more for you than that bitch."

"Don't call her that."

"What is she, then, torturing you, maligning you? Come home with me. I'll send my sister packing if you stay with me."

"So, you do know the rumor."

"Yes, I heard. But I knew it wasn't true from the start."

Soon after that, I fled from Vincent. I fled the city. The *New York Mail*, smart enough to buy a good reporter on the cheap, sent me out to cover an evangelistic conference in the Adirondacks. This kept me elated for days—it was like spending every waking hour in the midst of hundreds of replicas of my mother and her friends, oh, all these white-haired, round-faced ladies (I ignored the pasty-cheeked gents with hell-fire always at their backs). It also brought me the first real cash since the *Metropolitan* had purchased my last article, in January, and I sent a check to Portland on the double, hoping whatever angels I refrained from mocking in my article would speed it home.

I contemplated making the trip myself but could invent no project that would earn my way. Now that Europe burned, no editor had his eye on the route to China. There was a forlorn kind of passion in the way our boys were volunteering, my brother Harry included, as if each sought love in the death of the enemy or longed for love in the possibility of his own swift and shattering demise—shock of shell splintering body in a hundred pieces, like the shock of coming? Who knew?

I was growing hungry again when the *Mail* sent me to discover the truths of a dog-owners' convention in the Newark fairgrounds. When I posted mother the proceeds from that extravaganza, she informed me that, though I was still somewhat unpatriotic, she loved me anyway. I had to borrow the cash from Max for the fare down to Washington to attend an anti-war rally that blotted out the silliness of the New Jersey dog-owners' meeting. Crowds filled the Mall in front of the Capitol. Black flags, red flags, Yankee flags swirled about in a Potomac fog. When a cop tried to stop me from mounting the stage, he went down under a signpost. A pretty girl curled up next to me on the train ride home.

Then, in high spring, when the fruit trees were in blossom, and all varieties of birds sang in the woods outside our door—Lou returned.

She came in through the open door, set down her small suitcase on the sofa and smiled inquisitively at me.

"Are we at war?"

I shook my head.

"Do you want us to be?"

"The war," she said again. "Are we in? I haven't seen a newspaper in days."

"You sound quite anxious about that," I said. "Have you heard something I haven't? Were you down in Washington?"

"You know where I was, Jack. I just haven't seen a newspaper in days."

"Then I will fill you in on the news," I said, lifting my voice a bit since I was afraid for a moment that our hostilities would recommence right then and there. "I looked for you in Washington, looked long and deep into the crowds, but I didn't see you there. Well, my love, this is the thing—would you like to take your coat off and sit down?"

"I think I might."

"I'll take your case."

"Leave it. I'll move it later."

She sat on the sofa and crossed her legs.

"You're not talking."

"I'll talk. I'll tell you about the rally held by the People's Council. There were anti-war people from all around the country, maybe nine or ten thousand, or more. We filled one entire avenue for a block and there were several good speeches. When I got up to say my piece, there was a lot of cheering. People appreciate the fight we're making, the fight against fighting. They read our articles, they listen to the facts."

"Did you write your speech?"

"No, I just talked it out right then and there. But the crowds inspired me. It was a swell thing we did. Then came the conscription bill hearings. I went down there to testify, but it didn't do much good. Most of the senators wanted blood and one of them even wanted my home address. So he could send the army after me just as soon as I'd finished speaking, I suppose. I told them that I didn't believe in a war between capitalist traders, that when it came to defending myself I could be just as violent as the next fellow—they were trying to make us all into pacifists—but I wouldn't fight in a war that didn't make sense to me as an American. They wanted me to stop talking, but the chairman was a fair fellow, and he let me go on until I was finished. After Wilson's message to Congress and these hearings, I think I really am finished. We all are."

Lou stirred ever so slightly, shifting her legs one way and then another.

"So, we're not in yet but we're nearly in?"

"That's where it seems to stand at the moment. We're sliding in that direction, and pretty soon we'll be rolling and then we'll be in. Did you come on the train?"

"That's the only way I could get here from the city."

"You were in the city?"

"For the day only. I didn't stay over." Her voice faltered a bit. "Why did you buy all that new furniture? We certainly can't afford it. Did you do it out of spite?"

"No, not out of spite. I wanted—I wanted us to begin again with new things."

"And my clothes? Where did you hide them?"

"I want you to begin again with new clothes."

"Jack, what did you do with my clothes?"

"Let's take a walk and I'll tell you all about it."

"Yes, all right," she said, and stood up suddenly, losing all of the calm and solemnity which had marked her movements upon her entrance. She looked at me with such a passionate denial of her own helplessness that I dared not approach her. Other signals lurked in that glance: the joy that our separation had ended, at least for a time, and the fear that I might at any moment leap at her throat.

Watching her pull open the front door of the cottage, I pictured myself pounding my fists on her back. Her hair, freshly brushed and gleaming, lay bunched upon her shoulders—the scent of her surrounded me, led me toward the door, but she stepped through just as I arrived and kept on walking a foot or two ahead of me to where the path turned around the southeast corner of the cottage and continued on toward the trees. Clouds scudded in an easterly direction, borne on sweet winds flowing off the river. Now and then the sun showed itself, holding steady and bright beyond the curtain of mist, giving us light enough for a long talk in the woods. Odors arose from steamy boggish places. I studied plants, newly burgeoning buds, twigs bloated with splendid sap and cheery juices of the season.

Lou halted abruptly on the path in front of me and I nearly walked over her heels.

"Where do we begin?"

Against the high ferns that sheltered newly blossoming wood-shrubs, she seemed a figure painted all too carefully in pink, contrasting sharply with the high yellow and light greens of our bushy surroundings. Even here in the shadowy wood she glowed with a power that drew my blood to the surface, like water in a moontide or metal in a magnetic web.

"You begin," I said.

"You only wrote to me once."

"Wasn't that enough? I couldn't say anything more than what I said this week. The fruit trees are in blossom."

"You're speaking so cruelly to me. Don't you want me back?"

I shuffled up the path a bit, feeling leaves with twitching fingers.

"I think this is where you belong."

She smiled tentatively.

"It is, I know it is. But I don't know that I can stay if you're going to keep this distance."

She burst into tears, hugging herself, as she turned her back to me. She stumbled forward into the bushes and fell against a tree.

When I tried to take her in my arms, prying her away from the tree, which she hugged as though it were her mother or her savior, she suddenly whirled and flung herself at me as though she were throwing herself over an abyss.

I reeled back into the undergrowth and Lou came tumbling after. We were shoulder deep in weeds and leaves before I could recover my breath.

"I've hurt my ankle," Lou murmured, clinging to my arm as I staggered to my feet and nearly pulling me down again. I offered her two hands and she painstakingly raised herself to her full height, then shrank back. "My ankle!"

"Oh, it's mad!" I shouted, "us stumbling about in the woods when we've got so much to talk about!"

"It's not mad that my ankle's twisted. You invited me out here for a walk, and now you want to ignore my injury."

I slammed a fist against my chest.

"And what about my injury? What more do you have than hurt pride?"

I slapped her across the mouth.

She leaped away from me, shrieked, bumped into a tree, and then leaned, sobbing, against it.

"That's right, kill me, I deserve it."

Her eyes flashed heat, then cooled as she bowed her head as if in mourning.

"I don't know what you deserve!"

I moved to help her up, but she hesitated.

"I'm afraid—"

"I won't hurt you any more, darling, I promise."

"I think my ankle's really banged up."

"Take my hand."

She clung to me, sobbing, as we inched our way back onto the path.

"It feels a little better already."

"Then maybe it's not banged."

"Maybe not."

Her fingers digging into my arm pleased me terribly.

"Aren't you sorry that you hit me?" she said.

"Of course I am, darling."

"I'm sorry that I ran off."

We reached the edge of the clearing. It had been light when we had left, and though it did not seem that we had been a long time struggling in the woods, the sun had descended behind the roof, and most of our cottage squatted in shadow, the windows offering even deeper darkness. I did not want to go in just yet.

"This way we live," I said.

"This what?"

Lou rested against the door jamb.

"How do you explain those fairy stories I've heard about my impotence? Was that the work of someone who loves me?"

Lou opened the door and hobbled inside.

"Are you going to hit me again? I wish you wouldn't. But if you do, I'll understand." She sank onto the sofa in the darkest corner of the shadowy room. By contrast, the sky beyond the windows glowed with the unexpected brilliance of a stage set.

"Will you tell me now what happened?"

"Why I left?"

I nodded, squinting in the deepening dark to watch her face contract with the discomfort of a penitent.

"It would be easier just to shoot me."

"You wouldn't have to explain anything then. But I would have to tell the world too much."

"You don't like the world to see us like this, do you?"

"There's so much more important news for them to learn, Lou. And more important things for us to do. That's why I feel so sodden and used up. I thought that we loved each other and that we could do serious work." I sat down on the floor across from the sofa.

"We never stopped loving each other, Jack. I never stopped loving you."

"Lies!"

"Can I explain?"

"Yes. If you can. Do you want something for that ankle?" I reached out as if to touch it.

"I want to rest it. I think it's all right but I want to rest it."

"The way to make it better is to soak it. That will make you feel swell. I've been soaking myself quite a bit these past few weeks."

"I've soaked myself, too," Lou said.

"I'll bet you have," I said. "That soak you ran off with wouldn't let you stay sober for very long, would he?"

"He's got a terrible disease, Jack."

"Oh?"

"I know you wish he'd die of it, but it's more like a terrible lingering illness than one that will kill him quickly. If you want revenge on him, his life will be sufficient."

"I don't want revenge. At first I thought I wanted a little courtesy from the bum since we're the ones who found him crawling across the beach at Provincetown. Now I think I'd just like to forget about him for a while."

"I don't know that I will, Jack, and that's the truth. Can you take it? I'll tell you more. You've got to know about me if you're going to love me."

"I'm listening."

"You read my manuscript?"

"I don't want to talk about that again."

"You said you'd listen. Please do."

She sat up arrow straight, her legs tucked up under her, satiny knees reflecting the faint glow from the window.

"If you read it, even just dipping into the pages here and there, you know about my loneliness, the separation and the solitariness I felt when I was a little girl. All my life I've felt as though I've been closed up in a tomb of air and I've had to claw my way through to people. First to Trullinger, then to you."

"And now are you clawing your way past me?"

"I'm here and not there, aren't I, Jack? Isn't that answer enough?" She clasped her hands together in front of her, as if she were about to pray.

"I have no answer. I'm deeply hurt. That's the truth I know."

"Can I come closer to you?"

"Come sit. I don't believe you're all washed up, just a bit soaked."

She laughed, as I had hoped she might, and slid from the sofa onto the floor.

"My darling, I'm so sorry."

We took ourselves into the little bedroom, undressed like patients entering a hospital and made quick and brutal love.

"Can we talk now?" Lou asked.

"I wanted to talk from the moment you arrived. I just couldn't seem to work the words out."

I lay back in bed, turning her tumbling narrative into images in my mind: her first time alone with Gene in the theater on the wharf, the pity she felt for him, and how this reminded her so much of our own first encounter and yet how different, since when she approached Gene in sisterly fashion he backed away rather than moving forward (as I had done), and this engendered more desire in her than affection, and how she detested herself for the feelings that assailed her, and how she rushed out onto the dunes, plunged toward the surf, saw the moon slip behind a bank of high swirling clouds, and felt chilled to the bone; and Gene pursued her in his slumping, inebriated way, catching up with her at the water's edge, her shoes lapped by gentle, lolling foam, the tide rushing in from Europe. He was shy, she was the aggressor (which convinced me that she was telling me some piece of the truth since she did not accuse the drunken hulk of rape but rather of submission); she leaned against him, took his hand and lay it across her shoulder. Braving the reek of sour mash he coughed out into the wind, she calmed him, kissed his eye, licked the stubble on his cheek, remembered that I was home in the beach house waiting for her return, felt her heart stop, then start again, felt her knees buckle but not the fall that followed.

During the next few weeks, they met at the theater, which was legitimate, and as many times as they could in Gene's little lean-to on the dunes, which was not. Gene knew that, for as drunk as he kept himself, he could not douse the fire that licked at his brain and his flesh, the burning point of the passion between them which was too good for him not to enjoy. But seeing me at the theater each day and sneaking off with Lou at odd intervals—at sunrise, when she'd tell me that she was going for a walk on the dunes, at noon, when she explained that she had to try on a dress that was a bargain, walks and errands, walks and errands—all this began to torture him so that he lost what little sleep he usually, in any case, had to struggle to attain. So Lou, my loving Lou, invented the story of my impotence, explained that, because of my internal problems, I had not been able to make love to her for months and months. She told him we had been living together as brother and sister, and worse, that I was grieved, sorely grieved, that I could not give her the pleasure that I knew she hungered for, and would not care if she were finding her physical romancing elsewhere. It grieved me that much.

Oh, it grieved me—to listen to her outrageous and torturous tale! Which continued on into the fall when we moved the theater to the Village, blended into the time of my real and serious illness, carried on into the weeks when I was in the hospital, on into the month when I returned home and we began the quarreling that led to our separation.

"Now do I know everything that I should know?"

"I haven't told you everything yet."

"Tell me," I said, "Tell me and it won't have to haunt you."

Lou turned slightly in bed, and only then did I realize that she had been clinging as close to me throughout the telling of her passion as she had when we had made love.

"I was never going to leave you for long. I never wanted to leave you at all."

"But you did leave."

"I wanted to stay. I tried to keep myself from going. But every day I woke up, I found that I was split in two—there was part of me moving toward you and part of me moving toward Gene. I wanted both of you. I knew that I couldn't have both of you, and then I made it so I lost what I had with either of you. Our horrible battles, my awful time with Gene in Connecticut!"

"Well, you haven't told me about that."

Up to Connecticut on the train to his family's summer home on the north shore of the Sound, those lovers fled away. Once outside the city where Lou and I had made our little life, she thought it would be easier to escape from the guilt she had suffered for months and months—not so much the guilt attached to her action but the guilt that grew with her silence. She had been working on her manuscript for many weeks before I found it, leaving it lying about her desk in the hope that I might thumb through it, find the incriminatory passages, and force her to reveal the rest of the truth to me. But though she wished for that, when I had confronted her, she could not say what was true, cowering at the last and preferring the lie to the possibility of recrimination.

"You needn't have worried."

"After what you did to the apartment?"

"Who told you what I did?"

"The janitor showed me some of the clothes he'd salvaged from the trash. Would you have done that to me, Jack? If I'd stayed with you long enough? Would you have thrown me out with the trash?"

"Is that what you'd prefer? Is that what you think you deserve?"

"I hear it in your voice. You hate me!"

"I want to hear the rest."

"You know the worst of it now. The rest of it is bad for me alone."

"Finish telling me."

"Don't you have something to tell me about yourself?"

"No, I don't have anything to say about myself. I'm the same old person you left behind, just a little worse for the wear and tear that comes with suffering awhile."

"You don't sound like the same person. There's not much love in your voice."

"It's love, just a slightly damaged kind of love. Have you finished?"

"I can't tell you any more. I don't have the strength."

"Find it."

"Don't speak so brutally to me, please!"

"You want the bear to strike you down with his paw!"

"Don't tease me, I can't take it."

"But you did take it."

"What did I take?"

"You took my love up with you to Connecticut. What happened there?"

"God, nothing! It was an awful time. At first we were alone and Gene wouldn't stop drinking because he felt so guilty, and then his parents came up for a weekend and he couldn't stop drinking because they fought so much with each other—his father with his mother, because she behaves so strangely in front of company, and Gene with his father, because they just can't get along about anything—art, politics, religion—they argue with each other over the price of the newspaper! They're so much alike they can't stand each other—and Gene's mother quarreled with him because she was jealous of me! And his brother fought with both of us because he couldn't bear to see Gene having such a success on Broadway. Jack, it makes our own circle seem so peaceful! Your mother may write to you about what you say about the war, but she still loves you, her letters show it. What if she spit at you when she saw you and then collapsed because of what she knew she had done? And what if Harry reproached you for your stand on the war, what if he made nasty comments around the table? Bitter, bitter place. And the foghorns groaning on the Sound at night, the dampness of the house itself, we might as well have lived *in* the Sound as on it...."

She brushed her hand across my chest, and I shuddered as though some slithery thing out of nightmares had crawled my way.

"I repell you now, don't I?"

"My disgusting dopiness repulses me, my stupidity, my blindness, my own low-down ignorance, my incredible innocence, my bluster and bravado and hollow heroicalness—"

"Not you!" she broke in, grabbing my arm and holding tight so that after I flinched she was still gripping me. "Me!" she screamed, shaking me. "Me! me! me! me!"

"Why did you do it?"

I peeled myself from her and sat on the edge of the bed.

"I was split in two!"

"Why did you come back here?"

"Because I want to try and live with you!"

"You can't live with him, but you'd like to stay with him!"

"It's not that way! I don't love him! I didn't love him! It was something else I can't explain! He needed me more than I can say. He would have gone crazy if I hadn't been with him. You were sick but they could cure you. He was alive and there was nothing that could save him. Jack, it was tearing me in two. There was nothing, no one, not father, mother, brother, no one but me who could help him! I had to go with him!"

"You wanted to play nursemaid to a genius, but it looks more like you played whore to a drunk."

"Is that what you think I am? You with your free-and-easy vision?"

"I think he's a drunk."

"But he's also a genius, and you knew that when we first found him. Don't lie to me, Jack."

"So you're part nursemaid, part whore. That's the logic I see in all this."

She delivered one hard blow to my back and slid off the other side of the bed.

"I'm going now."

"Back to Connecticut? I thought you didn't like the foghorns and damp?"

"You fool! You're ruining yourself! You don't know what you're doing!"

"I've never felt like this!"

She clambered back up over the bed and leaned over me.

"I'd kill *you* if I could!"

I took a deep breath.

"Please sit, Lou. If we go on much longer, there'll be a double murder or a double suicide here and the world could never stand it."

She laughed lightly, as in the old days, and then without hesitation, sat at the foot of the bed, her body giving off a faint hue of light, as bodies sometimes do in the dimness of darkened rooms.

"Shall we begin again?" she asked.

"And how do we do that?"

I held on to the side of the bed, suddenly fearful that it might tip over and spill me into the pit below.

"I'll kill myself and save you the trouble," Lou said, hiking her knees up until she could rest her delicate chin upon them.

"Please, honey, don't torture yourself anymore. I'll try to get those awful things out of my mind."

"I feel like the worst kind of criminal," she said, "as though...I've just hacked with a hatchet at the most beautiful painting in a museum...."

"Is that our love? The most beautiful painting in a museum?"

"The most precious...yes...see, you still feel the same way I do!"

"I still do, Lou, yes, I do. We will do something to heal this up! Christ, I'll get myself trepanned!"

Slapping my hands to my eyes, as though suddenly blinded and made to see in the same calamitous instant, I left the bed and stumbled toward our tiny kitchen where the dishes had piled up and the garbage reeked.

"I'll cut it out myself! Our love has known the test of fire! Now I'll test it with the blade!"

"You're even more hysterical than I am, Jack. Come back!" she called.

I fumbled about in a drawer and found a dull-bladed vegetable knife. Lou had switched on my reading lamp, so when I staggered back into the room, she saw the blade and flinched as I touched the point of the knife to her neck.

"Don't you want to cut out the offending part?"

I flung the knife against the wall and dropped to my knees in front of her.

"I wish your comrades could see you now! You're so unbearable sometimes, Jack! You don't want to end this pain, do you? It makes you feel heroic."

I jumped to my feet, shaking as I stood before her, as though a cold draft of Arctic air had blown into the room.

"It makes me feel like garbage! It makes me feel like dying, like war, like carnage!"

"And I'm the enemy in this war?"

She laughed, a choked, forced laugh and opened her mouth to speak.

I hit her with my closed fist—her head snapped back with a cracking noise like that of a branch fractured in a windstorm. She clasped her face and spun into a corner quaking like a cowardly hound.

"Did I hurt you?" I heard myself ask, rubbing my hand which stung as though I had just slammed it against a thick wooden post.

"I'm sorry, darling, let me help you now, let me help!"

"You've done it now!" she spat out from between her fingers.

"Have I hurt you?"

"You huh huh huh!"

"I what?"

"You *broke my jaw!*"

"No, sweetness, I couldn't have done that!"

Lou closed her hands over her eyes and settled into a docile heap of hair and hands and knees. She remained this way even as I struggled to get her into her clothes for our long walk into the village.

"Is it getting any better? Squeeze my arm if it hurts bad," I said. "I know you might not want to talk. At least your ankle seems better. Is it?"

She shook her head and flinched as I slid my arm about her waist to help guide her around a turn in the downhill road.

"Well, I've really done it this time, haven't I?"

Lou stared down at her feet, up at the trees, any place but where I was. A few stars lingered above the pines. There was no longer a moon.

We'd only had my big illness since we lived in Croton, never an illness small enough to consult a local doctor. And so we were strangers to the white-haired gent in the bathrobe who opened his door at what was a rather early hour in the morning.

"She fell," I said.

"I feh," said Lou, staring the doctor in the eye.

"Fell on your face?" He showed Lou into his little examining room. They weren't in there long before he came out alone and walked right past me into another room. I thought he was going to telephone the sheriff or some such thing, but he returned dressed in a gray suit, accompanied by his wife, a stocky, sour-looking woman.

"Morning," I said as they walked past me into the examining room. It was a long minute or two before they came out.

"You're Reed, aren't you?" the doctor said.

I nodded.

"How is she?"

"Oh, she's not hurt too much physically. Bruised a bit, but the jaw's not broken."

"It was an accident," I said. "We both feel bad about it. You know who we are?"

The doctor's wife spoke up then.

"We know very well who you are, Mister Reed. We read about your escapades in the newspapers."

"Small place, Croton," the doctor shrugged. "Missus, you want to fetch the lady while I get something for her to take for the pain?"

His missus went into the examining room and closed the door. The doctor leaned close to me, and I could smell his minty breath and the rubbing alcohol on his neck where he had hastily shaved.

"I don't believe she fell," he said. "I also don't believe in hitting women. But—"

"Doctor—"

"—in a few months you're going to have your chance to do all the fighting you like, Mister Reed. Whether it's your war or not, you're going to be swinging punches at the Kaiser's boys instead of helpless American women. And there's no way you're going to get out of it either, because you're going to be taking your physical examination right here in this room."

He withdrew a few steps from me as though he had timed the end of his speech with the opening of the examination room door.

Lou's face had swelled up purply and hideous. She wouldn't look at me, but the doctor's wife wouldn't stop staring. Her husband pressed a bottle into my hand, recited some words over Lou and showed us to the door.

We walked slowly back up the hill. All the stars had now gone the way of the departed moon. Lou went on ahead of me into the cottage. I was standing there staring at our small garden in dawn light when I heard the village taxi chugging up the hill.

Lou came out of the cottage, her suitcase in tow, as the cab appeared around the curve of trees.

"I'll help you," I said.

"Yuh lee muh aluh!"

Her shriek, when I touched her, scattered birds.

"I guh," she called back over her shoulder as she went to meet the cab. "Yuh cuh et I kuh mysuh!"

"I'll stay here, Lou! I'll give you plenty of room!"

"Uh guh to huh!"

The driver got out and opened the door for her. He looked at me with suspicion, as though he had been reading the same newspaper as the doctor. He firmly shut Lou's door and returned to his seat behind the wheel. As he turned the vehicle around, I rushed onto the road. I grabbed the rear door handle, and he stopped the car.

"What're you doing?" The driver snarled at me through his open window.

"Druh!" moaned Lou from the back seat.

"Take me with you," I said to her.

"Guh!" she called to the driver.

"I'm getting in," I said, my hand still on the handle.

"Guh!" Lou grunted.

The driver understood her intent if not her words, because he sent the vehicle lurching forward, and I relinquished my hold on the door handle, dancing back and away from the smoky wake of the departing cab.

She'll tell him to turn when she reaches the bottom of the hill, I said to myself, finding a tree stump at the edge of the road and sitting down. She'll tell him when they reach the station that she's changed her mind and wants him to drive her home. I listened awhile for the noise of his engine but heard nothing but birds and the sound of the light spring breeze playing amidst the green-gold leaves above me. In a sentimental fiction, I might have heard the sound of my heart cracking a little at the center. But this was real life and I wept, but not as much as I would have liked to have wept. I kicked my heel against the stump. The stump remained still and I hurt my foot. Did I hear the sound of a train pulling out of the station? I kicked the stump a hundred dozen kicks. When the sun had crept up beyond the pines, I heard someone walking, walking and whistling up the hill.

I ran, laughing, down the road.

"Max!"

He was alone.

"She asked me to give you this note." I didn't like the way he was staring at me as I stuffed the paper into my pocket.

"Aren't you going to read it?"

"I can't bear to."

Max looked annoyed.

"I don't mean to Dutch-uncle you, pal, but if I were you I would at least read the note and figure things out from there."

"I know what she'll say!"

"Read it."

"I know what it says."

"Read!"

"I was rotten to her, I know. I shouldn't have made love with Vincent, I didn't have my heart in that. But Lou was already in thick with *him*!"

"Read the note."

"I treated her like a true pal, like a sister and a lover both. And she betrayed me! She sneaked around the corner on me while I was sick! She put out all those stories about me! The bitch! The filthy civet cat!"

"Read!"

I shook my head at Max, at the trees, at the promising sun.

"What's she going to tell me now? That she's been your lover, too, Max? Have you gone and done that with her?"

"You're a sad picture, Jack," Max said. "Come down to my cottage and we'll get you a drink."

We walked down the hill to the path that turned through the woods and led to his cottage. The sun felt pleasant on my face, but my guts froze, as though the Arctic wind that had blown in through our bedroom had roared up again and pierced my flesh and bones.

"You're usually like a whirlwind," Max said. "Get the hell out of this funk, brother. Read the note! I want to know the whirlwind again."

After a few drinks at Max's cottage, I could feel a little bit of my old self stirring again, and took out the note.

Lou claimed that she wasn't going back to Gene but wanted to spend some time alone in the city to think about the turmoil of the past winter.

"I'll give her that," I said.

"She's taking it whether you like it or not. New women don't ask. That's how she got you in the first place, wasn't it? So you better not fight against it. We need to send you off on assignment, some place that will take your mind off all this."

"Couldn't we find some sympathetic millionaire who'd send me to China."

"China? That's not news. If the *Metropolitan* wouldn't send you there, we won't be able to raise the cash. Eastern Europe is another story. There's a lot of rumblings along the Russian front these days."

"I'd go if you can get me there," I said. "I'm going to play drunk now, and when I get really stinking, I want you to prop me up at the desk and put a pencil in my hand and give me some paper. I'll write a play then, maybe two. I'll fill it with foul-mouthed sailors who are always drunk. The booze'll cover up their poor English, make it nice and slurred and easy to listen to. If any ideas show up, pitch them overboard. We'll just wheeze and sniff and lumber around the stage, scratch like monkeys and call it life."

June again. A time for commencement. The city smelled like a border town—everything steamed and dripped, and the streets reeked of excrement and refuse. On my way to the pawnshop to redeem my father's watch (since my wallet was now temporarily swollen with income from several silly news stories and features), the only vital signs I noticed on the streets were children brawling and a few full-bladdered horses gushing indifferently into the gutters.

"Where's the girl who used to work here?" I asked the balding man—he might have been thirty or three hundred—whom I found behind the bars.

"That firebrand? She went home to make the revolution."

"She went back to Russia?"

I gave him the cash and the ticket and he handed me the watch.

I wound the timepiece carefully and held it up to my ear to listen for a moment to the mechanism.

"You think she was happy here? I'll tell you, I wish she had gone sooner. Lectures on the evils of the capitalist system she threw in for free along with nearly bankrupting me on transactions."

"I may be heading for Russia soon, myself," I said, slipping the watch onto my wrist.

"Good. Tell Malka and her socialist friends anytime they want to bring the crown jewels, I'll be happy to see her."

Throughout this vexing time, Lou had been moving from place to place, spending a week with the Cooks, a few days with Mary Heaton Vorse, then over to the Dells, and then to Margaret Sanger's. She would stop in now and then at Patchin Place to pick up things as she needed them but only after warning me in advance, either through a friend or a telephone call, so that I could leave before she arrived. She claimed—through her intermediaries or over the telephone—that she wasn't afraid of me but just wanted to avoid any nasty encounters. I was afraid of myself. I spent a week in Washington (while Lou moved in to Patchin Place in my absence), I met Steffens at the Press Club and walked with him alongside the steamy Potomac. When I told him exactly how nasty I had been, he merely clucked his tongue.

"We've all been bad, and we'll all be good again," was what he had to say on the subject. His mind was on revolution—petty bourgeois squabbles mattered less to him than pigeon dirt.

"What are these affairs of the heart when compared with the great upheavals of the masses? I have a feeling, Jack, a great feeling that one day soon a wave of toiling people will wipe the slate clean and begin our culture over again."

I thought quite a bit about Steffens's vision while the train rolled me northward toward New York that evening. In the seat next to me was the seventeen-year-old daughter—I asked her how old she was, and so I knew exactly—of a congressman from Buffalo. With her perfect posture and crinkly white dress and gloves, she gave the impression of sweating not a bead. When I cleared my throat and asked her to move a bit closer to talk since I had spent the week in interviews with men of state and highest offices and had used the force of my throat to its limit, I broke out in goosebumps. I was so relieved when she was met at Pennsylvania Station by a starch-faced aunt that I invited them both to dinner. They respectfully declined.

I returned to Patchin Place to find sweet mementos of my lovey strewn about the apartment and, in the middle of the dining table, a note asking me to meet her at Polly's Restaurant the next afternoon. I had been a good boy on the train and I had been rewarded.

The inside of the restaurant was silent, empty I turned on

my heel and had one foot out the door when I heard her call to me.

She had been sitting all the while in the far corner of the room opposite the door, her body drawn up in the shadows against the wall.

"I didn't see you," I said, sitting down opposite her. "Have you been well?"

"If you're asking about the lumps you gave me, they're better. I miss you, Jack, but I don't think it's time yet for us to move back together again."

I reached across the table for her hand, but stopped when she would not return the gesture.

"You're my love," I said. "And also my wife. And yet you say that you don't want to live with me?"

I slumped back in my chair, disheartened.

"I understand how you feel. I feel the same way, Jack. But I need to be alone now."

"Alone! With him!"

"Not with him. Or anyone. Just alone. With myself."

"Darling! I'll be with you! We'll be alone with each other!"

"I'm still afraid of us, Jack. I need more time to think about what I've done...."

"And what I've done. I admit that I've had some part in this."

Lou showed me something resembling her old smile. "I'm glad that you can say that you've been at fault along with me."

"I know I have," I said. "I'm just not quite sure what it was I did that drove you to it."

"You didn't drive me to leave you. I never left you. You were always with me. Even tomorrow, you'll be with me, Jack."

"Tomorrow? What happens then?"

"I'm sailing for France. I've been asked to do some war reporting of my own."

"I'll go with you."

"You're banned from the country."

"I'm sorry I ever fired that gun."

"You're not truly, are you?"

I couldn't help but tell her the truth.

"But when you come back from France," I said, "by that time Max will have raised money to send me to Russia."

"China's off?"

"Yes, it's Russia where he thinks I should go. I crossed the border there once when I was in Eastern Europe with Robinson. It was a muddy place, blue skies, peasants always cheerful even with mud up to their mustaches and breasts."

"They have both mustaches and breasts?" Lou's somber mood showed another sign of cracking.

"And heads that grow beneath their shoulders."

"We'll see," she said.

"So we will," I said.

The next few months went by as in a dream or a lyric love song as I made preparations for the trip to Russia that, each day, seemed more possible. Rain fell on Manhattan a good part of that time, after dark, reminding me of the night when I first met Mabel and of all the evenings I had caroused down these Bohemian streets since then. Almost as though I were a character in one of O'Neill's boozy melodramas, I sensed the fall of the curtain on one act of my life and anticipated the raising of it upon another. I never felt more free than when I performed the simple chores that came before departure: arranging with Max to pick up the money for my passage—a Russian-born uniform manufacturer was putting up most of it—and other needs; finishing a few articles whose deadlines drew near; writing letters and sending them westward.

There was a letter postmarked from Paris waiting for me in the mailbox one night. My hands, which never trembled while holding a rifle or a pen, shook from fright as I fumbled with the page.

> . . . honeybear of my life, I can't stay away from you any longer. I've bought my ticket. I'll be home . . . .

Behind the Croton cottage, where vines drooped sleepily in the dense midsummer heat, a green snake, distant cousin to a rattler that once intruded on a boy who dreamed of kings, sunned itself on a flat bed of stone. I put down my book and studied its curving figure, dappled in leaf-shade. If I were a will-writing man, I might have made a note right then and there—after I was gone I wanted this garden to be his.

Postscript

*J*anuary 1, 1936
Hotel Liberia
Paris

Dear Max,

After all these years this voice in your ear and you're wondering why. Well, I've just shipped off almost the last of Jack's papers for the man in New York who's going to do his biography, and I feel so bereft again I had to write. It used to be that walking some hours along the Seine would help to cure me of these blues—they hit me so that sometimes I think of jumping in and never coming up for air—but what's a girl to do when even lovely old Paris doesn't help anymore to ease the pain of writing the rest of his story and mine, the two tales twined together like the plants that sprang up out of the graves of Tristram and Iseult? I put pen to paper, sitting far above the strife in the streets, the clash of warring factions right and left, the marching of the Popular Front that Jack would have opposed were he alive to speak out today—I sit and stare at the photograph that rests atop my bureau, the one you took of us one summer in Croton, Big and his Little. A little shiver runs up my spine when I recall how you and I cried out at the obituary that came over the wire that morning in early April.

> April 1,1920, Abo, Finland—*American journalist and war resister John Reed died here yesterday in front of a government firing squad. Finnish authorities announced that Reed had been detained for several weeks by customs officials in Abo after attempting to pass illegally through Finnish territory on his way to meet a U.S.-bound freighter.*

> Police said that at the time of his arrest Reed was carrying large amounts of counterfeit Finnish currency, jewelry, and other valuables. He was tried under a new Finnish law designed to deter smuggling and was executed in a police station courtyard a few hours after the sentence was passed.
>
> Author of scores of articles and several books, Reed was probably best known for his stirring account of the Bolshevik Revolution Ten Days That Shook the World. He had been traveling in Russia in search of material for a sequel to this volume. At his death he was several months short of his thirty-third birthday.

Remember how we wept and wailed when we first read this story? And only hours later did we look at each other and all at once begin to laugh. April 1st! What fools *we* were! And wasn't it just like him to send us a message of his whereabouts in this terrible but joking way? So I went to Washington and met the famous influential Mr. Bullitt who took me out to dinner and told me that he would do all he could to get Jack released.

Max, I've been a bad girl again and held back some papers from that biographer. I've kept the original of the obit, and also a stack of manuscript pages that Jack wrote while in the Abo jail—all those months!—and who knows who kept him there, the Americans? Zinoviev? both?—A Finnish SP member Madame Malmberg smuggled them out for him the same way she smuggled out the obit he wrote for himself, and the pages eventually reached Paris where the influential Mr. Bullitt got hold of them and turned them over to me.

"Another wedding present?" I said to him. "You're extraordinary, William." I meant that—then.

I've read them, Max, and been inspired by them to try again to write my own view of things. I've lost touch with Thomas Seltzer; I don't even know if he's still in the publishing business though I did see about ten years ago some novels by D.H. Lawrence that he brought out, and so I was wondering if you might make some inquiries for me about a publisher for my own memoirs. I have a good publishing record, Max, two books on Russia—it was the marriage to

Bullitt that slowed down my work, and having the child, and then the horrible period when I lost touch with things, as if all in one big wave the pain of Jack's death broke over me, and the divorce—those are other stories, Max, and I won't go into them here except to say that any publisher ought to relish having me tell, if not all, at least some of the juicier things about my marriage with Bullitt—the links I form between revolutionary society and high society ought to whet the appetite of a number of readers, don't you think?

Max, I've been a good girl again and I've been working. I've survived a bad year and I have stopped going out except to feed myself—the streets are dangerous again and you never know who you'll meet or what demonstration you might wander across—and so I have decided to stay in my room and write the rest of his story and mine. Shouldn't the world know what it was like to be with him at the end and how it was for him? and what it was like for me in the years beyond? It all could make a wonderful book, a true American story, Max, don't you think? His story in his own words and then my giving the rest of his story and then the rest of my story? Wouldn't they want to hear the woman's side of things? The stories I've got about Russia, Max! And the stories I've got about the Philadelphia Main Line! I've resolved to tell it all this year, Max. I've resolved to stop drinking and keep a steady hand.

Pent-Up Aching Rivers

(Max—Jack liked this line from Whitman—What do you think of it as a title? Or what about "Days That Shook Our World"?)

For Jack Reed, Russia meant great crowds massing in squares and marching on palaces where once the Czarist tyrants ruled—wave after wave of people and flags and rifles and pitch-forks and scythes and knouts and fists raised on high above the stream of heads and faces and shoulders, an army of Excaliburs flowing in a rush toward their homeland's destiny. Read *Ten Days* again. It's an opera, an epic ballet, an event so vast and far-reaching that no movie director but God Himself could have filmed it, and yet an event that Jack put into masses of words that move across the page with the inevitability of destiny.

"You know how come, little honey, I can write this when nobody else can come close?" he said to me one evening when he came down from the studio he'd rented at One Sheridan Square. "Because I'm a Westerner. All those phoney-baloney idea men, even Max, who grew up in the East, they were planted like trees in one place—but I grew up where even the earth moved if you stood still and the winds blew fierce and the rivers rushed toward the ocean and the folks just itched to get a move on no matter where they found themselves standing about. And if you're going to write about revolution, you've got to know real motion, not just movement—the real thing, the whirl, the flux, the shifting of things from night to day and day to night and back again." He pulled me close to him in a big bear hug—he smelled of cigarettes and absinthe and coffee and bitter sweat and food and ink and pencil shavings and God knew what, just about everything except (how happy I was to notice its absence) someone else's perfume.

He'd been racing through the manuscript, producing mounds of paper with the speed of a mad bricklayer—it had taken nearly a year to get his files back after customs took them away. And so he raced into the book, the opera, the real-life novel with an entire people as the hero, the epic ballet score, the movie only God could have made, raced with the speed of a man trying to keep up with his imagination, racing so fast sometimes that he left even his imagination behind and wrote out of that very thin but intense fire that comes into a writer's life only a few times, when the truth ultimately becomes what you write it to be, and the devil take the scholar.

"I met Max on the way home," he said. "He asked me how I was doing. Can you believe that? As though we'd passed on the path to the farmer's market. He asked me what I thought of the Series. 'Haven't seen you since then,' he said. I said 'I'm writing about a bigger game.' 'What's today's score?' he asked me. 'Workers six, capitalists two,' I said. 'And now we're three games up on the bloody landlords and factory owners. And tomorrow Lenin's on the mound.' 'Can't wait to read it,' he said. 'Neither can I,' I said."

"What *is* the score, Big?" I asked.

"Just what I told Max. I'm up to the Winter Palace, and the whole business is flowing like the Hudson in springtime. Except I've been getting the Petrograd freeze-ups just sifting through my notes—my hands shake, my toes turn cold, I can feel that I'm back there, hon, I can feel my way back to what happened then. Oh, Little, I'm so glad for my feelings. I couldn't write a word without them!"

We talked about the Winter Palace all through dinner, the way children talk about castles in fairy tales.

"Remember those soldiers with the chocolates?" he asked. "They'd never seen chocolates before in their lives. Talk about bears! Remember how they scooped up huge paw-fuls of those bon-bons direct from Paris and stuffed them into their mouths and their caps and their pockets? Ah, remember how we laughed about the way the candy wouldn't melt until the thaw! And the wine? Here were men who'd never seen a bobble of wibe leh alog tasted the stuff.

"Bear, don't talk with your mouth full."

"That's how we Westerners talk, ma'am, with a mouth full of meat and a paw full of chocolate and pockets stuffed with fancy wines and liquors!"

"Oh, I do love you! Oh, I can't wait for the whole world to read your book! They've all got to know what it was like!"

"Hell, yes, they've got to know! The world's got to know. All Americans got to know! They got to know what's happening to them before it's too late. They got to learn how to swim or get swept away in the great flood!"

Big Jack Bear brought his fist down on the table so hard he made the cups leap.

"Don't spill your coffee, Bear."

"And remember," he said, standing up and pushing his dishes aside, "remember how those Red Guards found those nuns cowering in the top attic of the Palace?"

"No," I said, "I don't remember that."

"Oh, yes, and they'd never seen nuns before, and they wanted to find out what was under those habits and they—"

"Bear!" I protested as he backed me up against the wall. "Bear! What do you have in mind?"

"How they picked them nuns up one by one and jiggled them to see what fell out of their pockets?"

"Bear!"

He hoisted me up until my head nearly touched the ceiling and held me by the hips and nuzzled his muzzle between my legs.

"You still have strength left after working all day and night?"

"All work and no play," he said, "makes Jack a—"

"Put me down!" I said.

"Yes, ma'am," he said.

"I mean, lay me down."

In those days when we slept it seemed sometimes that we dreamed in tandem of white nights, the great heaving flow of the ice-burdened river, the steady but glacial passage of an entire race—prince and soldier, artist and peasant—while the two of us soared like petrels on stormy winds, privileged as no two witnesses had ever been to the upheaval of a nation.

(Remember when I left for France? Jack couldn't stay for long in Croton without feeling that he had to do something about the world. Neither could you stand back and let the draft suck the best and youngest of the brood into the whirlwind. You both fought a good fight against recruitment, against the war.) And so when he returned from Russia, he used the only weapon he knew he could use effectively, his powerful speech. Not even the arrests for speaking out, which was his right and privilege at public meetings, shocked me like the trial that all of you suffered when he returned. We joked about it before we left Russia—we joked about it on the morning we went to court. But I saw the light change in his eyes midway through the first morning, when the judge made clear by his tone of voice that he did not think that the trial was the lark Art Young made it out to be. During a recess Jack took me by the hand and said, "I think I know what it was like back in Tombstone when the judge said 'Hang 'em!' and somebody stood up in the jury box and took a rope out from under his chair."

I'd never felt his hands tremble before—not when a squad of zealous young Red soldiers put us against a wall outside of Moscow and smoked our cigarettes while one of them tried to decipher the passes we showed them—not when Lenin himself threw up his hands after Jack denounced Zinoviev's position on American labor—not when I looked him in the eye and said, 'Yes, I went to bed with A—— D—— while you were away, and is it any different from the little *tovarischka* Malka that you kept in your room in Moscow before I arrived (but that was after his trip to Russia, and now I'm getting confused, and my hands are trembling)—and he leaned close to me and whispered, "I'm going to have to find a way out of this. I don't want to go to jail."

And I squeezed his arm to reassure him that whatever he did was fine with me.

"Just let me get *this* book done," he said. "Then they can cart me away."

'This book' was *Ten Days*, still unwritten—we still hadn't gotten the files back yet. But he was so full of his book, and when he spoke in court he dreamed the book aloud, talked it into our hearts and so it was almost as if he had already written it, and the hard labor to follow was somehow after the fact—he spoke of the wars he had witnessed and the dead he had witnessed and defended his article with the greatness of a knight of old—you were there, you heard him—it was as gallant a vision as any I've heard and moved the courtroom to silence and then to awe.

I think that I was the only one who could tell, though, that for all of his beautiful words Jack was thinking to himself all the while he spoke, thinking, What am I going to say when the judge asks me about recruitment with the war going on? What am I going to say? Am I going to tell him what I believe and go to jail? How will I fight while in jail? I've been behind bars and I know that a man can't fight when he's in prison. And I could see that he had learned a few things while in Russia, I could see that he had discovered how to put one thing before another, one important thing before a less important thing, and so he decided—well, he didn't formally decide, I'm sure—but he felt that staying out of jail and writing the book about the revolution was more important than saying what was his own personal truth this one time, and so when the Judge pushed him to the wall and asked him if he was opposed to the country obtaining military forces to fight the war, he said no, and when the judge asked him if he meant to use his article about insanity on the battlefield to frighten families into opposition to the war, he said no.

Remember the prosecutor's final speech, Max? When he spoke of his friend who died in France?

"Somewhere he lies dead, and he died for you and he died for me. He died for Max Eastman, he died for John Reed, for Floyd Dell...."

And Art sat up out of a cat-nap, looked about wide-eyed and asked, "Didn't he die for me, too?"

And our laughter continued on into the night as we celebrated, and then we went to Washington and I helped get back those files.

"William," I said, "won't you do this for me?"

"How can I possibly not?" Bullitt's chalky face reddened as though I had touched him where he had never been touched. His own hands went to his note pad and he jotted down the information. A few days later it was accomplished.

"I'll never forget you," I said.

"You...you Mata Hari," he said.

I clasped my hands to my chest.

"Oh, no one's ever said such a beautiful thing to me in all my life!"

For weeks afterward, Jack would turn to me now and then in the night and say, half in jest, half in earnest, "I'm a liar, but a revolutionary liar. How Mother would object!" He lay a large warm paw on my shoulder and paused, as if he were listening to the silence gathering in the alley outside. "I've always owned up to my messes before this, you know?"

"I know," I said, rolling close to him in bed.

"But there's more than my personal honor at stake here, isn't there?"

"Yes, Big darling."

"There are lives at stake, the lives of future generations, in Russia, here, all over Europe, all over the world."

"You're talking about it as if you have the choice yet to make," I said. "You've already given your testimony."

"I testify every day. I testify whenever I write a page." He sat up and lit a cigarette.

"And you're worried about whether you're going to become a liar in your work?"

"You understand, Little honey, you truly understand."

"There's the truth of life and the truth of poetry," I said. "And we've always known that the truths of life change with every day and every generation, but the truth of poetry always remains."

"Is that a truth that changes or one I can depend on?"

He wiggled his toes against me and sucked in smoke from his cigarette and I could see his eyes in the glow from the butt end.

"Our lives have become poetry, dear Big," I said.

"Do you really believe that?"

"I feel it. Don't you?"

"Most of the time. But certain things aren't poetry. The trial wasn't poetry, was it?"

"You made it poetry, Big."

"Did I truly?"

"Truly," I said.

"It's been different ever since Russia, hasn't it?" he said.

"Different, yes," I said. "More poetic, more beautiful."

"Everything led up to it," he said, "like stepping stones across a flooded creek. But now we're on the other shore, and it is different, I agree."

"One thing isn't different," I said.

"One thing?" he said. "No, that's different, too. It's better."

"How could it be better, Bear? Big Bear."

"It's changing for me," he said. "Each time it changes. It becomes something better."

"Can the best be bettered, Bear?"

"It can change into something better than itself," he said. "It has something to do with dialectics. I've been reading. I know that the world can change no matter how good it becomes. Why not our love?"

"It's going to have to change a lot to get better," I said.

"It will," he said. "And that's not a revolutionary lie, either."

"I believe it," I said. "I know that I've become a better person than I used to be. I believe that we could become better lovers."

"Even better," he said.

"Even better than now," I said.

He sat up again, this time to tap out his smoke.

"I've finished the poem."

"The 'America' poem?"

"Yes."

"Say some of it to me, Big."

"I'll try to say part of the beginning." He cleared his throat. "'By my free boyhood in the wide West,/The powerful sweet river, fish-wheels, log-rafts,/Ships from behind the sunset, Lascar-manned,/Chinatown, throbbing with mysterious gongs....'" He paused for breath, and I tried to imagine these things in the dark of our little Patchin Place bear cave, the towers of the city surrounding us like mountain peaks of some mysterious future earth. "'The blue, thunderous Pacific, blaring sunsets/Lost beaches—'"

"And lost bitches, don't leave them out," I said.

He laughed and cleared his throat again.

"Ahem," "'Lost beaches, camp-fire, wail of hunting cougars....'"

The poem made me weep, not for all the lost times it made me think of, but because of all the futures it made me wonder about.

"You're a Whitmaniac," I said.

"It's not an inch as good as Whitman," he said. "But do you like it?"

"I love it. I love you. Remember what I wrote to you that night in Moscow?"

"Say it, Little," he said, holding me close.

"Don't squeeze my ribs so tight and I will. There. 'I want you to know that sometimes when I am thinking/About you/I have a lump in my throat/And I am a little bit awed./You are the finest person I know/On both sides of the world/And it is a privilege to be your comrade.'"

He squeezed me again.

"I like that better than anything," he said. "Better than anything Vincent has ever written."

"Let's not talk about lost bitches," I said.

"Just lost beaches?"

"Yes."

"Want to hear more of the poem?"

"Yes."

"Well, you asked for it."

That next year he had little time left for poetry. And I think he began avoiding you, Max, because you reminded him, just by being yourself, that he was giving up poetry for other things.

"I saw Max again," he said one night in spring after he had finished the manuscript. "He wanted to talk about my poetry. 'What poetry?' I said. 'I don't write poetry. I'm too busy with reality. I have promises to keep.'" His eyes glowed when he spoke as though he were in a room in the dark, smoking a cigarette, and his pupils had caught the light.

This was after he'd gotten deeply involved in the Socialist Party struggle and in the fight to make the real communist party into more than just a pale imitation of a communist party.

"How can you keep 'em down on the farm after they've seen Paree?" he said one night at dinner in Chicago. "I've seen the Bolsheviks in action. You just can't make a communist party any other way." Fraina was there. They were still speaking then. And Sherwood Anderson was there. Fraina objected. Jack went out to the men's room and Anderson followed and when Jack came back I could tell by his face that something was wrong. As soon as we were alone I asked him what had happened.

"We were pissing," he said, "standing there at the urinal, and Anderson says to me, 'When are you going to give up this storybook version of politics, Jack, and get back to your writing?' I laughed it off, but I couldn't help feeling as low as I used to when I looked down and saw myself pissing red."

The struggle went on all summer. Jack had his victories and his defeats, though after the big Chicago meeting where he waded into the opposition delegates swinging his big fists, it was mostly defeats. He put up a good front—but I knew him too well not to notice the sadness in his eyes.

"They don't see! they don't see!" he stomped about the apartment, raving. "And I've got to make them, I've got to help them!"

These moods worried me. Anyone listening through the wall might have thought he was talking about visions of little green men or pink elephants big as the Ritz. Worse, there probably were people trying to listen through the wall since by this time the government had begun a big campaign to break up the activities of all of us dedicated to the revolution, and a large part of that campaign was spying on us to find out what our next moves would be. Fearful of agents taking down every word he said, I tried to hush him.

"Let them listen!" he said. "My words go out on the wind—let those who have ears listen to what I say about the world, about the fire that's building!"

At meetings of our faction, he spoke no less intemperately, and it was all I could do to help separate the poetry of his speech from the reality of the tactics the group had in the works. Then came the meeting where Jack was chosen to go to Russia to put the problem of recognition of the true and correct American communist party right on Lenin's desk. There was no way that I could go with him—the government would not grant either of us a passport and Jack was going to have to smuggle himself out of the country under a false name and then smuggle himself across Finland, where the white reaction raged, and sneak back into Russia.

What made me feel so low made him appear to take on new strength.

"I'll do it!" he said the night of that fateful meeting, "I'll go underground and fight the good fight! And woe to him who dares to get in my way!" He had rolled up a copy of our new newspaper *The Voice of Labor* and slashed away with it at the air.

A few days before his departure from the Brooklyn docks—disguised as a seaman and holding a passport with the name of "James Gormley"—I woke up with the worst stomach ache I'd ever had in my life, even worse than the pains that came with the disease I contracted from Gene that terrible winter Jack went into Johns Hopkins. I wanted to beg him to stay! I wanted to tell him about my pains!

"Big!" I cried in the night after he sailed away.

"BIG!" I shrieked into the wind that roared across the bridge where I walked alone for hours, staring out into the darkness toward the ocean.

I vomited blood. I went to a doctor.

"Have you ever thought of a psychiatrist?" this man said.

"It's somewhat experimental, but in a case such as yours...."

In a case such as mine, I went to see Gene, but he wouldn't let me in the door.

"I'm working!" he shouted from the other side.

I pounded and pounded on the door, but he wouldn't let me in.

In a case such as mine, I took the train west. Andy was in Taos. He talked a lot about the open spaces around us.

"My Christ," he said, "doesn't it engulf you? It's the best possible place for a painter to live...You've got an intangible world out here. Space—it's unbounded. How do you paint the drama of space? And look at the sky! It's a blank wall—the most powerful emptiness I've ever seen...Oh, Lou, how I love to paint deserts! It's like Marin says, you go down into your guts and haul up light. Oh, if I can be as bold as that! Half as bold as that!"

Mabel was there, filling up a lot of space. She was now Mabel Dodge Luhan, very square and fat and miraculously pale despite the sun. She had married an Indian named Tony from the town, a large rectangular fellow who seemed a match for her bulkiness. He built her a beautiful adobe studio across from their *hacienda*, and if only she had stayed in it. But she couldn't stay in it—she had to run the entire town. I thought that I would try to live quietly and while Andy painted put together a book about Russia from the articles I had already done. Being near Andy helped, the way baling wire holds together an old Ford. But whenever Mabel came near I trembled and quaked.

"When you write to Jack," she said to me one afternoon when I met her in the square, "tell him how much he has moved us all with his reports—tell him that I always knew he would grab the world around like an old pear tree and give it a few good shakes."

That night I got sick again and the sickness wouldn't go. For all the desert space around us the state was too small for

Mabel and me to be there at the same time, and since it was her corral and her *hacienda*, her little Mabelkingdom, I had to leave.

And so it was no use and it was no good and it was a hell of a thing, Max, the way a few months stretched into half a year and his letters became so discouraged and discouraging and then he said he was coming home and the word stopped coming, and then in mid-spring the obituary!

I went to see Bullitt again.

"This is becoming an annual event," he said, pouring me a larger drink than he poured himself. "But I don't mean to joke."

"It's becoming an annual joke, William," I said, throwing back the whiskey the way I'd picked up from Jack—and Gene.

As though he could scarcely bear to witness such an act, he went over to the window. It was the same hotel we'd met in the first time. It was just as well that it was necessary to leave Philadelphia and go to Baltimore to meet—he couldn't have felt right in Philadelphia or Washington, and I wouldn't have felt right in New York.

"It's only part of a joke to me, Lou," he said, staring out at the promising spring sky. "If the world ever stops whirling...."

"What?"

"If the world ever stops...never mind. Let's go over this once more..."

"Yes," I said, feeling the whiskey on my mind, "let's go over this."

Bullitt worked his charms again. He enjoyed this work all around, too. He wanted to be with me. And he wanted to make a study of the President—he thought that the President was a real study, and he enjoyed watching him under pressure—he wanted to know what made the man behave as he did. (In the end, I think, because he wanted to know about himself....)

"It's all too much like medieval court intrigue," I told him when we got the word from Colonel House that Jack had been released from the Abo jail and had crossed the border again into Russia.

"Modern...medieval...isn't it all the same?" Bullitt said.

"It's got to change," I said. "It can't always be like this."

He left his place at the window and crossed the room to kiss me on the cheek.

"And if it only goes on like this, then it only goes on like this," he said. "I don't believe that you change the nature of the beast. But should it ever change, Lou... should it ever...."

And I knew that we were no longer talking about politics. One dark night on the Baltic while hiding below decks—the Finns were searching the cargo holds for contraband—I thought long and deeply about all this. Guard dogs sniffed about the other side of the bulkhead where I hid and I thought calmly and clearly about my love for Jack and life. I don't remember the name on the passport I carried then—I couldn't have told any torturer if caught how I had come to be where I was—the creaking of the ship, the slapping of waves against the hull, the noise of the dogs, the clumping about of the thick-booted guards, police, customs inspectors, soldiers, spies—the smell of creosote, the stink of fish, the steam of my own long-unwashed self—why should it have mattered to anyone, let alone to Jack, if I struggled through all this filth and strife to meet him? And wouldn't I have been more suspect if I had appeared all soaped and sweetly perfumed on a barge with musicians, never having known any turmoil or any other lover? And would it have been possible for him to trust me when I finally found him again and told him how much I labored to reach his side? And the world and the years and the desert sky with a hundred million stars scattered about like the seconds of our lives, what would all this nature know if we did change and could make ourselves known to each other, lover to lover, man to man, woman to woman? Would the world care? Would nature turn over in its grave if, after crawling through muck and trenches stacked with the bones of boys and rats and flushed with poison gas and the propaganda of scurrilous princes, we found a way to be true to each other? And changed one small part of the world? And shifted the space around us to change?

I'd never known Russian spring, the season the people believe to be the most beautiful. On my first trip, the weather had been cold and rainy and then cold and full of snow—and with Jack still in Baku at the conference of eastern communist peoples when I arrived in Moscow this time, I found myself enveloped in early autumn, warm days, chill nights, and it seemed as though I was fated never to know the real Russian warmth, the heat that comes unfettered by cold air currents and distorting clouds—it was already cold in my hotel room, and though I'd suffered through the worst winter months the last time, Jack had been there to keep me warm. For the moment I was alone.

Or so I thought until the first morning after my arrival when I stepped out into the hall and found a dark-complexioned young man in a worn, dark suit leaning against the wall obviously waiting for me to leave the room.

"You're not the chambermaid, are you, comrade?" I said.

"Pliss?" he said. He held up his empty palms as if the ability to speak my language were something he might have grasped with his fingers.

I smiled my best official smile and walked off down the hall. I could hear his feet on the worn carpet behind me, but I didn't look back. That night I checked my things and discovered such matters as the fact that a finger or so of my best perfume was missing—perhaps it had been the maid who had done that except that it was clear from the condition of the room that the Dielovoy Dvor no longer asked women to do that sort of work. Could the dark man who had tailed me all around the city that day have a comrade who drank cologne? Or did he pour some into a handy flask and take it home to his wife or girlfriend?

I asked Emma some questions about this when I saw her a few days later. She immediately motioned for me to step outside the room and follow her down into the lobby of her hotel.

"Personally," Emma said, "I don't mind the diet, because all my life I wanted to lose this pot—" and with that she patted her tummy, "but the spying on their own I could do without."

"Who's behind it?" I wanted to know.

Goldman shrugged—she shrugged like a tough young kid from the streets of the Lower East Side.

"Who isn't? Everybody wants to know what's going on even with the people who find out for everybody else what's going on. I find it personally offensive and ideologically unbearable."

"It must be because we're foreigners," I said. "They have good reason to worry about foreigners."

"If I am foreign to the revolution," she said, crossing her arms and taking a stance as though she were about to complain to a neighborhood grocer about the quality of his produce, "then nobody is a native."

That night as I settled into a cold bed in a cold room the lights flickered incessantly, and finally I turned them out. Lying there in the dark, so close to and yet so distant from my beloved, I shivered awhile even with my coat piled on top of the blankets. And I lay there listening to what I thought were rats in the walls—and mourned the loss of the ideals of public health that the revolution had at first been instilled with—and then heard someone cough and then whisper and I decided that either the public health was worse than I thought or else Emma was correct and the walls had ears and the health of the revolution was failing. How I longed to have Jack at my side, not just to warm my body but to help me understand the strange turn things seemed to be taking.

At last he arrived from Baku!

There I was, sitting in my room reading about Whitman's noiseless, patient spider when Jack roared into the room.

"Did you bring it?" he said, flailing at me with a nearly stick-thin arm. He was trying to embrace me but it seemed that he had nearly lost control of his muscles and jerked about like the very scarecrow he resembled.

I tried to catch my breath, tried to hold back my tears.

"Did you bring it?"

He croaked when he talked, like a man who has gone a long time without water.

I lay my head on his shoulder. He smelled of tobacco and disinfectant and a strange odor that he later told me must have been the scent of the fierce tea he drank constantly while in Baku.

"I missed you," I said.

"And Little, how I missed you! Did you bring it?"

"Your father's watch wasn't there," I said. "Somebody must have bought it."

I felt a tremor run through his malnourished body and held tightly to him for fear of his striking out at me—I could feel the pressure rise in him, and then subside.

"Too bad," he said, almost in a whisper. "You had the pawn ticket?"

"Yes," I said.

"Well . . . I guess I went and hocked it one time too many." I could hear the disappointment in his voice, like a little boy who's just lost something from a collection he'd been keeping for years. "But I needed that extra bit of cash before I sailed . . . ."

"I have a letter from your mother," I said, pleased to change the subject.

"Good, good. I'll read it later." He drew back from me and as though he'd just spilled some invisible substance across his suit coat brushed herself off with long bony fingers more like those of a skeleton's than the firm big hands I knew. "As for now. I want to introduce you, Little Honey, to a few hundred thousand people."

He led me out the door, ignoring the stocky man with the salt-and-pepper mustache who lounged in the hall outside.

"Your bodyguard?" I asked, hurrying to keep up. Though Jack looked awful, he moved as swiftly as ever, and it cheered me to force myself to stay at his side.

"Thought it was yours," he said, glancing back over his shoulder.

"Why are they doing it, Jack?" I asked as we descended the stairs to the lobby.

"Doing what?"

"Watching me," I said. "Or is it us?"

"Don't let it get you down, Little Honey. It's epiphenomenal only. Back in the U.S., I'd be worse than watched—I'd be slapped back in jail, wouldn't I?"

"It's true, Jack," I said, feeling a sudden chill at the thought that my plans for him clashed rather violently with what the U.S. Government had in mind. "Perhaps it's better that we stay here until things cool off back in the States." I slid my arm about his waist. "I wouldn't want you to have to endure any more time in jail. What if we go to Mexico?"

He looked at me in a strange way, with eyes that appeared to be nearly burning in their sockets.

"My Little Honey, dear, I would do anything for you, but don't ask me to be a coward."

Right there in the middle of the lobby I began to cry.

"Sweet Little Honey," he said, taking me around. "Want to hear something?" And out of his shirt pocket he pulled a crumpled piece of paper.

"I wrote this for you in Abo." He focused with red and bulging eyes on the tiny sheet of writing. "Thinking and dreaming/Day and night and day/Yet cannot think one bitter thought away—/That we have lost each other/You and I. . . .'"

He was the one who was weak—I was the one who fainted.

A week went by before I found out just how strong I was going to have to be in order to survive. Jack made me keep up a wicked pace—we went to the theater each night and during the days he led me from office to office and meeting to meeting so that I could meet the important and wonderful people whose acquaintances he had made in his recent struggles. Though he had lost his attempt to get the CLP position endorsed—and locked horns with Gregori Zinoviev in several tumultuous public meetings—he lost none of his respect for those who had defeated him, and they seemed to have increased their admiration for him. Lenin himself spoke to Jack as though he were more than a comrade—almost a nephew or a son.

"You must both stay long here," he told us, "and you must learn how to speak Russian. Poetry gets lost in translation—so much that we do remains lost to you, Reed, and you know more about us than any other American."

He narrowed his small, Tartar eyes and looked at us with such understanding and intimacy that I melted. No one who sees that look could oppose him, I decided then. I asked if I could spend some time with him in the following week so that I could do an article about him, and he nodded. When I asked if I could meet Madame Krupskaya, his wife, he smiled broadly.

"Yes, you must do that because you will like her, she is so intelligent."

And we met Trotsky, and Lunacharsky, and all the others.

"Our lives are so amazing, Big Darling," I said to Jack one afternoon toward the end of that week as we strolled along the Moskva. "We've met so many of the people who make the world what it is and change the world into what it will become." We stopped and looked down at the dark and swiftly flowing water—rain splashed about the surface, rain that would soon turn to snow. There'd been no sun at all that week, but I had felt so warmed by Jack's presence that no weather however dreary could have bothered me. I had even stopped feeling annoyed whenever I spied the little men who followed us from place to place, though I couldn't help noticing that even now the same one who had been stationed outside my room on the night of my arrival now dawdled behind us on the embankment like a lover out of Dostoyevsky, lost in thoughts or feelings too powerful for words.

"One river leads to another," he said. "The world flows along, and soon all waters join in one great sea."

"And then?" I asked.

He laughed, his old outrageous grin smiling through his skull-like face.

"And then the gods turn off the faucet and you drink ambrosia with them up there."

He pointed to the blanket of clouds that dropped toward the walls and buildings of the Kremlin.

"Lovey," I said, slipping an arm about his waist. "What if before they turn off your spigot we watered my garden with your seed?"

He kissed me and I could taste Baku on his lips.

"Yes, it's time for that, isn't it?" He took a deep breath and drew back a little, gazing out over the river again. "And it's time for other things, too. I wrote a lot when I was stuck in jail in Abo, darling—a lot of scribbling but some pages that I don't want to throw away. I began a novel, a novel in the form of a memoir, I wrote quite a lot of pages—" He ran a hand through his hair, which had grown quite thin since his imprisonment. "Or is it a memoir in the form of a novel?" He raised his voice to a near yell. "Well, what the hell, to hell with form! Leave that to the bourgeois artistes!"

The small man in the dark suit approached to within earshot, as if Jack might be shouting slogans in favor of the Czar.

"'You of the mighty Slavic tribes and empires! You Russ in Russia!'" Jack hurled at him, and he turned away as if to contemplate once again the weighty matters on his dark-suited mind.

I laughed a lot, but Jack's face clouded over, and I could see something come into his eyes as he again turned to stare at the slurring waters.

"'From pent-up aching rivers,'" he said in a quiet and sombre chant, "'From that of myself without which I were nothing,/From what I am determined to make illustrous, even if I stand sole among men,/ From my own voice resonant, singing the phallus,/Singing the song of procreation,/Singing the need of superb children and therein superb grown people,/Singing the muscular urge and blending....'"

He paused, and I could see tears in his eyes, a sight most unusual.

"Is something wrong, Darling?" I asked, brushing my hair from my eyes. The wind had picked up along the river. The wind was blowing cold foam off the river.

"He's such a great poet," he said.

"He is," I said.

"I'll never be half as good as he is."

"But even to only be half as good would be pretty great," I said.

"Do you really think so? I want to try, Lou. I want to give my best time to writing now. There are a few things I need to clear up when we get back home, but I'm going to give up a lot of the work that kept me from writing."

"I'm so glad to hear that, Darling," I said.

"And if there's more jail ahead, well, it won't be half as bad as Abo, and I wrote a lot in Abo."

"Yes," I said.

"I might do a book about American prisons...and a lot of poems. And the novel. I'll finish what I began in Abo and then I want to do another. It came to me one night in Baku—imagine—" he dropped my hand and pointed to the buildings, to the sky—"I was sitting in a tent eating roast camel while outside musicians were playing and the dancing girls were hootchy-kootchy-ing it up, and it came to me, a new kind of book, a novel without a hero, a book about the masses, about the great tides of men, the mass ebbs and flows of human events, and all the millions of millions who live in those human rivers—and all time's a geography that these streams pass through!"

I clutched him by the worn lapels of his shredded scarecrow coat.

"You speak poetry to me, my darling! And I know you'll write what you say!"

"I'll begin tomorrow morning," he said, taking me by the wrists. "And now we'll go and hunt up some food—just like the frontier over here, that's why I think I love it so much, Little Darling—and then we'll go back to the room and let those pent-up aching rivers flow again!"

"'Singing the song of procreation,'" I chanted as we turned and marched back along the embankment.

"'Singing the muscular urge....'" answered Jack.

We left the little dark-suited man far behind, scratching his head in puzzlement. Jack eventually slowed up along the quay where a shriveled woman dressed all in black dipped up *kvass* from a little barrel.

"Let's drink to tomorrow," he said, raising the ladle to his lips.

I shook my head.

"Couldn't," I said, shrinking back from the barrel while the little old woman stared at me as though I were a specimen from another planet. I looked over my shoulder and saw that our shadow had caught up with us.

"It's just their equivalent of root beer," Jack said. "Come, I'll drink your share too," and he drank again.

Jack was always the better dreamer. But that night he slept like a stone washed on the bottom of the Volga while I soared and rushed above the earth, a bird, a bat, a bomb sent flying from an artillery batallion that would explode on impact—and when I awoke whimpering in the cold, I huddled closer to Jack and felt him burning.

"Lovey dear, don't you feel well?"

He stirred and looked about as though he had just come up from the bottom of the river.

"I've got an awful headache," he said, and lay back down again.

"You feel warm," I said. "I think you ought to stay in bed this morning."

"Yes," he said, closing his eyes, "you go on to the little Lenin household and interview the Mrs. for *Smart Set*."

"Don't get smart." I said. But I did have my tea with Krupskaya that afternoon, and it was a pleasant event—we talked of Kollontai and women's rights and what it was like to be a mover and shaker in her own right when her husband was always the one in the spotlight—but my mind was on poor Lovey all the while. Back at the hotel, he was burning—and tossing and moaning—his headache had sharpened—and he slept awhile and then awoke, crying out for news of a rooster he claimed he heard crowing right there in the middle of the city.

"I'm going to have a doctor come up and look at you," I said.

"Hell with that," Jack said. "They need doctors at the front—send him to the front."

"I'm calling one just the same."

Several hours later came a dour little man with a pince-nez and a bad limp.

"Influenza," he said. "Several days' bed rest, and he will feel fine," he added in German.

"What will you give him?" I asked.

He shrugged off my question. "Nothing will help except rest."

Jack got up the next morning and fell on his face.

"Several days," repeated the doctor later that afternoon. "You must follow my advice."

Jack stayed in bed a few days more. His temperature never

fell near the normal mark, though he found that he could get up and walk around without any dizziness for a few minutes each afternoon.

I took the opportunity to go off for my interviews with the staff at the Foreign Ministry. When I returned, Jack lay sprawled across the floor, breathing hoarsely.

"That's enough!" I said. "We're getting you to a hospital."

Easier said than done. The commandant at the hotel had to arrange for Jack's transportation and it took hours for us to get to the Marinsky Hospital. Jack's face fairly glowed in the rain when we helped him from the car to the entrance.

"Like a stove in winter," said one of the old women who aided the nurses when she first took a look at him.

A soldier barred my way to the wards. When I protested, he pointed to a door and I went to request permission to stay with Jack. The doctor in charge told me that that was impossible with typhus cases and I fainted at hearing the news of Jack's disease.

"You could die," Lenin said to me later that afternoon after I had made myself so impossible that his aides finally allowed me into his office.

"I don't care," I said. "I want to be with him."

"Very well," he said, squinting at me as though I were a difficult passage in very fine print in a book he was studying. "You're true comrades, aren't you? You two?"

I nodded, scarcely able to breathe.

"And did you enjoy talking with my wife?"

"Yes," I said with a cough.

"She enjoyed your company. You will come back some evening?"

"When Jack gets well," I said.

"Yes, of course, you will both come to see us."

When I returned to the hospital the atmosphere had changed—I was allowed to pass directly into Jack's room where, during the next few hours, a number of new doctors stopped in to have a look at his sleeping figure.

"Mrs. Reed," said one of these new physicians, a dapper fellow in an old but clean gray pin-striped suit, "May I speak with you?" His accent, from the Lower East Side, made me horribly aware just how far we'd come from home.

"Yes," I said, wondering if he could hear my pain when I spoke. We were leaning together against a window looking out on the cold rain, the gray stones of the October Prospect.

"I'm Dr. Moskowitz, and I grew up in Manhattan and recently returned here to help with the problems. . . ."

"Doctor!" I reached for his hand.

"I know, I know how it feels to have someone from your home near you. Let me tell you, one of my former associates is your husband's old friend Dr. Carl Binger and Dr. Binger once told me about the kidney operation. And so I want to tell you that in all honesty this does not help your husband's chances much in fighting the disease. I'm sorry to inform you about this, but I've learned revolutionary honesty is better than bourgeois illusion. I'm sorry to say it, but it's true."

"Isn't there anything—"

The doctor placed his hand over mine and squeezed.

"For typhus there is nothing to be done except wait and watch the struggle—and even if we had anything it would all be reserved for the front."

"Please," I said, pressing myself against him, "please help him to live."

"It's my duty to tell you what I did, but also my duty to try and do all I can. Lenin himself asked me to attend your husband!"

"What a good man," I said.

"They are both good men," he said. "They are all—most of them—good men."

I could feel the heat rising from his body and I warmed myself by it.

"I don't know what I'd do if . .if. . . ."

He pressed my face to his shoulder. There was tobacco on

his breath and disinfectant in his hair. All men in those days seemed to smell of either one or the other or both.

"Let's take this one step at a time," he said, and it made me feel good because of his American voice.

Several days went by, and Jack grew miraculously stronger while I suffered my period and felt unaccountably weak.

"Little Honey," he said, stroking my hand as we sat together on the edge of his bed. "You're so brave to stay with me."

"But we're winning, Jack. You seem so much better today."

"And you look depressed, little sweetheart. What is it?"

And I had to tell him about my period, and how we'd lost our chance that month to make our baby.

"Next month," he said, with a wink as wicked as any I'd ever seen.

"Oh, yes," I said, and began to shiver. "Oh, yes," and I went on shivering so much that one of the nurse's aides who stood at the door came toward me, as though she feared that I had suddenly come down with typhus myself.

That night Dr. Moskowitz presented me with a bottle of precious brandy, and I stayed in the hotel room and drank myself to sleep.

For several days before that, visitors of all sorts had come to the door of the room: Louis Fraina, who brought the minutes of the International Congress, which Jack had asked for so that he could go over his remarks; and a number of friends in the struggle of the last few years came too, including Emma G. and a young woman who wouldn't give her name but spoke to me in the corridor about the heroism of my stalwart husband who had made such a contribution to the understanding of the Revolution in English-speaking lands.

"Are you Malka, by any chance?"

Her eyes fluttered as though a small light had been passed across them, but she shook her head as if to say no.

"What does my name matter? I am a Russian woman, you

are an American woman, and together we must stand in solidarity against the forces of counterrevolution." She grasped my hands, kissed me once brightly on each cheek, and then raced away down the corridor like a schoolgirl who had just pulled off a nasty prank. She nearly collided with an armed militia guard at the end of the hall, danced around him and, cupping her hands to her mouth, called back to me, "We will always remember him and love him!"

"He's not dead yet, you little bitch!" I shouted at her. But she was already around a corner and out of sight. The dark-suited man stepped into view, almost as if she had tapped him on the shoulder and told him his rest period had ended. Although he lingered in the corridor as ill-at-ease as he had been in the halls of the Dielovoy Dvor, none of his superiors ever appeared to pay Jack a visit.

"How could they?" Dr. Moskowitz said to me when I tugged at his white coat and railed to him about this great discourtesy to one of the revolution's greatest supporters. "Should they put themselves in jeopardy of the disease? Louise, with all due respect, they have their work and it must go on."

"I'm ashamed for complaining," I said. "He seems better though today, doesn't he?"

Moskowitz nodded, wetting his lips to speak, but holding something back.

The next morning Jack slipped again into the fiery river of his fever.

"You know how it is when you go to Venice?" he whispered to me as I leaned over his bed. "You ask people—Is this Venice?—just for the pleasure of hearing the reply."

His eyes flickered open and a smile formed on his lips.

"We've never been to Venice, Jack," I said. "After you get well, we'll go. On our way home."

"Of course," he said, "while it's not a river, still the waters sing their little songs. . . ." He raised a finger toward the ceiling. "Like all good rivers. . . Cliff and Sox and Bates and me, we appeased that old genius...darling, I don't mean to be so melodramatic, but it was the spirit in the waters, don't you think?"

"Yes, darling," I said, biting down on my knuckles but feeling no pain. That night as I curled up in a chair in the corridor and tried to sleep I could still see my teeth marks where I had broken the skin.

Another dawn broke—this time without a sound, silent white young flurries falling past the window. Jack appeared to me as white as the snow, whiter than the sheets that covered him up to his neck. I recalled horribly the skull I kept back in Portland, and snatched myself away from his bedside.

"He cried out!" one of the old women in attendance said as she hurried after me down the hall.

"Please, dear God, God of gods, help him, help him this once," I said, clasping my hands together right there in the corridor. "He's never asked you for anything before. Give him this, Lord, and I'll be good, I'll be a better person, Lord, I'll do things for you, Lord, I'll give time to you, Lord."

"Missus?" The aide tugged at my sleeve. "I go to light for him a candle."

I could feel the sweat pouring off me—I could feel the blood flowing from me though I should have stopped bleeding a day or so before. I gnawed on the knuckles of my unmarked hand. I could see the new teethmarks when I reached his bedside and clutched at the sheets.

"Did you bring it?" he asked without opening his eyes.

I tried to speak but my throat closed up on me.

"Did you bring it?"

I whispered something, I don't remember what.

"Good show," he said, and began to cough so violently that at times he seemed to bounce clear off the bed.

"He's reached the front," said the doctor in attendance.

"Bully for you," Jack said when he stopped coughing. "Bully good all. We'll bring rockets, yes, and little..."

His voice dropped away. I leaned my ear close to his lips Something clicked in his throat.

"What's that?" I asked.

Out in the corridor some people had gathered.

"What has he been saying?" Emma Goldman asked. "Will he make a statement?"

"A statement! About what! He can't hear me!"

She pulled me close.

"Sorry, sorry, I was just wondering...."

"Wondering what?"

I freed myself and lurched violently against the doorjamb. My shoulder hit, but I felt no pain, only a dull gnawing, like rats or voices within a wall.

"There's a rumor going around that...this...." She pointed toward the bed inside the room. "That this...was the work of Zinoviev...that he sent him to the Baku Congress when he knew there was a typhus epidemic...."

"It's true," said Fraina, appearing at her side. "I mean, there is a rumor. I tried to explain to Emma that such a thing would be impossible, but she wants to believe in conspiracies. So Jack opposed Zinoviev. So we all have our differences within the revolution. We work them out. Wasn't he appointed to the Executive Committee of the International three days after he lost the vote on the labor question? Lenin is an honorable man, and Zinoviev follows his lead."

"So are they all honorable men," said Emma.

"*Ach*," Fraina said, spinning away from us and wandering back down the hall to where our dark-coated watch-dog stood, staring at an empty metal table.

"He never said a thing about Zinoviev?" Emma asked me. Her eyes appeared to dance from side to side, as though they were about to pop loose from her skull.

"Please go," I said. "This is where politics ends. This is my life, and my life alone."

Jack lay without moving in the center of the bed, but when I leaned close I could hear him reciting.

"'The old order changeth,'" he whispered, "'yielding place to new....'"

Several more hours went by, and he seemed to shrink into

himself each time I looked at him. He rambled in a loud whisper, saying old poems, and nonsense words, and sometimes talking of rivers in a quiet, sweet way. Before it grew dark, he gave a great shudder and I hovered over him.

"I want to tell you," he said.

"Yes?" I leaned my ear close. "Is it about Zinoviev?"

"I owe a cock to Asclepius," he said.

"Oh!" I fell to my knees at his bedside.

"I see it, a great wall winding like a serpent across the hilly countryside...."

"Oh!"

"...and so we've gained that shore...."

"Oh, no!"

"...and left only little Hairball behind!"